Pills for Pets

Pills for Pets

The A to Z Guide to Drugs
and Medications for
Your Animal Companion

Debra Eldredge, D.V.M.

CITADEL PRESS
Kensington Publishing Corp.
www.kensingtonbooks.com

CITADEL PRESS BOOKS are published by

Kensington Publishing Corp.
850 Third Avenue
New York, NY 10022

All Kensington titles, imprints, and distributed lines are available at special quantity discounts for bulk purchases for sales promotions, premiums, fund-raising, educational, or institutional use. Special book excerpts or customized printings can also be created to fit specific needs. For details, write or phone the office of the Kensington special sales manager: Kensington Publishing Corp., 850 Third Avenue, New York, NY 10022, attn: Special Sales Department, phone 1-800-221-2647.

CITADEL PRESS and the Citadel logo are Reg. U.S. Pat. & TM Off.

First printing: April 2003

10 9 8 7 6 5 4 3 2 1

Printed in the United States of America

Library of Congress Control Number: 2002113468

ISBN 0-8065-2436-7

Contents

◆

Foreword

Our pets are valued members of our families. We choose and raise them with care, similar to that given to the two-legged members that share our homes. Pets are eager participants in everything we do. They greet us with glee whether we're gone for an hour or for a day. They never, ever judge us and easily accept our being less than perfect.

They're such an important part of our lives that when their physical well-being is off a beat, we'll do all we can to insure their companionship for many more years. Sometimes we're upset when we take our sick pets into the veterinary clinic, and we don't listen as carefully as we should. That night, after our vet is tucked into bed, we wonder if we should put the prescription into the refrigerator or if a symptom is a side effect of the drug. Perhaps our pet vomits—should we redose? Or maybe we'd simply like to learn more about the disease or injury our pet is suffering.

This book eases our minds when we forget to ask questions or are unable to reach the veterinarian. The old saw about whoever acts as his own lawyer has a fool for a lawyer? The same can cetainly be true of acting as your pet's vet. But this book helps give you tips in working with your vet—even choosing your vet. It is not meant to replace veterinary care, but to supplement it. Debra Eldredge, DVM, has written this book to help pet owners better understand their pets' illness and the drugs used to help them recover.

Every pet is an individual and can react differently. Some animals might have a bad reaction to a medication. Older pets may respond more slowly than younger ones. A Siamese might require different medication than a Labrador or an Arabian mare—and certainly will need a smaller dose. What if you are on vacation and your pet suddenly becomes ill, what do you do? Dr. Eldredge advises that you should be *sure* that the vet-on-call knows what other meds your pet is taking.

Herbal treatments are not always 100 percent safe. Even herbs, improperly used, can be deadly. Our "house doctor" lists the pros and cons of each herb.

Who would have thought chamomile tea could be used to treat skin inflammation or hot spots? Dr. Eldredge tells us the possible uses of herbs, as well as the warnings about side effects.

How much do we give? If some is good, more is not better. What about using our medications or over-the-counter drugs? Can I give this drug in food? What can I do to prevent illness? The answers are inside these covers.

Debra Eldredge, DVM, gives us advice on various treatments available to animal lovers. From choosing a vet and health insurance, to methods of medicating and equipping a first aid kit, her experience as a veterinarian and animal lover helps us to do the best for the pets in our care. A mother of two human "chicks" with a menagerie of six dogs, four cats, one goat, two donkeys, six horses, sixteen sheep, one guinea pig, twelve ducks, and an occasional house bunny, who knows better?

This book is the next best thing to having a vet living in your house.

—Chris Walkowicz, award-winning author
and dog breeder, AKC judge and president
of the Dog Writers Association of America

Acknowledgments

———◆———

This book is a tribute to many people. It is a tribute to my agent, Jessica Faust, who believed in me and this book long before I did! It is a tribute to my parents, Dave and Vern Mainville, neither of whom went to college, who said, "Of course you can be a veterinarian!" It is a tribute to my professors at Cornell and colleagues over the years who have shared information and stressed the need for, above all, "doing no harm." It is a tribute to the fellow members of the dog writers list who have pushed, prodded, and laughed together over our works. It is a tribute to my husband, Chuck, and my children, Kate and Tom, who have cheerfully (well, cheerfully most of the time) eaten cereal, helped with chores, and lived in less than Martha Stewart splendor while I worked on this book. And most of all it is a tribute to the many wonderful animals who have shared my life over the years and the ones who share my life now. That includes the patients I have cared for as well as my own wonderful family of pets.

Special thanks go to Pembroke Welsh Corgi, Susan, and Belgian Tervurens, Beep and Dani, who have stayed faithfully on the floor near me as I worked away at the computer. Special mention should also be made of Samantha my nineteen-year-old cat who has *not* helped by walking across the keyboard at inappropriate moments! My thanks to all of you!

Introduction

———◆———

First, I should say what *Pills for Pets* is not. It is not intended as a substitute for your regular veterinarian. It is not intended as a guide for "do-it-yourself pet pharmaceuticals." It is also not the definitive guide to the chemical structure and exact physiologic effect of pet medications.

What *Pills for Pets* should be is added knowledge for the concerned pet owner: a guide to how some medications work, what they might be used for, and what possible problems to watch for. It should help you to understand why that particular medication is being used for your pet and to be more involved in your pet's medical care. It should keep you alert to drug interactions and make you read directions carefully. After all, *you* know your pet better than anyone else!

Do not get caught up in the exact dosing schedules included for many of the medications. We now know that exact doses often need to be customized. A young puppy and an older dog with kidney failure may have the exact same bacterial infection but require very different dosing regimens or even different drugs. The routine dosages included here are guidelines only. Dosages for cats and dogs are given in mg/lb while those for birds, reptiles, rabbits, and pocket pets are given as mg/kg since those are the common ways we weigh these pets. While many drugs were initially tested on animals, much of that data is not generally available. Many of the dosages used in veterinary medicine are extrapolated from human dosages, which may or may not be ideal.

Veterinarians usually have a group of medications they are very familiar with and get good results from. They may choose to use a medication in a way that is not included here, but which is also very successful. Trust your veterinarian, or if you don't trust him, change to a different clinic.

Be aware that new medications and new drug interactions are being discovered every day. Medical information starts to become obsolete almost as soon as it is written or published. Check for newer research and newer drugs frequently. Knowledge is power. Advances and new knowledge about herbs and alternative treatments are coming out every day. Understand that many medications used for our pets are not FDA approved, but have stood the test of time and trial. You are your pet's health advocate and you need to stay informed.

I have included some general information on pet health, drugs, and pet care to aid you in providing the best possible care for your beloved animal companions. I have tried to switch pronouns off and on so both sexes receive fair treatment.

Having said all that, I hope that you will never need most of the information in this book—that your pets will be happy and healthy and take only the necessary preventative medications.

PART I

◆

General Drug and Medication Information

CHAPTER 1

Types of Medications

———◆———

There are many different types of medications. Medications can destroy unwanted invaders such as bacteria or can affect the way our own tissues react. Some medications may have multiple uses. While most medications are quite safe, virtually all of them have the potential for causing side effects. Medications should be used only if needed and always under the guidance of your veterinarian.

Antimicrobials

This group of medications includes the drugs that fight small invaders of your pet's body—bacteria, protozoa, rickettsia, chlamydia, and mycoplasma. Their purpose is to destroy those invaders or inhibit their growth, and ideally these medications should work in concert with Fido's own defensive mechanisms.

Within this class, the most common group is the antibiotics. These medications use a substance produced by one microorganism to fight others. Penicillin is the "grandfather" of this group—growing from a mold and capable of destroying many bacteria. Antibiotics may be bactericidal (killing bacteria outright) or bacteristatic (inhibiting the growth of bacteria).

Bacteria can fight back—with either acquired or natural resistance. In the case of natural resistance, for example, the bacteria may be missing an enzyme that is the target of the drug, so that drug can't harm it. Acquired resistance is becoming a very important factor in the medical fields. In this situation, a drug initially works well against a certain bacteria. Unfortunately, if the drug is not used correctly—the dose is too low, the medication is not given for the full course, or the medication is used at a low level very long term—some bacteria will survive and develop resistance. This may occur through mutations, which are then passed on to future generations of that bacteria. Suddenly the antibiotic is no longer effective. For this reason, we should use our medications very responsibly and carefully. Always follow the directions on a medication exactly!

Some antibiotics are now manufactured synthetically and may have new molecules added to increase their range of action. Sulfonamides and quinolones are two groups of primarily synthetic antimicrobials.

Antifungals

Antifungal drugs attack fungae—including both mild skin forms such as ringworm and serious internal forms. Some of these are very powerful medications with serious side effects. They should always be used under the direction and guidance of your veterinarian.

Antivirals

While vaccines and our pets' own immune systems are the primary defense against viruses, there are some antiviral medications now available. These tend to be very expensive and often have multiple undesirable side effects. Many viruses do not have efficacious medications at this time. Antivirals are virtually all prescription medications and should be used only under the guidance of your veterinarian.

Parasiticides

Drugs to harm parasites come in many types. Internal parasites include both worms in the gastrointestinal tract and parasites, such as heartworms, which live in the heart, lungs, and bloodstream. Protozoa are often controlled by these drugs as well.

External parasites come under the control of this class of drugs too. So fleas, ticks, and mites are all treated with special parasiticide medications. It should be remembered that these medications are basically poisons—intended to poison the parasites and not your pet! While most of them are quite safe, they should always be used with care and by following their directions exactly.

Chemotherapeutics

Treating cancer has come a long way in veterinary medicine. Along with surgery, pets may receive radiation or chemotherapy drugs. These are extremely powerful and dangerous medications and should be used only under the supervision of your veterinarian. While ideally they destroy only unwanted cells, sometimes normal tissues are affected as well.

Steroids

Steroids can accomplish a wide variety of tasks. While we commonly think of them as anti-inflammatory drugs useful in autoimmune problems (where your pet's body reacts against itself) or for arthritis, many hormones are also steroid based. Depending on your pet's problems, these can be almost miraculous. They are not free of side effects, and long-term usage can have serious effects. You should use these medications only under the guidance and direction of your veterinarian and use them exactly as directed.

Nonsteroidal anti-inflammatory drugs

These are medications developed to reduce inflammation, often help with pain, and are very commonly used by people. Think of aspirin and acetaminophen. Like steroid anti-inflammatory medications, these are not free of side effects and should be used only under the guidance of your veterinarian (even the over-the-counter ones).

Antihistamines

This class of drugs covers the medications used to deal with many allergies. While they don't deal with the allergy itself directly, they limit the effects of histamine—the cause of many symptoms of allergy victims. In people these drugs tend to cause drowsiness, but pets seem to be more resistant. Many antihistamines are available over the counter, but you should check with your veterinarian for dosage and safety before using any of these in your pets.

CHAPTER 2

Drug Approval

◆

Drug approval is a very serious business in the United States. Our government takes its job of keeping us safe very seriously. Our country is known for escaping many of the tragedies caused by not carefully testing drugs (very few babies with thalidomide damage were born in the United States compared to Europe, for example). Sometimes our testing and review procedures seem to have as their goals the creation of bureaucratic jobs and paperwork, but overall the system does work. While pet medication procedures aren't quite as stringent as human medication procedures, they are still quite strict. There are provisions to help in emergency cases, though.

While we may moan and groan about some government programs, including the slow pace of drug approvals, the United States has one of the best records for drug safety. Our procedures are long and tedious, to say nothing of requiring extensive paperwork, but for the most part our medications are safe. This is one of those reasons to avoid ordering medications from overseas websites, where the countries of origin may not be so stringent. (See Chapter 7: "Pill Purchasing via the Internet.")

The bottom line for drug approval by the Food and Drug Administration is proof of safety and efficacy—the drug must be reasonably safe and must do the job it is labeled for. This requires clinical (in vivo) testing as well as laboratory testing (in vitro). Animal medications require stringent testing just like human medications.

To gain approval, a new animal drug must first be listed with the Center for Veterinary Medicine. Laboratory tests must be clearly outlined, and the application must include which species it is to be approved for and the route of administration (injectable, oral, etc.). The tests must be conducted in approved facilities and provide a set of required information. All information on adverse effects, toxicology, and a full environmental assessment are part of the process.

Medications that have undergone other approval testing and are now being tested for new and unique treatments may be expedited. Under the NADA program (New Animal Drug Approval) system, the verdict on a medication takes about 180 days—this is, after all the testing has been completed and the application is sent in.

A medication that is approved for dogs will not get automatic approval for cats. Also, a medication approved for oral use may need further testing to be approved as an ear medication. As you can see, this makes it expensive to get medications FDA approved. Many companies do not feel it is financially worthwhile to do full FDA approval on some of their drugs, especially for species like birds, reptiles, or pocket pets like hamsters. It is felt that only between 10 and 15 percent of the medications we need and use in veterinary practice are fully FDA approved.

Sometimes extensive testing has been done on a medication for humans using animal models. This information may help with a drug approval for pets. Veterinarians may also use "unapproved" drugs as long as within a patient-client relationship, this is explained to the client. This is called "extra-label use." Many of our best veterinary drugs are used under those circumstances. While there may not be formal FDA approval stamped on some of these medications, many of them have been used safely in pets for years and there is a wide collection of information on their use, safe dosages, etc. Extra-label use includes any time a drug is used at a different dose, different frequency, different route (orally versus injection, for example), different indication, or for a different species.

Veterinarians will share information about successful medications at seminars, in journals, and via professional Internet groups. For unusual pets such as many exotics, this may be the only way to find treatments. Even then, what works for one species may not work in another species and may even be harmful.

This same "information network" comes into play even for common pets such as dogs and cats when they get unusual diseases. Your veterinarian may consult with human physicians and/or drug companies to try and find treatments. Pets may get into experimental protocols at veterinary colleges just like people sometimes do. Research about unusual diseases in pets may help people and vice versa.

These situations also cover what are labeled "orphan drugs." These are the medications that may be very helpful, even life-saving, for certain rare diseases. It is often not economically feasible for companies to go through approval for a medication that would not be used very often. Pets receiving these treatments must show that there is no known safe alternative medication and then they may be added to any clinical trials being done. Any unapproved drugs should always be used under the guidance of your veterinarian and with a full knowledge of your pet's health history and any other medications she is taking.

Your veterinarian may choose to get an INAD (Investigational New Animal Drug) request to use a drug that is not approved yet for any animals or people. Sometimes drugs that are not yet approved for certain uses but have been used successfully clinically may be used under "regulatory discretion." These drugs have been shown to be safe and efficacious in clinical settings. An example would be the use of potassium bromide for aiding in seizure control.

Remember, whenever you are using a drug that is not FDA approved or that requires a prescription, there must be a relationship with a veterinarian who knows your pet.

Guidelines for a Valid
Veterinary-Client-Patient Relationship

- The veterinarian must make the clinical judgment that this drug is important for the health of your pet.
- The client must follow the directives of the veterinarian.
- The veterinarian must have at least a preliminary diagnosis on which to base the use of this drug in this pet.
- The veterinarian must have examined the pet and have personal knowledge of the pet's health history.
- The veterinarian must be ready and able to provide follow-up in the case of drug reactions.

CHAPTER 3

Drug Compounding

———◆———

Drug compounding may be one of the most helpful developments in veterinary medicine in recent years. While progress has been steadily made in developing new drugs and refining treatments for illnesses, no one has come up with a better method to pill a cat yet. Compounding can possibly give us easier alternatives to dosing our recalcitrant pets in the future.

Compounding is under fairly strict guidelines itself, but studies are under way to look at alternative ways to get medication safely and easily into our pets. An example is the study using transdermal methods to get methimazole into hyperthyroid cats. Using a gel or patch would be dramatically easier than catching a hyperactive, aggressive cat and trying to poke a pill down her throat. The dangers to both of you would be greatly reduced!

Drug compounding involves changing drugs or medications. There are three basic areas:

Reformulating: changing an injectable into an oral form, for example, or adding flavors.

Mixing drugs: combining medications into one to make it easier to dose a pet.

Novel delivery: incorporating drugs and medications into biscuits or gels to make it even easier to treat a pet. Ear, eye, and inhalant methods may also be used.

Drug compounding is not without some controversy. When drugs are ordered through compounding pharmacies, you still need a prescription for most medications. That prescription should be from a veterinarian with whom you have a valid client relationship. For example, you can't simply get a prescription over the phone from a veterinarian who has never examined your pet.

Compounded medications are still required to fit FDA guidelines. So drugs that are not FDA approved for pets can be used, but must be used under the supervision and guidance of your veterinarian. If a medication is not FDA approved, switching it from an oral drug to a gel form will not change its status. If the medication is FDA approved, however, switching the form may remove its approval.

With any compounded drugs, it must be shown that they are still safe and efficacious, they are being used for a monitorable disease, and there is no other suitable method.

It can be more difficult to assure quality control when reformulating a single dose, and there have been discussions about the efficacy of some medications when used in gel form (to apply to the inside of a pet's ears, for instance, instead of giving orally). Obviously if drugs are combined in one product, the drugs must be compatible.

The pluses to compounding can be great. Fish-flavored liquids for cats can be a great boon. Medications in flavored biscuits could help elderly people treat their rambunctious pets. Rubbing a gel onto an earflap is much simpler than trying to pill some pets!

The compounding of medications for pets and people is likely to come under greater scrutiny in the future. Hopefully the methods will stand up so that medicating our pets can be even easier!

For further information about the FDA standards and concerns about compounding, see www.fda.gov/fdac/features/2000/400_compound.html.

CHAPTER 4

General Medication Guidelines

There are some basic rules that should hold up for any medications, no matter where you get them or what illness they are being used for. The guidelines listed below are simple and straightforward. Always make sure you have this information and clearly understand how and when to use your pet's medications. You should never hesitate to question your veterinarian or ask to have something clarified. *You* are your pet's best health advocate and she is depending on you!

- Know the medication or supplement you are giving—packages or bottles should be labeled clearly. If you have trouble reading the labels, ask your veterinarian or pharmacist to type out a sheet in large print for you.
- Know how much medication you are to give and when and how to give it to your pet—this should be on the labels as well. If your pet needs to fast or this medication goes better with food in the stomach, you need to know that.
- Ask for guidance in how to medicate your pet—even a demonstration if need be.
- Know how much medication or supplement is in the bottle or package— this is important information in the case of poisoning and should be on the label.
- Make sure that *you* understand why your pet is receiving this medication— what condition is being treated and what changes you should see in your pet's clinical signs.
- Use all of the medication as directed—don't stop treating your pet until it is finished or your veterinarian advises you to.
- Do not use a medication after the expiration date—which should be included on the label or the package.

- Make sure your veterinarian is aware of *any* other medications or supplements you are giving your pet—two products that are safe alone may be deadly in combination.
- Make sure you are aware of any common side effects.
- Keep medications and supplements in their original, well-labeled containers. Most veterinarian hospitals and pharmacies will put drugs into childproof containers unless expressly requested not to.
- Store medications and supplements safely and appropriately. Dispose of medications as directed.
- Prescription medications should come only from your veterinarian or a pharmacy (possibly Internet). These medications *must* always have a prescription as part of their order form written by a veterinarian who has examined your pet and knows your pet or be purchased directly from your veterinarian who knows your pet's health history.

CHAPTER 5

Prescription Medications

———◆———

Prescription medications may simply mean "more hassle" to you. These medications cannot be picked up at the corner market on a Sunday morning, but require a prescription generated by a veterinarian who has examined your pet. Try to remember that there is a good reason for this. These are powerful medications that could do harm if used improperly. Having a prescription is an extra guide to the use of the drug. There are guidelines included as to what information should be on your prescription. Also look at "Medical Abbreviations" in the appendixes if you don't understand anything written on the prescription. Prescription medications may make the difference between life and death for your pet—use them with care!

Most of the medications discussed in this book and that your pet will encounter over her lifetime are prescription medications. That means the medications can only be purchased directly from your veterinarian or from a pharmacy (either local or Internet) with a written prescription attached to the order form. Medications that should have prescriptions will say: "Caution—federal law restricts this drug to use by or on the order of a licensed veterinarian."

This requirement of prescriptions is for the safety of your pet. Many medications have "qualifying factors"—they may not be safe in certain species, they may be dangerous in pets with certain health problems, etc. Having a prescription shows the pharmacist that your pet has been examined by a veterinarian and the veterinarian feels this medication is important for and safe to give to your pet. The veterinarian presumably knows your pet's medical and health history and is also aware of any other medications or supplements your pet may be taking. Obviously if you are purchasing your medication directly from your veterinarian after an office call, no written prescription is needed. The report in Spot's medical record covers that.

If you are taking a prescription from your veterinarian to a pharmacy, make sure it is legible. Many practices now type up or at the very least print the pre-scriptions. The prescription should include the medication, your pet's name, the amount of the medication, how much to dose your pet and how often, and the contact information for the veterinarian in case the pharmacist has any questions. Medications that are "controlled substances"—drugs with the po-tential for human abuse—have special prescription forms.

Prescription forms now include a space to mark whether your veterinarian feels a generic form of the drug your pet needs is acceptable or if your pet should receive a certain brand. Some brands may be easier on Fido's stomach or taste better. Sometimes certain brands seem to be more effective. There are drugs that don't have a generic form. Other drugs tend to be available only in the generic form. On the prescription will be a space marked DAW to be checked off. That stands for "Dispense As Written." If that box is checked, the pharmacist should use either the brand name or the generic version of the medication, whichever your veterinarian indicated.

The prescription will also indicate if your pet will need refills. This is most common for long-term medications such as seizure medications. Some drugs can be dispensed only a month's worth at a time and refills are limited for up to six months total on one prescription. This is used to limit the possibility of human abuse with some of these medications.

Prescription Information

* Name of your pet.
* Name and contact information for the veterinarian who wrote the pre-scription.
* Date when the prescription was written.
* Name of the drug being dispensed—this may be the generic name or a brand name. If a brand name is mentioned, the veterinarian will generally check off a box labeled DAW (Dispense As Written), meaning that he wants that exact brand dispensed.
* Size of the drug to be dispensed and what dose to be given to your pet—both amount and frequency. So it might say: "50 mg given orally twice daily." If the pills come in a 25 mg size, that means two pills given twice daily. If the pills come in a 50 mg size, that means one pill given twice daily. Be *sure* you understand the exact amount to give your pet and how often.
* How many pills or how much liquid is included.
* Whether or not there are to be refills and, if so, how many refills.

CHAPTER 6

Over-the-Counter (OTC) Encounters

We are accustomed to self-medicating many of our minor health problems with over-the-counter (available without a prescription) medications. It seems that we ought to be able to do the same thing with our pets. Unfortunately our pets have different metabolisms and different physiology, which makes it difficult to just extrapolate from our experiences.

While there are over-the-counter medications that are safe for our pets, many of the medications are quite dangerous. Even with the "safe" medications, determining a correct and accurate dose may be difficult to do. Breaking adult human versions of some pills into Chihuahua-size doses is virtually impossible.

The over-the-counter option may seem simpler and cheaper, but make sure it is safe and not going to be more expensive in the long run—check with your veterinarian first!

Naturally we all love to be able to treat our pets with a simple over-the-counter treatment—maybe even a medication we already have in our bathroom cabinet. It is easy and relatively inexpensive—and unfortunately could be fatal to our pet! Some drugs that have become household words for treating people such as acetaminophen (Tylenol) can actually be fatal—in this case for cats.

It is important to discuss the use of any OTC drug with your veterinarian before trying it for your pet. Any preexisting medical conditions your pet has may influence dosage or use of a certain medication. The dosage given for people may be totally inappropriate for a dog or cat. It should also be noted that most of these medications are not FDA approved for use in animals and should be used only with that understanding and under the guidance of your veterinarian.

The common painkillers are an excellent example. Acetaminophen can be used with care in dogs, but is fatal to cats. Aspirin is fairly routinely used in dogs (the buffered version given with food) but should be used only very cautiously and at a greatly reduced dose in cats. Ibuprofen is not recommended for either dogs or cats.

Since these over-the-counter medications are usually not approved for use in pets, the exact safe dosage may not have been determined through clinical studies. Instead, veterinarians use dosages that have been developed anecdotally or through experience. These dosages are often passed on at seminars and via veterinary journals, along with cautions noted by the veterinarians who have used these drugs. Those dosages may have been used in a pet with only one health problem and your veterinarian may feel the dose needs to be adjusted or that drug removed altogether from the treatment protocol due to other health considerations in your special friend.

I can't emphasize enough how important it is to have a good relationship with your veterinarian and to keep in touch with him about the use of medications. The pharmacist at the local drugstore is very knowledgeable about human drug usage but doesn't know animal physiology. A voice over the phone or an e-mail address over the Internet doesn't know that Spot has a chronic liver problem as well as his acute case of diarrhea you want to treat.

There are many OTC medications that can be helpful, however. Antihistamines for allergic reactions are generally safe; for example, diphenhydramine (Benadryl®) can be used in both dogs and cats. Hydrogen peroxide makes a wonderful emetic if you need to make your pet vomit after eating something inappropriate. Psyllium (Metamucil®) can be very useful in a constipated dog or cat.

With OTC medications there should be directions for use and an expiration date on the container just like your prescription medications. Do not use these drugs past their expiration dates. Follow any special directions, such as taking on an empty stomach, as well as the directions given by your veterinarian. If possible, get a written dosage schedule and directions from your veterinarian so you know exactly how to use the medication.

Always let your veterinarian know if your pet is taking any over-the-counter medications! Drug interactions could be fatal, and some over-the-counter medications could be dangerous in pets with chronic health problems.

CHAPTER 7

Pill Purchasing via the Internet

It seems that almost every family has a computer these days, and Internet access is very widespread. People search "the Web" for everything from books to clothes, so checking out the Internet for medications seems a natural step. There are many precautions you should take here, however!

Many of the medications your pet may need over her lifetime are "prescription" medications. This means that these drugs are available only directly from your veterinarian or by purchase elsewhere with a prescription. A prescription is a legal document signed by your veterinarian that lists exactly what medication your pet needs, what dose and how to give it, how much and how many refills you might need. It will also show if the drug can be dispensed in the generic (non–brand name version) or if it should be dispensed exactly as written—including the brand of medication.

Certain precautions need to be taken if you choose to purchase any medications over the Internet. First, the site should require a prescription from *your* veterinarian. Getting a prescription from a veterinarian online who has never examined your pet is a violation of many state and/or federal laws. That includes getting a prescription after merely filling out a survey on a website. The veterinary professional needs to see and examine your animal and take a thorough history—impossible over the Internet. An Internet pharmacy that sells prescription medications without a valid prescription is in violation of the law. An Internet pharmacy that refills a prescription that has run out and should not be renewed may be putting Fido in danger if his health conditions have changed. Those qualifications apply to regular pharmacies as well, of course.

If you have a prescription from your veterinarian, you can check out sites for best values. Beware of foreign sites. The medications may not be exactly the same as those in the United States, and if you have problems, there is no way to get recompense. It may also be illegal to import certain drugs. A good site should have a pharmacist available for consultation and who will check which other medications your pet may be taking to prevent problems.

Generics are suitable for many treatments, but there are cases where a certain brand of medication has advantages. This can include being FDA approved, so there is some known data about safety and drug interactions. Be aware that some medications need special storage and shipping arrangements. If a medication should be refrigerated and yours arrives a week after ordering in an uninsulated package, it should not be used.

If a pharmacy (anywhere) pushes a "miracle" drug or treatment, look elsewhere. As your grandmother said, "If it sounds too good to be true, it probably is." Stick to exactly what medication your veterinarian feels is best for your pet.

You can check out pharmacies by going to the National Association of Boards of Pharmacy at www.nabp.net or 847-698-6227. They can let you know if a certain pharmacy is licensed and in good standing. Some sites will display the NABP VIPPS (Verified Internet Pharmacy Practice Site) seal, which indicates they have met state and federal requirements. If you do try to purchase medications online and have problems, you should report the pharmacy site to the FDA at www.fda.gov/oc/buyonline/buyonlineform.html. By doing so, you may put an illegal operation out of business and save someone else from the heartache of harming their pet.

It is important to realize that there are many pet healthcare sites on the Internet. Some of them are excellent, but some freely give out incorrect and possibly even harmful information. Try to stick to sites run by veterinary colleges and associations. If you come across an article on a medication or health problem that you feel applies to your pet, print it off and run it by your veterinarian. Often articles deal with only one problem and the treatment may be very different for a pet with multiple problems, of a different breed, etc. Your veterinarian can guide you to excellent websites that deal with any chronic problems your pet may be experiencing. Don't try a new treatment based solely on an article on the Internet without checking with your veterinarian first—that new treatment could very well be unproven and could harm or kill your pet!

Fad diets and treatments crop up on the Internet with great regularity. Do your research! What worked for one pet may not actually help your pet at all. Very often owners are not aware of the complete treatment their pet was receiving. Most reputable veterinarians online or with websites stress the need for a physical examination of your pet and a complete history before trying any treatments or changing treatments.

Veterinary advice should be given out only in the context of a valid veterinary-client-patient relationship.

Guidelines for a Valid
Veterinary-Client-Patient Relationship

- The veterinarian must make the clinical judgment that this drug is important for the health of your pet.
- The client must follow the directions of the veterinarian.
- The veterinarian must have at least a preliminary diagnosis on which to base the use of this drug in this pet.
- The veterinarian must have examined the pet and have personal knowledge of the pet's health history.
- The veterinarian must be ready and able to provide follow-up in the case of drug reactions.

Having given all these caveats, I can now say that sometimes you can find helpful information online about your pet's problems. You may have more free time than your veterinarian when it comes to surfing the Net (remember your veterinarian may be trying to research problems for multiple pets). Just keep the warnings mentioned above in mind!

CHAPTER 8

Disease Considerations

Rarely do we have an ill pet who has only one problem. More commonly, even our middle-aged pets already have some arthritis or mild changes in their liver or kidney functions. Sometimes a problem has been present for so long or is so mild and well controlled that we forget about it. Underlying health problems can influence the way medications work, though, so we need to keep track of any problems our pets have and any treatments we are giving them—even something as simple as a dietary supplement like glucosamine for arthritis.

I recommend that families keep an up-to-date file card for each pet with any ongoing problems or major problems in the past. The file card should also list any drug reactions and any supplements or medications your pet takes chronically. My sixteen-and-a-half-year-old cat is a diabetic and on daily insulin. I have to always keep Tiger's diabetes in mind when I treat her for any other problem. She also gets diarrhea from amoxicillin (an antibiotic) so I know not to use that for her.

Along with uncomplicated age factors, many pets have underlying disease considerations when it comes to determining drug choices and dosing schedules. Most dosages you see have been determined by trials with healthy adult animals or were extrapolated from human dosage schedules. If your pet has chronic health problems, those have to be taken into consideration. Keep in mind that pets with chronic problems are often on long-term medications or dietary changes. Always make sure your veterinarian is aware of these things when you add another medication to your pet's treatment regimen.

Renal or kidney problems can significantly affect the medications used for your pet. Many drugs are excreted via the urine. With kidney diseases, the rate of blood flow through the kidneys is almost always decreased. This means less time for the kidneys to filter or bind substances. Slower excretion can lead to toxicity. Many drugs will need to have either the dose or the dosing frequency reduced or both. In addition, you may need to make extra efforts to keep your pet well hydrated.

Liver problems can be exacerbated by lower blood flow and changes in protein binding. Many drugs are metabolized (changed) in the liver and some are excreted in the bile. If the liver is not working efficiently, drug dosages may need to be lowered by as much as 50 percent!

Obviously if your pet has heart problems, the blood flow to all of the tissues and organs is affected—normally the flow will be decreased. With age, blood flow is already redistributed to the heart and brain preferentially. With decreased flow, there is greater danger of toxic levels of some medications building up.

The liver and the kidneys will get less blood flow, possibly slowing the excretion of some drugs. Drugs that are given by injections into the muscle will be absorbed more slowly and some medications may need to be given by intravenous injection simply to be sure the drug gets to where it needs to work. Dosages may need to be reduced.

If your pet is suffering from an acute gastrointestinal problem and is vomiting, giving oral medications may not help very much. Diarrhea can cause medications to move rapidly through the intestinal tract and decrease the amount absorbed.

Hyperthyroid pets will have an increased rate of metabolism and may "burn up" medications faster than normal. Diabetic pets may be very sensitive to any medications that influence the blood glucose or insulin levels. Some medications affect the urine glucose tests, so you must be careful about adjusting your pet's insulin dose based on the urine tests.

All of these things must be taken into consideration as well as any interactions between medications or supplements your pet may be taking. Be sure your veterinarian is aware of any supplements or medications your pet is on long-term—even something as simple as glucosamine added to the diet to help with arthritis. Drug interactions can lower the efficacy of the medications you are prescribed for your pet or even lead to harmful results.

CHAPTER 9

Treating the Young and the Old

◆

Old pets and young pets often have special problems that must be taken into consideration when you are going to medicate and treat them. Your veterinarian takes the age and health of your pet into consideration when determining drug choices and when planning the dosing schedule. The dosages listed in the drug section are guidelines only—your pet's doctor will customize the treatment just for her.

Geriatric Pets

Older pets often have some disease problems (which will be discussed below) but even healthy older pets have some changes in their metabolism. These changes can influence the way drugs are handled by the body.

Cardiac (heart) changes that we expect are a slight decrease in output each year. This means your pet gradually has to work harder to move the same amount of oxygen-rich blood around to all the body cells. Also, as pets age, the blood flow is redistributed a bit so that the heart and brain (very essential organs) still get their full amount. The muscles may lose some blood flow and so our pets tend to slow down or have to work harder to accomplish the same runs they used to do easily.

Meanwhile, the respiratory system is also changing. There is a decrease in the residual lung volume and a slower response to lower oxygen. Older pets have trouble breathing as deeply as they did when younger and need special care under general anesthesia.

We see some changes in the gastrointestinal tract as well. Most older pets have less salivation (though some drool extensively if they have dental problems). The stomach and intestines have slower motility and less absorption so many older pets don't make efficient use of their food. Special care needs to be taken if you use nonsteroidal anti-inflammatory medications in older pets to be sure the gastrointestinal tract does not become irritated.

The liver of a mature pet is often slower and less efficient at metabolizing medications. This can require lower dosages and/or less frequent dosaging.

With decreased blood flow, possibly the kidneys are not as fast or efficient either. Drugs may take longer to be excreted in the urine, again requiring lower dosages or less frequent dosing schedules. Special care must again be taken with the nonsteroidal anti-inflammatory medications and the aminoglycoside antibiotics.

While some older pets stay quite fit and trim, most have a decrease in muscle mass and an increase in body fat. This change in body composition can influence fat-soluble drugs.

Older pets do tend to have a decrease in receptor sensitivity. This means that they may not clearly show signs of pain even when they could benefit from pain medications.

Mature pets are more likely to be on multiple medications and to have underlying or obvious illnesses. Balancing their medications and treatments can be difficult at times!

Pediatrics

On the other end of the spectrum are the very young patients. In puppies and kittens, twelve weeks or so is considered to be the cutoff for pediatric considerations. Some factors are in play for longer, however, including any medications or supplements that might interfere with bone growth and development.

While very young (forty-eight hours or less) puppies and kittens have fairly open absorption in their gastrointestinal tract (to absorb colostral antibodies), absorption then slows. Very young pets tend to have a neutral pH in their tract at first and the presence of milk with calcium and proteins to bind drugs can interfere with medicating them adequately. Some drugs are actually best absorbed from the rectal mucosa (as enemas) at this age.

Very young pets have a smaller muscle mass for handling injections of medications. They are greatly influenced by environmental temperatures and by the state of their hydration. Young pets need to be well hydrated and kept appropriately warm at all times.

Both kidney and liver functions take time to mature so drugs are slower to be eliminated. Lower dosages and/or less frequent dosing schedules may be needed to safely medicate very young pets. Anesthesia monitoring requires special attention.

Pregnant and Nursing Pets

Obviously the youngest patients of all are the unborn fetuses, the neonates (newly born), and the still nursing pets. Many drugs can pass through the placenta and may influence the development of the fetuses. If your pet is pregnant, make *sure* your veterinarian knows this when determining medications! Obviously you may have to make choices sometimes between the health of the mother and the chance of injuring her babies. These same considerations apply when looking at treatments that can pass into the milk.

CHAPTER 10

Viva la Différence—Different Species, Different Drugs and Dosages

———◆———

When it comes to veterinary medicine, variety is the spice of life. Most veterinary clinics deal with animals of multiple species, to say nothing of the wide variety of sizes and shapes just within the canine companions. And along with mammals ranging from Great Danes to mice, we also might have pet birds or reptiles to contend with. This can make finding safe medications and determining safe dosages very difficult.

Cats and dogs are the primary pets we deal with. Even though both are classified as carnivorous mammals, there are some differences in how they react to and handle medications.

Cats have a smaller blood volume so it is easier for them to reach toxic levels of medications. They dehydrate more easily, also making toxic levels easier to reach. Since cats are smaller and with a higher metabolic rate than most dogs, the effects of disease may be greater. For example, overweight cats have more trouble with fat-soluble drugs than overweight dogs do.

Many medications are metabolized in the liver. This process often includes glucuronide conjugation, a series of chemical reactions involving enzymes called glucuronyl transferases. Cats have a deficiency of these enzymes, so they either are very slow at metabolizing some drugs, or can't keep up at all and have serious toxic reactions. Two examples here are aspirin and acetaminophen. Dogs can be treated with aspirin twice daily. If cats need aspirin, they get treated every forty-eight or seventy-two hours. With acetaminophen, cats can't keep up at all and can die from just one pill, due to damage to their livers and red blood cells.

Cats can sometimes metabolize drugs with a different pathway (using sulfates instead of glucuronides, for example) but that doesn't always work. Sometimes they just need to totally avoid certain medications.

Feline red blood cells are very sensitive to oxidation. This easily leads them to the disease state of methemoglobin, in which the tissues of the body do not get their normal amount of oxygen delivered.

Some medications work best when given at the time a pet is most likely to be active. That means dogs get steroids and aminoglycoside antibiotics in the morning while cats get these dosed in the evening.

Even within dog breeds we see some differences. (Note that all dogs are the same species—from Great Danes to Chihuahuas.) Beagles have been the classic research dog, but they may not be truly representative of all dogs. Sighthounds, such as greyhounds and Salukis, are notorious for having very little body fat. With their lean body weights, they may actually get overdosed with some medications. It can also be easy to overdose them with drugs that are redistributed to tissues, especially fatty tissues.

Brachycephalic dogs (with short faces, like Pekingese and English bulldogs) are more susceptible to cardiac (heart) arrhythmias if given medications like the sedative acepromazine. Many collies have a genetic mutation which makes them prone to overdosing with ivermectin.

When it comes to reptiles, we are often making guesses as to what will work. Reptiles are "cold blooded," so they depend on the environment to adjust their metabolic rate. Since reptiles are somewhat dependent on the ambient temperature (the temperature of the environment around them), they need to be kept at the high end of their normal temperature range when they are ill. This not only keeps their metabolic rate up and lessens the risk of toxicity from any medications, but also seems to be beneficial in stimulating their own immune defenses. Increasing the cage enclosure temperature needs to be carefully monitored. When reptiles are sick, they also need to stay well hydrated. This can be more difficult with the increased temperature, so make sure you monitor humidity as well as temperature. Provide drinking bowls for reptiles who will use them or spray the cage more frequently for reptiles who lap drops off surfaces.

We come across idiosyncratic reactions here, too—ivermectin should not be used in turtles. If you have a sick reptile, try to find a veterinarian who enjoys working with reptiles and preferably one who belongs to the Association of Amphibian and Reptile Veterinarians. Often herpetologists will work with a veterinarian to increase their mutual knowledge of a certain species.

Birds tend to do better if kept warm while ill even though they are "warm-blooded" animals. With their pneumatic (air-filled) bones, they are very susceptible to respiratory problems, including toxic fumes. Canaries were used as sentinels in mines, as they would die from toxic gases in time to alert the miners to leave.

There are huge differences in size, diet, etc., between a great horned owl and a chickadee and we just don't have enough specific information for each species.

Birds range from complete carnivores (meat eaters) to pure herbivores (plant eaters) and many species in between. With the different dietary habits come different gastrointestinal tracts. That can affect the way that oral drugs are absorbed and processed into the tissues.

Much of the medical information on birds that was available in the past came from poultry producers. We now have more veterinarians specializing in the unique needs of pet birds. There is a wealth of knowledge being developed that will eventually trickle out to the general public. In the meantime, if you have a sick pet bird, try to find a veterinarian who enjoys working with birds and preferably one who belongs to the Association of Avian Veterinarians. Many pet bird breeders will work closely with a veterinarian in an attempt to increase their mutual knowledge of different species and their care.

Rabbits and many pocket pets have unusual gastrointestinal tracts. Their digestive systems and well-being depend heavily on helpful intestinal bacteria. Using antibiotics or other medications that upset the normal bacteria can be very harmful, even fatal. Supplements (such as *Lactobacillus*) to keep these bacteria healthy in the face of antibiotic usage is common. Guinea pigs are notorious for their anaphylactic reaction to penicillin. It is difficult to keep all these interactions in mind when planning treatment for a pet!

Modern veterinary medicine has made great strides in developing medications for our pets and determining dosages and treatments. It can be reassuring to see how far feline medicine has advanced in just the last twenty years owing to increased research funding and the interest and dedication of many cat fanciers. We still have a long way to go, but there are lights shining out there in the various forests.

PART II

◆

Alternative Therapies

Introduction

While feng shui has not hit the dog kennel business yet, many Eastern therapies and Old World alternative therapies are breaking new ground in veterinary medicine. We see more pets being treated with acupuncture and herbs. These are ancient treatments but are just now being researched in modern veterinary medicine.

At this point in time, many of these treatments do not have clinical research to back up their treatment claims. Does this mean they don't really work? Not necessarily. It means that they might work but we aren't sure. Right now we want to be sure these treatments are safe first of all, then hopefully efficacious. We need to see if they will work on pets with a variety of illnesses, not just healthy pets or pets with one small problem.

Just as with conventional therapies, alternative medications aren't panaceas. A drug or herb that works well in one patient may not work in another. Medicine is not an exact science like mathematics—it is more a combination of art and science. What the alternative therapies offer us and our pets is another chance, another way to fight illnesses and health problems.

CHAPTER 11

Bach Flower Remedies and Essences

———◆———

Flower essence therapies and remedies use extracts of flowers to help treat "emotional" problems. The healing principle behind these is that many physical illnesses have an emotional component and improving the emotions should help with the physical problem.

At this time, there have been no controlled studies, no actual mechanism of action described, no proof of real effects, and no proof of definite success. Most of the information on this subject is based on anecdotal accounts. Does that mean it is total quackery? Not necessarily. These may actually help or they may only give a placebo effect (in this case for the owner). There do not seem to be bad side effects, so they are quite safe in most circumstances. Do be careful with alcohol-based flower essences in cats.

Dr. Edward Bach was the first to study flower essences and he identified thirty-eight that he felt were of value. His work is based on flowers as beings of "energy" and that their "vital force" can be distilled down and put to use in other beings. Flower essence oils are mixed with water and/or alcohol. They can be added to drinking water, given straight, or rubbed inside a pet's ears. Since alcohol is in many of the mixtures, as mentioned above, you need to be very careful when using these medications on cats.

The most common flower essence compound is the "Rescue Remedy," which is a mix of a variety of essences. This combination is considered to be helpful with dogs suffering from fears or shock. Owners report it being useful for dogs hit by cars or suffering other traumas as well as dogs with thunderstorm phobias. Dog show competitors have picked up on this to help with show nerves (sometimes for both dog and handler!).

Essential flower essence of aspen is another version felt to be helpful with fears, including fireworks.

Proponents of the flower essences stress that ideally these are used as adjuncts to therapy—not in place of all other treatments. Essences can be combined and the combinations are more commonly used than the single essences.

Before using flower essences, you need to thoroughly research which companies have a record for standardized ingredients and be sure which things can be safely combined. Flowers can contain some powerful compounds such as digitalis, which comes from foxglove. Always check with your veterinarian before you add any supplements or treatments such as these to be sure you aren't heading for a bad drug interaction or exacerbating one of your pet's health problems. Many of these medications may not be appropriate for older pets with multiple health problems.

CHAPTER 12

Food As Medicine—Prescription Diets

◆

While many women have long maintained that chocolate is medicine, it has taken quite a while for human medicine to recognize the benefits of diet and foods as an integral part of health care. Dogs and cats with health problems can easily eat specially balanced diets that help to compensate for a multitude of illnesses. Special diets exist for pets with diabetes, kidney or liver problems, urinary stones of various types, and even aging! And of course, it is easy for us to feed our pets only the "right" foods while we still sneak our "bad" treats.

With multiple companies now making veterinary/prescription diets, your pet even gets a choice of flavors and brand she prefers. My diabetic cat goes back and forth between her two favorite diets while my healthy nineteen-year-old cat sticks to her standby favorite—no substitutes accepted!

We are actually a little late getting on the bandwagon in human medicine by looking at foods as health aids. Historically, veterinarian Mark Morris developed a special diet for the kidney disease of one of the world's first guiding dogs for the blind. From there, veterinary/prescription diets have taken off.

We now have multiple companies making special diets for ill pets and diets to cover a wide range of illnesses. Prescription diets are available only from your veterinarian or with a prescription from your veterinarian to use at other sources.

These are diets specially formulated for health problems. While certain protein levels may be just what is needed for a pet with kidney problems, that same diet may not provide adequate nutrition for a growing or young pet. These diets should *only* be used for pets with diagnosed health problems and as prescribed by your veterinarian.

Since these are "prescription" diets, you need to plan when you travel or board your pet. The foods can be purchased only with a prescription or directly from your veterinarian, who has your pet's complete heath records and history. If you are traveling cross-country, you need to carry a prescription with you so you can purchase food as needed. If you are leaving Spot at his favorite resort, you need to bring along his special diet.

Prescription diets can help with problems from simple weight loss to reducing the risk of various types of bladder stones. There are dog and cat versions of most foods and they should be used only for the designated species and the designated problem. Many of the diets come in both dry and canned formulations. If your pet resists one brand of a veterinary diet, you now have the option of trying other brands. Most pets will happily eat at least one of the prescription diets available.

Most prescription diets are designed to be used for the rest of a pet's life. For example, the latest diets for diabetic cats are to be fed daily until the cat passes away. Some diets are geared more for short-term use—diets to help dissolve bladder stones, diets for weight loss, even bland diets used short term to help your pet recover from a bad bout of gastrointestinal illness.

You need to discuss the use of the diet with your veterinarian. Many pets should not receive *any* treats or supplements while on their prescription diets. Some medications may interfere with the diet as well. Giving an acidifying agent as well as putting your cat on a special diet to acidify the urine may be harmful. That would include herbs and nutraceuticals, so as always, make sure your veterinarian is aware of any supplements or other medications your pet is receiving.

Special diets make it easier for busy pet owners to provide their ill pets with the extra nutritional support they need. And having that nutritional support may cut down on the medications your pet needs to take and the bouts of illness that need to be treated. Many dogs with severe skin allergies who had previously survived on special baths and corticosteroids can now eat the hypoallergenic diets and look great. Pets with heart or kidney disease now live longer due to the "right foods." Prescription diets have been a major step forward in veterinary care.

CHAPTER 13

Herbal Treatments

———◆———

While herbal treatments have been used for thousands of years, they have grown in use in veterinary medicine just over the past two decades. It is extremely important to realize that just because something is herbal, natural, or organic does *not* necessarily mean that it is safe. Herbal remedies may cause problems for people with allergies and may even cause death if used improperly or at the incorrect dose. Very few herbs have undergone controlled testing to determine safe and efficacious dosages, efficacious uses, and interactions with other medications. The FDA (Food and Drug Administration) classifies most herbal therapies as nutraceuticals—sort of in between nutritional supplements and medications. This class of compounds does not have the extensive regulation that prescription medications do.

Many of these treatments do not come under the jurisdiction of the FDA so the quality is not always assured. The exact amount of the compound you want from an herb may vary greatly from batch to batch. Herbs may have pesticide contamination and even be affected by growing near roads where the fumes can be absorbed. Since herbs are not currently patentable under law, most companies have no desire to put a large amount of research and testing into them. Be aware that very few herbal producers have veterinary knowledge and labels may not be at all accurate for pets. Willow is used for its salicin (the primary component of aspirin). This medication can be deadly for cats. Yucca is used by some pet owners as a substitute for arthritis medications. What they may not realize is that yucca is broken down into a steroid in the body—the very substance owners may have been trying to avoid. Mixing herbs can also lead to dire consequences. Digoxin (from foxglove) and hawthornberry used as a heart tonic can be fatal.

On the plus side, many herbs are safe and it is felt that using the entire herb may have positive effects that simply isolating the desired compound and using that alone will not produce. Many of our current medications have botanical origins—such as digoxin mentioned previously. Before giving any herbal medications to your pet, talk to your veterinarian about interactions with medications your pet may be taking and what problems you need to watch out for. In the future it is likely that herbal medications will play a larger part in veterinary medicine, but right now their use is still being studied.

It is felt by many serious herbalists that fresh herbs are preferable to dried herbs, but getting fresh herbs may not always be feasible. If you are collecting herbs yourself, be *sure* you can identify the plants! If you want portions of the plant from aboveground, such as flowers, you should collect them before the flowers are in full bloom. If you want the whole aboveground plant, try to collect them before they start to flower. Roots are best collected in the fall. Many herbs are not tasty and owners may need to put them in capsules to treat their pets.

Information is included below about some of the most commonly used herbs. Note that there is no dose noted. Inclusion here does not signify safety for use in your pet or that the herbs are safe and efficacious. *Always* consult your veterinarian before using any of these!

Alfalfa

Alfalfa is a legume commonly fed to livestock. It is rich in calcium, magnesium, iron, potassium, and vitamin K. Alfalfa has been used to treat arthritis and kidney problems. Alfalfa does have some antioxidant activity as well. It can lead to bloat, anemia, and miscarriages if used improperly.

Aloe

Aloe is a plant widely used for topical treatment of burns and sores. It can be used topically on inflamed ears as well. Many people will keep an aloe plant in their home and simply break off part of a leaf to rub over sore areas.

The extract acemannan is considered an excellent immunostimulant. Acemannan is often used as part of the treatment protocol for fibrosarcoma tumors in pets and for feline leukemia treatments. While acemannan is used orally, oral aloe vera itself can be dangerous and should not be used without veterinary supervision. Aloe should be used with care in cardiac patients.

Arnica

Arnica is one of the most commonly used herbs. Also known as leopard's bane, the active ingredients are sesquiterpene lactones. It is useful for reducing inflammation and pain. As part of those functions, arnica increases the activity of white blood cells, increases circulation, and improves wound healing. It is used topically for bruises and sore muscles. Arnica is quite toxic if ingested in its normal state. It is used as a dilute homeopathic medication to treat shock and trauma. If ingested at full strength, it can cause weakness and an increased heart rate. Remember that cats often lick off substances used topically!

Astragulus

Astragulus is an herb used to improve immune function. It is considered to be very safe and is sometimes added to regimens to treat viral infections and cancers. Astragulus does interact with some chemotherapy and immunotherapy medications, so always check with your veterinarian before giving this herb. In cats, this herb has been used as part of the treatment for hyperthyroidism. There is one species which is safe, but some are toxic, so always consult a skilled herbal medicine practitioner before using this herb.

Burdock

Burdock is used as a tonic for liver problems, to help with urinary problems, and for some cancer treatments. Burdock is felt to have some antioxidant properties. It can cause calcium oxalate crystals and stones in the bladder and urine if used incorrectly. This herb should be used with care in diabetic pets as it can affect the dose of insulin needed.

Chamomile

Known as a "tea" herbal treatment, chamomile has been used for nervous or fussy dogs. It may also be used topically for skin inflammation and "hot spots" (moist eczema). Chamomile has been touted as an herbal dewormer for some intestinal parasites. This is related to ragweed, so watch for any allergic responses.

Dandelion

Dandelion is primarily used as a tonic and as a diuretic. Dandelion does contain potassium, which makes it attractive as a mild diuretic. Allergic reactions may be noted. Beware of use in pets with gallbladder problems. Dandelion may lower blood glucose (sugar) so it should not be used in diabetics or patients with blood glucose problems. This is a plant that should not be used if growing near a road as it can absorb toxins from auto emissions.

Dong Quai

Dong quai is a volatile oil mix known for its hormonal effects. It is related to carrots and parsnips, so considered to be quite safe. It has been used as a tonic for post-whelping bitches and for dogs with chronic ailments.

Echinacea

Echinacea is a derivative of the purple coneflower. It has developed a wide following for use in viral infections (primarily colds) in people. It is also used for chronic upper respiratory problems in people. It is considered to be an immune stimulant with no direct bactericidal effects. Echinacea may interfere with some immunosuppressant drugs so it should be used with care in pets under treatment for immune problems. It is sometimes used topically on burns and chronic skin conditions. Echinacea may also be used as "mouthwash" for pets with gum problems. Historically echinacea has been used to treat snake bites as well.

Echinacea should not be used on pets with sunflower allergies or in patients with immune problems.

Slippery Elm

Slippery elm has been used to treat constipation and coughs, primarily in people. The outer bark can be toxic.

Ephedra

Ephedra is an herbal treatment used for asthma in people. It is *not* to be given to cats—since it has caused fatalities. This is a very powerful herb and should not be used without guidance, if at all. Short-term usage under supervision is recommended if ephedra is to be used for your pet. Pets with glaucoma, hyperthyroidism, and heart disease can all suffer serious consequences and it should not be used for them.

Garlic

Garlic has long been considered an adjunct to flea and parasite control in pets. Some feel it has antimicrobial properties as well as its parasticide qualities. Garlic is included in some arthritis treatments and for constipation. Garlic may be helpful in pets with cardiac disease as well. Garlic can cause serious problems if used long term or at high dosages and is falling somewhat out of favor. While gas is a minor side effect, anemia can be quite serious. Garlic may influence the dose of insulin needed for diabetes treatment so you should consult your veterinarian before using this herb on diabetic pets.

Ginger

Ginger has been used anecdotally in people for car sickness and to help with gas and diarrhea. It is felt that ginger may help with the nausea associated with some chemotherapy treatments in pets. Ginger also has anti-inflammatory effects and can be used as a treatment for arthritis. Extracts of ginger might interfere with blood clotting.

Gingko

Gingko has been a much-vaunted memory stimulant in people. This has been anecdotal so far. A major problem has been the differences in active ingredients between batches. Gingko may be used for some cardiac problems in pets and sometimes as part of the treatment for kidney problems. It has been associated with anticoagulation problems (bleeding disorders). Gingko seeds may be toxic.

Ginseng

Ginseng has a variety of uses. American ginseng is considered to be a tonic for women and older people. Siberian ginseng is felt to protect against the effects of stress. Ashwaganda is a strong Indian version. None of these should be used long term and it should be noted that many preparations are tinctures and so contain alcohol. Ginseng may decrease blood glucose (sugar) so it may conceivably be of use in diabetic pets. This would require careful veterinary supervision. Ginseng may interfere with digoxin levels.

Goldenseal

This herb is used in some cancer treatment regimens and also for gastritis (inflammation of the stomach). It can be made up as a "mouthwash" to use in pets with gum inflammation as well. If goldenseal is used for any length of time, your pet should be given additional vitamin-B complex as this herb can drain the body of these vitamins. Special care should be taken using this herb in cats. Goldenseal can have cardiac effects and should be used only under veterinary supervision for pets with heart problems.

Peppermint

Peppermint can be used to help treat vomiting or coughing in dogs. Ideally enteric-coated capsules should be given to prevent any localized irritation.

St. John's Wort

St. John's wort has gained fame for the treatment of depression and to a lesser extent arthritis. It can be extremely dangerous if combined with any other monoamine oxidase inhibitor and serotonin reuptake inhibitor (such as Prozac®). In pets, St. John's wort has been used for separation anxiety. It can cause photosensitization. There is less anecdotal information on this than some of the other herbs. St. John's wort may interfere with digoxin (for heart patients) and some other drugs. This herb should be used only under veterinary supervision.

Valerian

Valerian is sometimes used in dogs for behavior problems. This herb can be toxic if used long term and should not be a substitute for behavior modification. It should also not be combined with other sedative-acting medications. Some pets may show gastrointestinal upsets as a side effect.

CHAPTER 14

Nutraceuticals

———◆———

Nutraceuticals are substances that fall into a gray area between nutrition and drugs (medications). This group can include some vitamins and minerals as well as some rather unusual things like shark cartilage. Ideally, you are not covering up a deficiency in the diet with these substances but instead are supplementing to help treat medical conditions of varying severity.

Owing to their "gray area" status, nutraceuticals are not under FDA regulation in the strict fashion that drugs are. This means you need to be careful where you purchase these supplements and try to establish that processing and packaging are done well. You want to be sure that the dose and the quality are the same in each unit. This can be difficult to determine on your own, so ask friends and your veterinarian for reputable sources.

While most nutraceuticals are extremely safe, some can have dangerous side effects or should not be combined with certain medications. With some substances, "more is not better," and you don't want to upset the balance of nutrients your pet is receiving. *Always* check with your veterinarian before giving your pet any supplements, and make sure they are aware of all the medications and treatments your pet is receiving.

Alpha-Lipoic Acid

This is an antioxidant which is considered to be quite safe. It has been used to treat cataracts, glaucoma, and the polyneuropathy seen as a sequela to diabetes mellitus. Cats may salivate or become ataxic with this substance so it should probably not be used in cats.

Aminocaproic Acid

Aminocaproic acid is a supplement that has been used to help cases of degenerative myelopathy. This problem is well known among German shepherd dog fanciers with the older dogs who lose control of their rear ends. It is not a cure, but may slow the progress of the disease.

Arginine

Arginine is an essential amino acid which is found in many foods. It would be unusual for a pet to be deficient in this. It has been supplemented to boost the immune system and for cases of liver lipidosis and hepatic encephalopathy.

Biotin

Biotin is one of the water-soluble B vitamins. It works in energy metabolism and is considered to be important for healthy skin and hair. Pets often receive extra biotin in the form of brewer's yeast. This supplement has fallen a bit out of favor in recent years though it was once considered to be part of organic flea control. Biotin is bound up by raw egg whites so it should not be given with raw eggs (actually, feeding raw eggs is not a great idea anyway!). There is some question of biotin helping in cases of diabetes mellitus. (See also vitamins.)

Chondroitin Sulfate and Glucosamine

These two supplements are included here together as they are often combined in pet medications. Glucsoamine comes from shellfish and chondroitin is from animal cartilage. These are considered to be extremely useful in treating damaged joints and helping to repair cartilage.

Coenzyme Q

Coenzyme Q, also known as CoQ10 or ubiquinone, is a fat-soluble antioxidant that is present in virtually all of our pets' cells. It is important for cell energy usage and to decrease the presence of free radicals, which contribute to aging. Coenzyme Q is best known for its use as part of cardiac treatment regimens. It is used in congestive heart failure and may be useful for cardiomyopathy care.

Coenzyme Q has been shown to help decrease blood pressure, decrease the incidence of blood clots, and help to stabilize arrhythmias. Some feel it can help overweight pets with their weight loss programs as well. Coenzyme Q is best given with food and is a common supplement for older pets to help counteract aging.

L-Carnitine

L-carnitine is an amino acid that is important for energy metabolism. In people, carnitine has been touted as helping with weight loss and improving athletic performance. In dogs, it is used in treating hepatopathy in American cocker spaniels and it has become part of the "mainstream" treatment of dilated cardiomyopathy, especially in boxers, though it can be an expensive supplement. Other suggested uses are for hepatic lipidosis and cognitive disorders in dogs and cats.

Taurine

Taurine is an essential amino acid, which means that it is an important building block of the proteins in our pets' bodies. While dogs can manufacture this amino acid in their bodies, cats need an outside source of taurine. Taurine is found in animal tissues and is a requirement for feline nutrition.

A deficiency of taurine can lead to retinal degeneration and dilated cardiomyopathy in cats. While a true deficiency state has not been shown in dogs, American cocker spaniels who develop cardiomyopathy are also helped by treating them with taurine supplements.

Taurine is also important for pregnancy and growth so it is included in feline diets for kittens as well as adults. Cats on commercial feline diets should have adequate amounts present in their diets.

CHAPTER 15

Vitamins, Minerals, and Electrolytes

———◆———

Vitamins, minerals, and electrolytes are a group of substances that fall into the gray zone between nutrition and medicine just like nutraceuticals (and, in fact, some get classified as nutraceuticals). These are substances that our pets require for good health, even though the actual amounts may be quite small. Usually these are present in more than adequate amounts in commercial pet foods, but owners who supplement or feed home-cooked meals should be very aware of these substances. I recommend anyone doing a home diet should have the diet checked by a veterinary nutritionist to be sure all the essential ingredients are present and in balanced and proper amounts.

The amounts of certain vitamins and minerals are standardized for pets (at least cats and dogs) and those guidelines are used in manufacturing commercial pet foods.

Biotin

Biotin is one of the water-soluble B vitamins. It works in energy metabolism and is considered to be important for healthy skin and hair. Pets often receive extra biotin in the form of brewer's yeast. This supplement has fallen a bit out of favor in recent years though it was once considered to be part of organic flea control. Biotin is bound up by raw egg whites so it should not be given with raw eggs (actually, feeding raw eggs is not a great idea anyway!). There is some question of biotin helping in cases of diabetes mellitus. (See also nutraceuticals.)

Calcium

Calcium is a mineral that is extremely important for healthy bones, nerves, teeth, and muscle functions. In bone, calcium works in concert with phosphorus and the exact amounts need to be balanced carefully for different growth stages and for different species.

Calcium is present in many different foods, including dairy products and bones. If bone meal is used as a supplement, care should be taken to check lead levels. If calcium is being added to a diet, the chelated form is best absorbed but can be quite expensive. You should never add a calcium supplement (either calcium tablets or calcium in the form of dairy products or other sources) without consulting your veterinarian and/or a veterinary nutritionist. Calcium is *not* one of those substances where if a little is good a lot is better! Rabbits eating large amounts of calcium in the form of alfalfa can develop urinary crystals and stones.

Calcium tends to be low in our pets' diets only if the animals are eating an all-meat diet. Calcium levels in the blood may become low around whelping time and during nursing and sometimes secondary to kidney problems.

Calcium levels can become dangerously high if your pet has been exposed to the newer vitamin D–type rodenticides and with some types of cancers. If you feel your pet has been poisoned with one of these rodenticides, contact your veterinarian and the National Poison Control Center immediately! Expect a prolonged course of treatment to try and save your pet.

The use of calcium in the body is tied to vitamin D as well as phosphorus. In reptiles it is particularly important to be sure that your calcium and vitamin D sources are proper. Ideally consult with a veterinary nutritionist or a veterinarian with exotic experience when formulating a diet for any reptile.

Calcium interacts with many other minerals as well as some medications. It will decrease the absorption of the tetracycline and quinolone families of antibiotics. It may also interfere with absorption of chromium, iron, manganese, magnesium, and zinc.

Remember, never add a calcium supplement of any type without checking with your veterinarian or a veterinary nutritionist!

Choline

Choline is another component of the vitamin B complex. This is one of the few components that is derived from the liver, not from intestinal bacteria. Choline is important for nerve impulse transmission, in hormones, and in the healthy functioning of the liver and the gallbladder.

Choline has been included in the treatment regimens for seizures and cognitive functioning disorders. It may cause anemia if given in very high doses.

Some natural sources of choline are egg yolks, meat, milk, and soybeans.

Gold

Don't think of riches here! Gold is a mineral used to treat immune-mediated and autoimmune diseases including rheumatoid arthritis and pemphigus. It can be given either orally or via injection and is often combined with corticosteroids. Gold "beads" may be injected and left under the skin for long-term treatments.

Gold is not FDA approved for medical treatment in pets and pets do not have a health requirement for gold as they do for some of the other minerals. A test dose should be given to check for any reactions. Any pet receiving gold therapy should be watched for bone marrow changes and kidney problems.

Care should be taken when combining gold therapy with other medications. While it is compatible with corticosteroids, it can cause problems with drugs such as azathioprine, which might also be used for these immune-mediated diseases.

Overdosing with gold can lead to gastrointestinal problems, skin problems, kidney problems, and changes in the bone marrow. This is a mineral which should be used only under the guidance of your veterinarian.

Iodine

Iodine is a trace mineral that has multiple uses for our pets. It is an important part of the thyroid hormones and is also used as a disinfectant. Iodine both influences normal body functions and acts against outside infections and infestations.

Iodine in the povidone version is a disinfectant that is antiviral, antibacterial, and antifungal. It is used topically as a treatment for skin problems, including ringworm. The povidone version is less likely to cause skin irritation. Potassium iodine is sometimes used to treat chronic coughs.

As a radioactive element, iodine is used to treat cats suffering from hyperthyroidism. Iodine is present in many common foods and rarely needs to be added to a pet's diet. Care needs to be taken with the topical forms of iodine when treating large open wounds. In those cases, excess iodine may be absorbed and could cause thyroid problems. Excess iodine may be a factor with heavy use of supplements with kelp. Again, always check with your veterinarian or a veterinary nutritionist before adding any supplements to your pet's diet.

Common brand names for topicals:
  Xenodine
  Betadine

Magnesium

Magnesium is a mineral that is important for bone formation and maintenance and that also influences the movement of calcium into and out of cells. Heart function is influenced by magnesium and there is some feeling that it could be useful for treating epilepsy and diabetes mellitus.

Magnesium, like so many other minerals, is influenced by some medications and by other minerals. Magnesium supplements should be used only under the guidance of your veterinarian or a veterinary nutritionist.

Manganese

Manganese is a mineral that functions mainly as an antioxidant. It is used as part of some arthritis treatment regimens and helps glycosaminoglycans be processed into glucosamine. Manganese may be influenced by other minerals.

Potassium

Potassium is an electrolyte that is very important for the proper functioning of cells, including the heart muscle cells. While potassium is normally adequate in the diets of our pets, pets with renal failure and pets taking certain diuretics may need supplemental potassium. Bananas are a good natural source but pills may be easier for most pets.

Side effects of the improper amount of potassium can range from gastrointestinal signs to life-threatening changes in heart rates. Cats with urinary blockages can develop seriously high levels of potassium and need emergency treatment.

Many pets that suffer from epilepsy are currently being treated with potassium bromide. This antiseizure medication may be used alone or to reduce the dosage of drugs such as phenobarbital. Potassium bromide is not being used for cats, but only in dogs at this time. Potassium bromide should be used only under the direct guidance of your veterinarian.

Selenium

Selenium is a trace mineral that works with vitamin E as an antioxidant and an important aid to glutathione peroxidase. Selenium has been used in the treatment protocols for pancreatitis, heart disease, and thyroid problems. It may decrease shedding (probably due to its thyroid influences). Some feel it is an aid in preventing cancers. Selenium requirements in the diet may increase if your pet is on long-term corticosteroids.

Natural sources of selenium include wheat germ, nuts, eggs, liver, and fish. Selenium can be toxic if given in large doses. Signs can range from hair and nail loss to nervous behaviors and even acute death. Selenium supplementation should be done only under the guidance of your veterinarian or a veterinary nutritionist.

Sodium

Sodium is an essential mineral that we most commonly think of as salt—sodium chloride. Sodium and chloride act together to help in maintaining the proper fluid balance in our pets (and ourselves!). Sodium may need to be limited in pets with heart problems. Too much sodium or too little can lead to toxicities.

Sodium is also used medically as sodium bicarbonate to treat acidosis in pets, as well as hypercalcemia (too much calcium) and hyperpotassium (too much potassium). This should be done only under the guidance of your veterinarian, as serious side effects can occur, including too little calcium or potassium.

Sodium also may interact with many drugs, especially in the sodium bicarbonate form, which changes the pH of the body fluids. Again, this is a medication which should be used only under close veterinary guidance and supervision.

Vitamin A

Vitamin A is an essential fat-soluble vitamin. Dogs can manufacture this from carotene but cats cannot so they need a dietary source of vitamin A itself. Vitamin A is well recognized for being important for vision, antioxidation, reproduction, and to aid in cancer therapies.

Vitamin A is present in many animal tissues including liver, fish oils such as cod liver oil, and green foods like alfalfa. Many people feel that the synthetic retinoids (not exactly like vitamin A but very close) are safer. All versions should be given with a fatty meal.

Vitamin A is definitely a vitamin that should not be overdosed. Side effects can include dry eye syndromes such as keratitis sicca, gastrointestinal signs, and decreased appetite in cats. Pets taking drugs that could potentially damage the liver and pets taking tetracycline are at risk for problems, as are diabetics. Vitamin A supplements should be given only under the guidance of your veterinarian.

True overdosing with vitamin A can lead to bone malformations and fractures, dwarfism, anemia, and skin problems. Supplementation is not recommended for pregnant pets as this can cause problems with the developing fetuses. Puppies and kittens do not need vitamin A supplements either.

Vitamin A has actually been used as a medicine for some problems. American cocker spaniels may show a skin problem which responds to vitamin A treatment (this is not a true deficiency). Sebaceous adenitis, another skin problem, is also sometimes treated with vitamin A, as is idiopathic seborrhea.

Vitamin B Complex

The term "vitamin B" covers a large complex of substances (including biotin and choline—mentioned previously). The separate components may have both numbers and names. These are all water-soluble vitamins so it is difficult to overdose them (pets can just urinate the extra out as opposed to fat-soluble vitamins where the extra may be stored in fat tissues and cause problems). Most B vitamins are manufactured by intestinal bacteria.

VITAMIN B₁ (THIAMIN)

Thiamin is important for processing nutrients and is involved in making ATP—an energy source for cells. Brain cells, smooth muscle tone, and circulatory tissues all depend heavily on thiamin.

Deficiency of this vitamin is rare in pets on commercial diets. Previously when some cats ate only raw fish, they would develop neurologic signs, including ataxia, holding the neck down, and seizures. Thiamin is present in many green plants, including alfalfa and spirulina. Pets on diuretics may need some thiamin supplementation.

Thiamin has been included in treatment regimens for epilepsy and cognitive function disorders in older pets.

VITAMIN B₂ (RIBOFLAVIN)

Riboflavin is important as a coenzyme (assisting enzyme function), for healthy red blood cells, and for the production of antibodies. It can be found in dairy products, egg yolks, alfalfa, and organ meats. Most pets receive plenty of riboflavin in their food.

VITAMIN B₃ (NIACIN)

Niacin is an important vitamin for healthy skin and nails (claws). It may be combined with tetracycline to treat some immune problems such as pemphigus and lupus. Cats have a very strict requirement for niacin.

If very high levels of niacin are given, side effects may be seen. These can include itching, skin disorders, bloody feces and seizures. Care should be taken in giving niacin supplements to pets with liver inflammation.

Previously, niacin deficiency was seen in some animals. Deficiency causes a syndrome called pellagra or black tongue. Animals would show skin problems, diarrhea, dementia, and eventually death. Niacin deficiency is rarely seen nowadays with pets on commercial diets. Sources of niacin include nuts, seeds, turkey, and milk.

VITAMIN B₅ (PANTOTHENIC ACID)

Pantothenic acid is considered to be an "antistress" vitamin. It is found in organ meats and is present in commercial diets.

VITAMIN B₆ (PYRIDOXINE)

Pyridoxine is strictly required by cats. It is important for water regulation in the body and red blood cell production. It helps to inhibit homocysteine, which affects the heart. It is currently being tried as part of the regimen for treating pets with kidney failure. Pets on seizure medications or theophylline may need some supplementation.

Pyridoxine is found in yeast, beans, and legumes and is present in commercial diets.

VITAMIN B₁₂ (CYANOCOBOLAMINE)

Cyanocobolamine is important for red blood cells and in preventing anemia. It is felt that pets taking stomach acid medications may need a vitamin B_{12} supplement. Normally there is plenty of vitamin B_{12} in commercial diets. Food sources include animal tissues, eggs, and organ meats.

FOLIC ACID/FOLATE

This B vitamin is well known for its importance in human prenatal care. It is essential for the healthy function and development of the nervous system. Supplementation must be done with care in pets receiving any seizure medications. It is present in adequate amounts in most commercial diets and can be found in yeast, legumes, such as peas, and fish.

Vitamin C (Ascorbic Acid)

Vitamin C is a required vitamin for the health of rainbow trout, Coho salmon, guinea pigs, the red breasted bulbul (a bird), and primates (including man). Most of our pets do not require any supplemental vitamin C.

Vitamin C is important as an antioxidant and for collagen and tissues. It has been used as part of arthritis treatment regimens and included as part of the treatment for copper toxicity. Ester C is the chelated mix most often used for arthritis treatments.

It is currently being questioned as to whether or not vitamin C is truly an effective urinary acidifier. It is felt that too much vitamin C might increase the risk of certain urinary stones such as urates and oxalates. Gastrointestinal problems can also arise from high doses.

Vitamin C is water soluble, so it should not accumulate in the body. Many dog breeders feel supplementing vitamin C helps prevent hip dysplasia but that has not been shown. In contrast it has been questioned if too much vitamin C might make bones osteoporotic. As with most things, moderation is the safest and makes the most sense.

Vitamin C is present in most fruits and many vegetables. Guinea pigs should receive guinea pig pellets which have vitamin C added, but since the vitamin is not stable for long periods of time, fresh foods such as berries, fruits, and vegetables should be given daily or the guinea pig should receive a chewable vitamin C tablet once or twice weekly. Guinea pigs can develop full-blown scurvy if they do not receive enough vitamin C, and ill guinea pigs seem to recover faster if supplemented with an injection or two as well as the fresh foods.

Vitamin C is often used with vitamin E as a fat preservative/antioxidant in pet foods.

Vitamin D

Vitamin D tends to work in partnership with calcium and phosphorus to help build healthy bones. Ultraviolet light (sunlight) is an important part of this partnership as well. Reptile owners, particularly iguana owners, need to consult their veterinarian, a veterinary nutritionist, or an experienced herpetologist to be sure they have the diet and cage setup done correctly for these pets.

Sources of vitamin D include fish liver oil, dairy products, and liver. Pets are rarely deficient (see reptile note above, though), but deficiency is marked by rickets (deformed bones).

Vitamin D in the form calcitriol is used in the treatment of pets who lost all or part of their parathyroid during thyroid surgery and sometimes as part of the treatment regimen for pets with chronic kidney disease.

This is another of those vitamins where just the right amount is the best. Overdosing with vitamin D can mimic some of the newer rodenticides and also cause neurologic signs, bone problems, and soft tissue mineralization. Do not give a vitamin D supplement unless you are under the guidance of your pet's veterinarian or a veterinary nutritionist.

Vitamin E (Tocopherol)

Vitamin E is a fat-soluble vitamin and an antioxidant. It is often combined with vitamin C as a fat preservative/antioxidant in pet foods.

Vitamin E also works in concert with selenium. Deficiency of both can cause "white muscle disease"—a weakness that may lead to death. This is seen more commonly in ruminants that our usual pet animals.

Vitamin E has been used in treating immune problems, exocrine pancreatic insufficiency (lack of pancreatic enzymes to digest food), for some skin problems, and as part of the treatment of cognitive function disorder in older pets. Vitamin E should be given a couple of hours before or after meals.

Care should be taken using vitamin E in pets with any clotting problems and, if it comes in a preparation with selenium, to avoid selenium toxicity. Food sources include dark leafy vegetables, liver, and eggs.

Vitamin K

Vitamin K has several components—the best known being K_1 or phytonadione. In most pets, adequate amounts of this vitamin are made by the intestinal bacteria. Pets with malabsorption or maldigestion syndromes or severe liver problems may need supplementation.

Vitamin K is also used in the treatment of anticoagulant overdoses, including the new rodenticides. Pets can be poisoned by these rodenticides by eating the rodenticide itself or in some cases eating the poisoned mice or rats. Treatment may be for prolonged periods of time to prevent clotting problems. The oral vitamin K should ideally be given with a fatty meal. Legumes are a natural food source of vitamin K.

There are many drug interactions with vitamin K, and this should be given only under the guidance of your veterinarian.

Zinc

Zinc is an essential trace mineral, which can be toxic in high levels. Zinc itself is used to treat copper poisoning, but it should not be supplemented without veterinary guidance.

Zinc has been used in the treatment of immune problems and is important for healthy skin and hair. A zinc-responsive dermatosis occurs in Siberian huskies and Malamutes. The acrodermatitis in bull terriers may also respond to zinc treatment, though injections may be needed if oral medications are not working. Diabetic pets may need a little extra zinc in their diets as well.

Zinc should be given with food but not dairy products, as calcium and zinc interfere with each other's absorption. Some medications are also affected by zinc supplementation. This mineral should be supplemented only under the guidance of your veterinarian or a veterinary nutritionist.

PART III

Caring for Your Pet

CHAPTER 16

Choosing the Right Vet for Your Pet

◆

Choosing a veterinarian can be as involved or as simple as you want. Many people are happy going with the closest veterinary clinic they can find in the phone book or the least expensive clinic in town. To truly be a partner in your pet's health care, however, you need to do a bit of research.

Many states have certification programs for veterinary clinics and sometimes even programs to verify continuing education for individual veterinarians. On a national scale, the American Animal Hospital Association (AAHA) is renowned for its strict standards for its member hospitals. You may not have any AAHA clinics in your area, and many noncertified clinics are still exceptional (they just may not have all the "extras" of an AAHA hospital), but the AAHA hospital listing can be an excellent place to start your search for a veterinarian.

If you just have cats, you may choose a feline-only practice. If your household has a little of everything from birds to dogs to cats, you want a practice that has experience in exotics. There are even some hospitals now that specialize in birds, reptiles, ferrets, and small "pocket pets" such as mice and guinea pigs. Veterinarians with exotic experience may be the hardest to find—your local zoo may be able to give you some references. You may even end up with multiple veterinary hospitals on your list just so you can cover all your pets!

Ideally each pet should have a relationship at one clinic. This way the records are all up to date and a complete record is kept with all of your pet's problems over their lifetime, any medications they have taken, and all their diagnostic test results. All of my animals have records at our clinic including referral forms returned by specialists when they have needed care outside our hospital. I can quickly check out vaccination histories, medication histories, and all laboratory work done on my pets. If you use one veterinary clinic for vaccines and a different one for an ill pet, you may not have a complete medical history in any one place. This can lead to dangerous health problems if you mix medications or forget important health history information. If you have a referral to a specialist, they should always send a full report back to your "home" clinic to keep your pet's records up to date and complete.

When investigating veterinary hospitals, you need to decide what is most important to you. Are you in some tough financial times and simply want the best you can get for the least cost? Is Fido as dear to you as any human family members and you have no financial considerations? Will the clinic of your choice accept a variety of payment options including a payment schedule or pet health insurance? Many clinics will make payment arrangements for their regular clients, but you may have to earn that privilege.

Is travel difficult for you or your pet? If you live in an area with rough winters, can you travel twenty or more miles in bad weather? Does your pet routinely get carsick or get upset traveling in a car? Factors such as these can help you to choose between two clinics that you like.

Do you prefer a "homey" atmosphere, or do you want an efficient clinical atmosphere? If you have a cat, do you want a separate area for your cat to wait in or can your cat handle hanging out with the dogs?

Are you comfortable with a general practitioner, or do you feel having a specialist available is important to you? While only a few clinics may have a specialist on hand at all times, most clinics now have access to specialists— either visiting their practice on a regular basis or as referrals. If you feel strongly about alternative medicine options, you need to find a veterinarian who has that expertise. If you are a breeder, you may want to be associated with a clinic that has a solid reputation for reproductive work, possibly even freezing semen.

The truly important features you need in a clinic are competent care, cleanliness, and good communication. Cleanliness should be a given, but check to see that examination tables are cleaned between each pet. Doctors and staff should wash their hands between pets as well. There should not be urine or stool in the exam rooms or the waiting area. Any instruments used on your pet should be clean (as in otoscope heads) or new (as in new syringes for any injections).

Competent care can be more difficult to judge at first. Ask about the continuing education of the doctors and staff (there may be certificates on the walls). Check with other people who use or have used this clinic to see if they are satisfied with the care their pets have received. When your pet has a problem, do some homework yourself so you can ask relevant questions and see if your veterinarian offers more information. Not every veterinarian will be an expert in every area, but your veterinarian should offer to look into problems for you if she isn't familiar with your pet's illness. A competent veterinarian will not feel threatened by your desire for a second opinion or a referral to a specialist. Many clinics will provide client education handouts on everything ranging from housebreaking your puppy to urinary problems in cats.

Some clinics are basically outpatient care only and will not have full facilities such as a surgical suite or radiograph (x-ray) equipment on site. While some mobile clinics come quite well equipped, many will refer you to nearby veterinary hospitals for involved care or advanced diagnostics.

Communication is extremely important. If your veterinarian does not have the time to answer your questions or is not willing to answer your questions, you need to look elsewhere. You should not feel intimidated by your veterinarian, and your veterinarian should be willing to research some health questions for you if he or she does not know the answer immediately. Ideally your veterinarian will be able to explain health situations in easy terms so you know what is going on with your pet. Your veterinarian should be comfortable with your pet and appear to enjoy your pet (though this can be strained with an aggressive pet!). The veterinarian should have a genuine interest in and love for animals as well as a strong medical background. Don't hesitate to ask questions or even ask your veterinarian to write things down for you. If you need to, write down any questions you have ahead of time and bring the notebook or paper with you.

You should get clear estimates of any procedures that need to be done (though realize that an estimate is just that—a best guess at the costs involved. Unexpected findings on surgery can add quite a bit to a bill, for example.) Make sure you understand the costs involved and always leave a way to be reached if decisions need to be made partway through treatment.

The staff at a veterinary hospital is very important as well. Everyone, from receptionists to veterinary technicians to kennel staff, should be willing and able to help you and your pet. People who genuinely care about animals are more important to your pet's care than amenities like coffee and doughnuts in the waiting area.

Emergency coverage can be done in a number of ways. Your clinic may cover all of its own emergencies. The plus to this setup is that you know where to go and the complete records for your pet are available. The minus is that the veterinarian on call may be exhausted and not at his best. Many clinics will cover only the emergencies of their own established clients.

Coverage for emergencies may be provided by an emergency clinic. These clinics are staffed overnight and on weekends and have a fresh, full-time staff available. They can be more expensive and they won't have your pet's full medical history available, so your responsibility in being up to date on your pet's care is greater. Emergency clinics often require payment up front since they don't have a steady relationship with you as a client. If your clinic has an arrangement with an emergency group, make sure you know the correct phone numbers and clear directions to get there.

Another emergency coverage situation is when veterinary hospitals in an area cover emergencies for each other. So if your pet has an emergency on Monday, you might be referred to clinic B, on Tuesday to your own clinic, etc. Again, you need to be sure you know what phone numbers to call in an emergency and make sure that you have clear directions and understand any payment arrangements. These clinics will often not have access to your pet's records, and again, you must be on top of your pet's healthcare history.

Today some veterinary hospitals have websites, newsletters, and possibly even allow e-mail questions to their doctors. If those items are important to you, ask when you call.

Things to consider in choosing a clinic:

Finances
Travel distance
Availability of specialists
Atmosphere and "petside manner"
Alternative options such as herbs, acupuncture, etc.
Cleanliness
Competent care
Communication
Emergency coverage

CHAPTER 17

Preventative Health Care for Your Pet

———◆———

The goal of preventative health care is to keep your pets so healthy and happy that they don't ever need most of the medications in this book. Proper diet, along with regular exercise, lots of loving attention, and good health care combine to give animals long, healthy lives.

Real preventative health care starts even before you acquire your pet. If you are planning on purchasing a purebred pet, the breeder can give you a big leg up on health care by screening their breeding stock carefully. Inherited health problems can appear in any animal from any source (and that includes mixed breeds, contrary to popular belief). The plus to a purebred pet is that the inherited health problems are becoming well known for certain breeds and pet owners have united for research to screen for these problems.

An example here is the Norwegian forest cat. Dedicated owners learned that their cats have the possibility of suffering from hip dysplasia. There is now a set procedure and a registry (the Orthopedic Foundation for Animals) which certifies cats free of this problem. So your cat can get a radiographic exam (x-rays) of the pelvis. If the hip joints appear normal, the cat receives an OFA certification number. If both parents are certified free of hip dysplasia, the likelihood of any kittens being dysplastic is greatly reduced.

Most purebred dog breeds have certain genetic defects that reputable breeders screen their breeding stock for—helping to reduce the incidence of that problem in their breed. Do your homework! Learn what problems may be common in a breed you like and then be sure the parents of any pet you want to purchase have been screened. I have Belgian Tervurens and I expect the parents of any puppy I purchase to be free of hip and elbow dysplasia, clear of any eye problems, and be seizure free themselves (unfortunately there is no test for epilepsy at this time).

If you are adding a house bunny to your home and going to a breeder, again you need to do your research. Lop bunnies seem prone to bite problems, so check that the parents are normal as well as inspecting the bite on your new rabbit. Other rabbit breeds can have similar predispositions.

With reptiles and birds, you always hope to find captive-bred parents and hand-raised babies, if possible. Check that the source of your new pet is clean and the animals all seem healthy, clean, and well fed. Try to avoid very unusual species that might be endangered in the wild and that don't have well-established diets and care regimens.

If possible, try to meet both parents of your new pet. This may not always work out as shipping semen is becoming more common for dogs and cats, but you should at least get to meet the mother. Observe her personality as well as evaluating her health. A healthy but mentally unstable pet is no fun either.

A reputable breeder will back up their pets and will also be a mentor, helping you with any questions or problems that come along in the life of your pet.

Beware of "new, unusual, rare, or highly exotic" claims. Often these pets are genetic freaks and not normal animals at all. This includes rare "teacup" dogs that may not be very healthy or mutant amphibians with extra limbs.

Having said all that, you may choose to adopt a pet from your local humane society or animal shelter. The same basic rules apply. Look for a clean facility, with animals that are clean and well fed. Obviously some of these animals may not look their best if they were strays, but you can evaluate the care. Try to avoid the pull on your heartstrings from the animal cowering in the corner or the ill animal. These pets may come with a boatload of problems that you may or may not be prepared for—both emotionally and financially.

So let's assume you chose a healthy pet to start with. Where do you go from there? For any new pet (that includes birds, pocket pets, and reptiles), a physical examination to check for any problems and stool sample (fecal) check should be routine. Try to get a diet sample from the breeder or store where you purchased your pet so you don't upset your pet's eating habits. Make sure you have clear information about what to feed your pet. This can be very crucial especially with some reptiles, whose diets change over their lifetimes. New canines may need a heartworm test and cats may need screening for feline leukemia. Pet birds may need fecal checks and screening for chlamydia. Check with your veterinarian about any special testing they feel is important for that particular animal. Your veterinarian can also guide you on basic care for your new addition.

Think about identification for your pet. Clear photos can be used to identify a lost pet, but even more importantly, dogs and cats that go outside need some identification. A tattoo or a microchip provide permanent identification—allowing you to prove an animal is a member of your family and helping to trace your pet back to you if he gets lost. There are clinics for tattoos and microchipping at many pet events or ask your veterinarian or local shelter. You must register your microchip or tattoo for it to work in helping to trace your pet.

Collars and identification tags are important, too. They are an easy way for someone who finds a lost pet to contact you. In some states, lost pets who are turned into shelters get a longer time in the shelter if they have an obvious identification on them—tags, tattoo, or microchip. That buys your pet time while you are diligently searching. Of course, best of all is not to lose your pet and to keep it leashed. (See "Leash=Love=Life," on page 235.)

House Rabbit and Pocket Pets

Make sure you have a safe setup for your new bunny. That means a cage where she can be confined for her safety and the safety of your home. Rabbits are social creatures, however, and don't do well locked away in a back room. Make sure your rabbit gets plenty of time out free with you. Rabbits need exercise to stay fit and trim. Most rabbits don't do well staying on wire cages for long periods of time. Their feet can develop very bad sores. If your cage is wire bottomed, make sure there is a resting area where Bunny can lie down or sit on something solid. Rabbits can be easily litter trained and given more freedom in your house. Just bunny-proof carefully, especially for wires!

Pocket pets can vary in their cage requirements and their social needs. Cages should be kept clean with fresh water available at all times. Do *not* use cedar chips for bedding as the volatile oils can cause liver problems in many of these animals. Hamsters often do best alone, while rats may enjoy companions.

Discuss spaying and neutering for both rabbits and some of the pocket pets with your veterinarian to prevent unwanted pregnancies and to avoid some health problems. This can be especially important for female rabbits, and if you want to have more than one house bunny, there are fewer behavior problems if the rabbits are spayed or neutered.

There are not established vaccines for pet rabbits or pocket pets at this time. They should all be screened for both internal and external parasites and be sure you are feeding a correct diet. Rabbits should get some real hay, and most of these animals do best on a varied diet with fresh food added in. Guinea pigs need a dietary source of vitamin C—this can be drops, chewable vitamin C tablets, or plenty of fresh fruits and vegetables. Too many seeds or nuts can make some of these animals quite pudgy.

Birds

Birds also need safe cages for when they are confined. Make sure the cage is large enough and of safe materials so that if your bird chews on it, there won't be health problems. Cages, including perches, should be cleaned frequently. Birds often do best with more than one perch and perches of different sizes. Do not use sandpaper-covered perches as these can irritate the feet. As mentioned above, cedar chips are not safe for bedding materials.

Temperature and humidity considerations are important for pet birds. Make sure your birds are warm enough and not in drafts.

Birds are uniquely sensitive to many toxic fumes, including those given off when nonstick-coated pans are overheated. Insecticide sprays and cigarette smoke (cigar smoke too!) can cause respiratory problems in birds.

Many birds will be happiest with toys or nesting sites in their cages. Check out the special requirements of the birds you chose. Some birds will have sensitive temperature and humidity requirements as well.

Birds also vary in their need for companionship. Many do fine with human company, but some birds such as the finches, need fellow birds to be happy. Taking on a large pscittacine such as an Amazon parrot may be a lifetime commitment. Many of these birds live forty or fifty years, and they do not do well unless they have plenty of human attention.

Vaccines have been developed for use in pet birds. You need to check with your veterinarian about whether your specific bird needs any vaccines.

Diets can also vary a great deal between bird species. Most birds do not do well on a steady diet of seeds, and you need to be sure you are meeting your bird's nutritional needs. Remember that, if your bird is moulting or laying eggs, the dietary requirements will change somewhat. Most birds require some fresh fruit or vegetables and they may need added vitamins during times of stress.

Regular physical examinations along with any laboratory work your veterinarian feels is necessary will go a long way toward keeping your bird healthy.

Reptiles

You need to know suitable cage size, type of cage, and temperature and humidity requirements for your pet. Many reptiles require special lighting to simulate the UV rays of the sun. Be sure you have the correct setup for your species. Cages need regular cleaning, and you should be careful about the bedding used. Corn cob and cedar shavings can cause problems. Newspapers (especially if you can get rolls without any ink) are often the safest cage substrate. Remember that many reptiles will need "hiding houses" for privacy and be sure you provide fresh water.

People tend to forget how large some of these reptiles can grow. A boa constrictor can be quite cute at twelve inches but at six feet you may run out of space. Most zoos are already full with reptiles and can't take in people's "outgrown" pets. As always, think *before* you purchase a pet!

There is a wide range of diet and habitat requirements in reptiles. Snakes often do well fed whole prey such as mice, but iguanas have dietary requirements that vary throughout their lifetime. We still don't really know the exact dietary requirements for most species, so you really need to research a reptile pet carefully and thoroughly.

There are currently no vaccines for pet reptiles, but screening for parasites is always important, especially with any wild caught animals.

Salmonella is a health problem that appears from time to time with pet reptiles. This is a bacteria that can pass to people (a zoonosis). While salmonella is present on the skin of many reptiles, keeping the housing for your pet reptile clean and practicing good personal hygiene such as washing your hands after handling your turtle can greatly reduce the risk of this problem.

There are now well established protocols for preventative care for dogs and cats. We will look at those here.

Dogs

Any dog, young or old, being added to your household should have a fecal (stool) exam done. There are parasites that are zoonoses (spread from animals to people) as well as interfering with the health and growth of your companion. A yearly fecal check is a good idea. Ideally any new dog being added to your family should have a check for external parasites too. It is much better to bathe Fido on his way to your house and get rid of the fleas than to discover them after he has settled in for a day or two and left flea eggs in your house!

Heartworm has spread throughout much of the United States now. All dogs should have a blood test to detect heartworm infection and then go on a preventative schedule as worked out with your veterinarian. This will vary with the area of the country you live in, with the weather a factor, since heartworm is spread by mosquitoes.

Good nutrition and grooming are important. If you keep your dog healthy and clean, it will be less attractive to external parasites. You may need flea and tick preventative medications, depending on the area you live in. Twice-yearly trips to the local groomer for a shave down may cover most of your grooming duties or you may need to brush out your pet daily.

Spaying or neutering should be part of every dog's life unless you are a knowledgable breeder (or under the guidance of someone who is) or are showing your dog in conformation. Spaying removes the hassles of heat periods, reduces the chances of your bitch ever getting breast cancer, and saves her from ever getting uterine infections or cancers. Neutering makes male dogs less likely to roam (with fewer chances of getting hit by cars or in fights), less likely to lift their leg to urinate and usually better with other dogs. It also saves them from testicular cancers. There are *way* too many unwanted pets in the United States, and you don't want to contribute to the overpopulation problem!

Vaccinations are an important part of your pet's health care. Rabies vaccination is required in virtually every state and country. Most areas require a first vaccination at twelve to twenty-four weeks of age, followed by a booster a year later, then boosters every three years. Rabies is a fatal disease that can be spread to humans, and this vaccine should be in every owner's health plan for their dogs.

Once we move beyond rabies, the waters tend to muddy a bit. Distemper is a serious, usually fatal virus that infects dogs. Generally puppies receive a series of three to four distemper shots (usually in combinations) from eight to eighteen weeks of age. The reason for a series of vaccines is that you want to make sure the puppy gets a dose after the maternal immunity has worn off and when his own immune system has kicked in. Traditionally, the pups have then gotten a booster a year later and annually for life. At the time of this writing, that booster schedule is being questioned. Some owners are electing to check titers (using blood samples) and vaccinating only when needed to increase the immune response. Other owners are going with every three years on booster vaccinations. You need to discuss this with your veterinarian and customize the vaccine schedule for your pet. A pet who travels extensively may have a different vaccination schedule than a dog who rarely leaves home. Young dogs and older dogs may have different regimens.

These questions about when and how often to vaccinate come up for virtually every canine vaccine with the exception of rabies, which is mandated by law. Be prepared to discuss this with your veterinarian so that your pet is kept safe.

Parvo is another virus that can have serious effects on dogs. It can be fatal in young pups, causing either a severe vomiting and diarrhea problem with blood loss included, or even a rapid heart failure called cardiomyopathy. Older dogs can become quite ill as well, especially if they get dehydrated. The vaccine for parvo is often combined with the distemper vaccine and given on the same schedule. Some breeders and veterinarians will separate it out and vaccinate for this problem every other week in puppies, alternating with distemper. The questions about frequency of boosters in adult dogs have arisen here too. Consult with your veterinarian as to the best schedule for vaccinations for your pet.

While virtually everyone agrees that dogs need to be vaccinated for distemper, rabies, and parvo, the other vaccines often included or offered may be more optional. Hepatitis (or adenovirus) is not seen that commonly but can be serious in young pups. Parainfluenza virus and *Bordetella bronchiseptica*, a bacteria, are both involved in the canine cough syndrome (sometimes called kennel cough). These vaccines may not be necessary unless your pet travels, is boarded, is groomed outside the home, or competes with other dogs. These vaccines may be automatically included in your dog's booster, though. I might add that one version of the *Bordetella* vaccine comes in an intranasal form so don't be surprised if your veterinarian puts drops in your pet's nose!

Corona virus and the protozoa *Giardia* both now have vaccines. Unless your dog is having a problem with these gastrointestinal diseases, you probably don't need to vaccinate for them. Sometimes local water supplies can become infected with *Giardia*, or if your dog goes camping in the wilderness, you may want this vaccine for protection if she drinks from streams in the woods.

Leptospirosis is a spirochaete that can cause kidney or liver problems. It has a variety of serovars (sort of like species), and a vaccine against one serovar does not seem to protect against the others. Technically called a bacterin since it is not a virus, the vaccine for Leptospirosis is the main cause of allergic reactions in dogs to vaccinations. Since this was not a widespread disease problem, many veterinarians and pet owners stopped using this bacterin. Leptospirosis is a zoonosis (disease that can be passed to people), however, and recent outbreaks of new serovars in the Northeast has caused people to rethink this position. A new vaccine is out that uses only a subunit of the Leptospirosis (so it should cause fewer reactions), and which has been designed to cover the newer serovars. You need to discuss the use of this vaccine with your veterinarian.

The Lyme disease vaccine carries some controversy with it also. Protection does not seem to be complete so dogs who have had the Lyme vaccine may still get the disease. They seem to get a milder form, but they can still show clinical signs. Most veterinarians will treat a dog with signs of Lyme disease, even if it has been vaccinated, so some veterinarians and pet owners are electing to pass on this vaccine. Again, check with your veterinarian about the incidence of Lyme disease and ticks in your area and whether vaccinating for this makes sense for your dog.

While these vaccination guidelines may seem quite loose, it has become standard to customize the vaccination schedules of our pets. Different dogs will have different disease exposures and need different types of protection. It makes sense to provide all the protection our pets need, but not overstress their immune systems.

Good nutrition, plenty of exercise, and lots of attention and training are important to keep your dog fit and happy. Dogs are social animals and don't do well if they are left alone for long periods of time. Fresh water should be available at all times and dogs need shade in hot weather and protection from wet and wind in cold weather.

An annual physical examination (possibly twice yearly for older dogs) is one of the best preventative care plans you can have. Ideally I suggest that pet owners go over their pets themselves once a week (possibly while you are grooming) to see if you find any new lumps, bumps, or problems. This includes lifting up the ears on a drop-eared dog and checking the mouth gently for any problems.

If health problems are noted early on, they almost always have a better chance of being easy and less expensive to treat. Your veterinarian may suggest blood tests and urinalyses for older dogs, possibly even an EKC (electrocardiogram). While some aging problems cannot be cured, if they are caught early, you can slow down their progression and give your pet a longer life of quality time.

Cats

Cats have flown to the top of pet popularity charts. They are easy-to-care-for pets for people on the go, not needing daily walks and not as socially demanding as a dog.

Perhaps one of the biggest preventative care programs you can do for your cat is to make it an indoor-only cat (or outside only on leash with you, or in a screened enclosure). Free-ranging cats have a high incidence of being hit by cars, attacked by other animals, and contracting serious illnesses. Feline longevity increases dramatically if cats are kept inside.

Any new cat, kitten or adult, should have a fecal test done to screen for internal parasites. Some of these such as the ascarids are zoonoses and care must be taken to treat for these parasites and practice good hygiene in cleaning the litterbox.

All cats should be tested for feline leukemia and feline immunodeficiency virus. Both of these tests can be done with a small blood sample—often right in your veterinarian's office. If your new feline companion tests positive for either of these viruses, you need to have a frank discussion with your veterinarian about prognosis, possible treatments, the chance of spread to any other cats you might own, and the fact that these problems are basically noncurable. (Some cats' own immune systems seem able to throw off the feline leukemia virus, but we have not managed to accomplish that with veterinary medicine yet.)

As with any new pet, a quick check for external parasites is important too. A flea bath *before* your new kitty comes home is much better in the long run for all of you than discovering fleas a day later! Depending on the situation with any other pets (who may go in and out), your cat may need some flea and tick protection. Discuss this with your veterinarian.

As with dogs, spaying and neutering should be part of every cat's life unless you are a knowledgable breeder (or under the guidance of someone who is) or are planning to show your cat in conformation (and there are some classes for spayed and neutered cats). Spaying relieves your cat of the hassles of heat periods, reduces her chances of getting breast cancer, and totally saves her from uterine cancers or infections. Neutering greatly decreases the likelihood of a male cat spraying urine in the house and lessens the chances for fights. Please remember the pet overpopulation problem!

Vaccinations are an important part of your cat's care. Cats are somewhat of a "sentinel species" (meaning they develop problems before other species) for vaccinations. Vaccination schedules for cats have been reduced recently and may continue to be adjusted. This reduction in vaccinations is a response to some vaccine-related cancers that appeared in cats. Some cats are apparently sensitive to the adjuvants (substances added to vaccines to increase the immune response and make the vaccine more effective) and developed sarcomas at injection sites. Vaccine manufacturers have acted very responsibly to reduce these and change their vaccines.

So what vaccines does your cat really need? Rabies is required by law, even for cats that are totally indoor kitties. Most states suggest a first vaccine at three to six months, followed by a booster a year later, then boosters every three years. Remember that bats do sometimes get into houses, and if they test positive for rabies, your cat must be strictly confined (sometimes boarded) for up to six months or euthanised if she is not current on her rabies vaccine. Rabies can be spread to humans and is fatal in cats and people so this is not a vaccine to avoid.

From there, things get less clear. You want to minimize the vaccines your cat gets, but still make sure Kitty has adequate protection. Ideally kittens receive a series of boosters to cover them as their mother's immunity wears off and their own immune systems take over. This is often a series of two or three doses of the vaccines needed. Traditionally cats got a booster at one year of age, followed by annual boosters. It is now felt that most feline vaccines can be safely given every three years after the initial booster at one year. If you have an outdoor only cat, you may want to discuss whether this will be adequate with your veterinarian.

Using the above recommendations, there are still choices to be made for feline vaccinations. Feline distemper (parvovirus) is recommended for all cats. This is a serious disease that can kill cats and you don't want to take chances. This disease can show up with a variety of clinical signs.

Feline herpersvirus and feline calicivirus are two of the most common respiratory viruses in cats. These can both cause very serious respiratory problems, residual eye problems, and even lead to pneumonias. This is another vaccine that all cats should receive (most often these are combined with feline distemper).

There is a vaccine for feline leukemia virus in cats. If your cat is an "only cat" who lives totally indoors, she does not need this vaccine. If you have multiple indoor-only cats *and* you test and screen any new cats for feline leukemia before adding them, you should not need this vaccine. If your cat goes outdoors, if you frequently take in stray cats that have not been tested, or if you foster untested cats, you need to use this vaccine.

Vaccines have been developed for *Giardia, Chlamydia, Bordetella,* and *Microsporum.* These cover diarrhea-causing protozoa, respiratory pathogens, and skin fungae respectively. None of these vaccines is needed for the average household kitty. If you have a cattery with recurrent problems and treatments are not clearing the problem, these vaccines may help. Some shelters and boarding facilities use these vaccines as well.

Last, but not least, there is now a vaccine for feline infectious peritonitis. There are still some questions being raised about how effective this vaccine is, and at this time it is not recommended for most cats.

The vaccine recommendations above are certainly not written in stone. You need to discuss the needs of your cat(s) with your veterinarian. Customizing vaccine schedules for individual pets is becoming the norm, not the exception, in veterinary medicine.

All cats need good nutrition and plenty of fresh water available at all times. Cats should get foods designed for cats, not dog food, as they have very different dietary requirements.

While cats may not demand attention like some dogs do, cats do need daily interaction. Many cats can and do learn tricks and enjoy playing with their people. Exercise can help to keep your kitty fit and trim. Regular grooming is important, particularly in long-haired cats, but even short hair cats enjoy being groomed with a slicker brush at least once a week. If you are not up to keeping a Persian or other long-hair coat groomed, have your cat professionally trimmed or shaved periodically to reduce matting.

One of the most important preventative care items on your list should be an annual physical examination (or more frequently in older cats). Ideally I suggest, as with dogs, that pet owners go over their pets themselves once a week (possibly while you are grooming) to see if you find any new lumps, bumps, or problems. This includes looking in the ears and checking the mouth gently for any problems.

If health problems are noted early on, they almost always have a better chance of being easy and less expensive to treat. Your veterinarian may suggest blood tests and urinalyses for older cats, possibly even an EKC (electrocardiogram). While some aging problems cannot be cured, if they are caught early, you can slow down their progression and give your pet a longer life of quality time.

CHAPTER 18

Basic First Aid for Your Pet

◆

Hopefully you will not ever have to face any emergencies with your pet. Most likely, however, at some time you will have to deal with a wound or injury. This information should help you to handle basic emergency care. It is best if you read this chapter ahead of time so that you are prepared—just like a good Boy Scout would be!

If you are someone who tends to faint at the sight of blood, don't worry. When faced with someone else's injury (in this case your pet's), I find that most people rise to the occasion. You are so busy working on the problem that you don't have time to feel ill yourself! When the danger is over and the problem under control, then you can sit down or faint.

The first, most basic rule of first aid should be: *Do not panic!!!* A calm owner will calm the injured pet and is much more effective at treating the pet. Many local Red Cross units now offer pet emergency first aid courses and pet CPR courses. Sometimes local animal groups such as kennel clubs or cat clubs will offer speakers on pet first aid. Take advantage of these opportunities.

If your pet is badly injured, such as being hit by a car and having obvious fractures, do not hesitate to use a muzzle. An injured, frightened animal will often bite without regard to whom they are biting. This applies even to very gentle animals who would not normally ever bite. At the very least try to wrap the animal up in a large towel. Do *not* get bitten yourself! An injured owner will have trouble helping an injured pet.

Allergic Reactions/Anaphylaxis

Allergic reactions can be caused by a number of things—insect bites, foods, medications, vaccines, even new household items. Hives are a common way for pets to show allergies. As long as your pet is breathing fine, your veterinarian may simply prescribe some antihistamines.

More serious allergic reactions are called anaphylaxis. Pets with anaphylaxis may show vomiting, breathing problems, shock, and collapse. This requires immediate, fast action, and you should contact your veterinarian right away. If your pet is known to have anaphylactic reactions, you should get an injectable epinephrine kit (they make them for people who have serious bee sting reactions) and have your veterinarian show you how to use it and what dose to use for your pet. Pets can die from anaphylactic reactions—guinea pigs receiving oral penicillins are a good example.

Abdominal Swelling

Abdominal swelling can be the result of a chronic problem such as liver failure or a heart problem or it can be acute such as gastric dilation or torsion (commonly called bloat). Puppies who rapidly gulp their food or drink large amounts of water can get swollen bellies. Puppies with heavy parasite infestations may also show a swollen belly.

A dog with a serious abdominal distension such as bloat will be very uncomfortable. She will often walk around uneasily, attempting to vomit but having only nonproductive retching. The gums may get pale or look darker in color with a slow capillary refill time. Bloat can be fatal, so if your pet is showing these signs, call your veterinarian.

Rarely, cats with urinary blockages will also appear distended. These cats often strain in the litterbox or have small accidents in unusual places. Both bloat and urinary blockage are serious conditions that need veterinary attention and as soon as possible.

Burns

If your pet has a burn, do *not* put any greasy substance on it. Just apply water and quickly get your pet to the veterinarian. Burns are serious trauma and can easily get infected or lead to dehydration. The hair around the burn may need to be trimmed, and depending on the severity of the burn(s), your pet may need to be treated in the hospital with intravenous medications and fluids. Mild burns respond well to aloe—either the plant or a water-based cream.

Choking

A choking pet may have something stuck in his mouth. Pets with objects stuck in their mouths often drool or paw at their mouths. Some will rub their heads in an attempt to dislodge the object.

You can try to open the mouth and carefully remove anything there—such as sticks caught across the roof of the mouth—but you must be very careful not to get bitten. A ball stuck in the throat may come out if you do a Heimlich-type maneuver on your pet's belly. Some pets will require tranquilizers or mild anesthetics before the foreign objects can be removed.

CPR (Cardiopulmonary Resuscitation)

CPR is actually something most breeders are familiar with—at least in puppies and kittens. Any pet may need CPR, though, and any pet owner can do this. The cardiopulmonary part of the name refers to the heart and lungs.

When a newborn pup or kitten comes out without crying or breathing, you instinctively do some of the parts of CPR. You start to clear the airways—cleaning off the nose and gently swinging the pup to remove fluid from the nose, mouth, and lungs. You might even gently blow into the nose or carefully compress the chest. You have covered the ABCs of CPR! A for airway, by clearing the nose and getting fluid from the lungs. B for breathing by blowing into the nose. And C for circulation by compressing the chest to stimulate heartbeats. With any luck, the pup or kitten starts breathing and its heart starts beating strongly almost immediately.

Our adult pets may sometimes need CPR as well. Pets are much less likely to have heart attacks like people do, but drowning, choking, or electrical shock are also very effective at causing the heart and lungs to stop. Certainly many pets who have been injured by such trauma as being hit by a car may also benefit from CPR. Always be careful with a trauma case to check for fractured ribs before you start compressions, though.

With an adult pet, many of the same principles are followed. You need the same ABCs. The airway has to be free of any debris, so you need to wipe out any vomit or saliva you can. (Remember, the pet is basically unconscious, so you needn't fear any bites. If your pet feels strong enough to fight you, he probably doesn't need CPR anyway! Do *not* get bitten yourself!) Close the muzzle and hold it closed so you can breathe into it. You may want to cover the nose with a clean handkerchief. For small pets like some reptiles or birds, you can use a small funnel or cut the top off a plastic soda or water bottle. Just remember that time is of the essence. The longer your pet goes without oxygen to the brain, the greater the chance of permanent neurologic damage, even if you save his life. Five or six quick breaths may be enough to get your pet breathing again. If not, go to fifteen or twenty breaths per minute. (The number of breaths here is what would be standard for a dog. For a cat or rabbit, perhaps a few more, for small pets, many shallow breaths would be best.) Don't blow full force into a pocket pet! Obviously, how hard you breathe in depends on the size of the pet. Try to see the chest move a little.

Hopefully you have help, so another person can be doing the chest compressions if your pet is too big for you to do everything at once. Lay your pet on its right side. For a large dog, put the heel of your hands just above and behind the elbow—with one hand on top of the other. Try ten quick compressions, and if that isn't successful, go to sixty to eighty per minute. For a smaller dog or cat, a tiny puppy or kitten, or pocket pet, put your fingers on either side of the chest and compress gently. Remember that birds need their chest wall to breathe, so compressions should be very gentle. To be honest, the pets most likely to need or receive CPR from their owners are dogs, cats, and possibly rabbits.

If you are alone, it is suggested that you do five or six breaths, then ten compressions. Continue alternating, so that your pet will get oxygen into its lungs and then the compressions will help to spread the oxygen through the body.

There is an additional technique which is not part of classic CPR that has been found to be very helpful. There is an acupuncture site on the soft skin below the nose (the skin where the wet part of the nose ends). Sticking a sharp needle here seems to stimulate breathing and help to get the heart working. This would work with newborns that are slow to breathe as well.

I would certainly work on a pet for ten to fifteen minutes before giving up hope. If the gums have a bluish color (not a help with heavily pigmented breeds), the pupils are dilated, and your pet does not blink when the eyes are touched, you know you have lost the battle.

A dog model for teaching CPR has been developed and some of the Red Cross offices offer one. They can also request to borrow one from other areas if there is interest. The training class is shorter and less expensive than the human CPR class. Some use a feline mannequin as well. I hope that you never need the information included here, but if you do, remember that time is of the essence. Start right in, stay calm, and hopefully you can save a life!

Diarrhea

While diarrhea is certainly not a pleasant situation, it is rarely an acutely life-threatening problem. If your pet is very young or has had diarrhea for a period of time and is becoming dehydrated, it can become very serious. Any diarrhea with blood should lead to a visit to your veterinarian.

A soft stool in a pet who is eating and drinking and acting normally may be treatable at home. Put your pet on no food for twenty-four hours (only if there are no health problems that would be exacerbated by a short fast), then gradually start your pet back on a bland diet. You should be in contact with your veterinarian and they may have you bring in a fecal sample to check for any parasites. Keep your pet's rear clean (this may involve trimming hair on long-haired dogs or cats). Pepto-Bismol® can be helpful but check with your veterinarian before giving any medications.

If your pet is vomiting and has diarrhea, has bloody diarrhea, is acting depressed, or is getting dehydrated, you need to contact your veterinarian.

Drowning

Most pets who drown fall into the family pool and, even if they can swim, simply can't figure out how to get out of the pool. Eventually they become exhausted and drown. Pools should always have pet-proof fencing and pets should never be left alone near a pool.

If your pet has fallen in, hold him upside down to help drain any free water from the lungs. Gentle pressure on the sides may help. These pets may need CPR (see page 76) and immediate veterinary care to help stimulate the heart and lungs.

Ear Problems

A swollen ear could have a hematoma (buildup of blood along the cartilage of the ear) and these often require surgery. An ear with foul discharge could be badly infected. Gently flush an ear with discharge or one that your pet is shaking (just in case there is a seed in the ear canal, which the flushing might remove). Then call your veterinarian.

Electrical Shock

Electrical shock deserves a visit to the veterinarian to be sure everything is okay. Do *not* touch the pet or the chewed cord or you could be shocked too. Pull the cord out using a wooden broom or some other object. Shutting off the power by using the circuit breaker will work also. Once the cord is un-plugged, you can check your pet. Some pets will have electrical burns in their mouths from chewing cords.

Check your pet's breathing and make sure she is not going into shock. See "CPR" and "Shock."

Foreign Bodies

A foreign body is anything that doesn't belong in your pet. This can range from thorns to porcupine quills. If your pet has a thorn in the paw or a fish-hook in the lip, you can try to gently remove it. Thorns should be pulled out carefully. Fishhooks need to be pushed through the skin (or lip) so that the hooked barb can be cut off. Then the rest of the hook will easily slide out backwards.

Porcupine quills need to be carefully removed. Trimming the ends off does not help and may actually make it harder to pull them out. If your pet has only a few quills, you may want to remove them at home with a pair of pliers, after muzzling your dog or wrapping him up in a towel or blanket. You will need a helper to restrain the dog. Beyond just a few quills, your dog should go to the veterinarian to have all the quills carefully removed under sedation. Your vet-erinarian will carefully check for any broken or chewed-off quills and may put your dog on antibiotic therapy. Missed quills can migrate under the skin into tissues and cause abscesses. Ideally, keep your pet on a leash in areas where por-cupines are seen.

Fractures

Broken bones often results from trauma such as being hit by a car. While a dangling leg may be a horrifying sight to you, the internal damage to lungs or liver may be much more serious. If your pet has a fracture, first calmly get con-trol of the animal. Tie a muzzle or wrap small pets up so they don't move and cause more tissue damage.

Check for shock (see "Normal Values," page 85), make sure your pet is breathing and has a pulse, and do CPR (cardiopulmonary resuscitation) if necessary. Put pressure on any bleeding wounds. Then deal with the broken bones.

If you have help, applying a temporary splint will keep the fracture steady. Even newspaper rolled to form a sturdy pad or a cardboard roll will work. Keep the splint as lightweight as possible and place the injured limb in the most natural position you can. Even with a splint on, your pet should be carried, if at all possible, to minimize additional trauma. Get to your veterinarian as soon as you can.

Frostbite

Frostbite occurs when your pet is out in very cold weather too long and the extremities such as the toes, ears, and tails may be exposed to low temperatures and thus develop decreased circulation. The skin may appear white or red and rarely a pet will show signs of shock. Tissues that may be frostbitten should be slowly rewarmed in tepid water. Do not massage the tissues while thawing as you may cause more damage.

It is also important not to let tissues refreeze after thawing. It may take days before you know if the damaged tissues will dry up and slough off. Pets may lose parts of their tails, ears, or some toes if the frostbite is severe enough.

Pets with frostbite may need extra veterinary attention such as antibiotics and shock therapy. See also Hypothermia.

Hyperthermia/Heat Stroke

Heat stroke is most often seen in pets that are too active in hot, muggy weather or pets left in cars on warm days. Cars will rapidly heat up and pets should not be left in closed cars at all (even with windows slightly cracked) in warm weather (over seventy degrees in my opinion, especially if the car is not in the shade).

Pets suffering from hyperthermia will pant and show labored breathing. They may be disoriented and show diarrhea or vomiting. Their heart rates go up as does their internal body temperatures and they may go into shock. Our pets sweat via panting and their footpads, so those are areas to work on.

Overheated pets need to be cooled—ice cubes in the groin area, ice wiped on the feet and cool water to drink or even just flush their mouths will help.

Pouring cool water over them seems to help or getting them into a cool water tub or bath. A fan blowing air will also help. Try not to cool the pet down below 103.5 in temperature as the body will continue to cool down with time. (If your thermometer reads 103.5, in a few minutes your dog will actually be lower than that.)

Contact your veterinarian, as secondary effects such as kidney damage may show up even a day or so later.

Always make sure your outdoor pets have shade and fresh water available in warm weather.

Hypothermia

Hypothermia is when the whole pet is colder than normal, with body temperatures dropping. You should notice your pet shivering and possibly acting weak and disoriented. Breathing rates and the heart rate will slow. These pets need to be gradually warmed up. A tepid drink or some warm (not hot) food or even warm enemas will help.

Lameness

An acute lameness maybe just a pulled muscle or bruise. If your pet is suddenly limping, check gently to make sure you don't detect any fractures (broken bones). If there are no broken bones or obvious wounds, you can run a cold hose over the affected leg for about five minutes. Then give an anti-inflammatory medication recommended by your veterinarian. That will take care of most minor lamenesses.

If your pet stays lame more than twenty-four hours or has bruising, you need to contact your veterinarian. Pet massage can help heal torn muscles and stretched ligaments. There are excellent books and videos available for massage for dogs and cats.

Nail Problems

While broken toenails are not life threatening, they can be very sore. You may need to pull any remaining pieces of nail which keep rubbing and making your pet even more sore. That is a painful operation and you should have help and restrain the pet with a muzzle and/or a thick towel. A nail cut too short can be cauterized with your styptic powder or silver nitrate stick. Sticking the toe into a bar of soap can also help to clot off the bleeding. Bleeding nails are not dire emergencies, but as Fido walks around, he can make a small amount of blood look like a major blood loss. Keep him quiet until the bleeding stops.

Broken or misshapen nails may have a fungal infection. You will need to have this checked by your veterinarian and your pet may need a long course of therapy.

Ocular (Eye) Problems

If your pet suddenly runs up to you with a squinted eye, try to flush the eye carefully with artificial tears. Then, take Fido or Fluffy to the veterinarian. Eye injuries can quickly go from mild to serious and I consider them emergencies worth being checked out by your veterinarian. A small scratch can go on to become a corneal ulcer. Get your pet to a veterinarian as soon as you can.

Seizures

Seizuring pets are best observed. Do *not* worry about them swallowing their tongues—they can't. We joke that many seizuring dogs get dropped off at the veterinarian (and most have stopped seizuring by that time) while their owners drive on to the hospital emergency room to have their bite wounds treated. Unless the seizure lasts more than five minutes (and time this by your watch—five minutes is actually a long time), simply observe your pet, keep other pets and children away, and make sure that your pet is safe. If the seizures last, you need to try and carefully pick up the animal to bring it to your veterinarian. Having some diazepam handy to give by enema is very useful for these "status" seizures. Normally the seizures are over fairly quickly and you can then safely bring your pet to your veterinarian.

Shock

Shock can have a number of causes. Shock itself is a syndrome whereby the movement of blood and oxygen to the tissues of the body is disrupted. This can have a number of causes—trauma, heart failure, blood loss, electrical charges, etc. Your pet will have pale mucous membranes, possibly shallow breathing, and a weak pulse. Pupils may appear dilated. Capillary refill time will be delayed. Emergency CPR may be called for.

For treating a pet in shock, you need to keep them warm and well hydrated and get them to your veterinarian or an animal emergency clinic as quickly as possible. A safe method you can use to stimulate the breathing and heart rate is to put a sterile needle (this can be the needle from a syringe) into your pet's tissues between the nose and mouth. This would be the upper lip in a person. Do this right on the midline and right under where the nose tissue ends (before the haired skin) and it should stimulate some increased breathing efforts. This is acupuncture site GV 26 and is very useful in resuscitation, including newborn puppies or kittens after a C-section. Be careful that your pet does not try to bite you!! If your pet feels strong enough to try to bite, he probably doesn't need this technique anyway.

Urinary Blockage

If your pet (most often a cat) is seen straining in the litterbox or leaves small accident puddles of urine around the house, contact your veterinarian right away. Some pets first show blood in their urine or you notice them licking their genital areas more than usual. Some pets may vomit as well.

Urinary blockages can be fatal as they prevent the body's waste products from leaving. These can build up to toxic levels. So don't hesitate to call your clinic!

Vomiting

Vomiting is often not an emergency. Cats in particular can vomit with ease and often leave hairballs around for us. On the other hand, if your rabbit appears to be trying to vomit, contact your veterinarian right away.

Do not feed a vomiting pet for twenty-four hours (unless your pet is very young or has a medical condition that a short fast would exacerbate). Then start back on small, bland meals. Your veterinarian may suggest something like Kaopectate® to soothe the stomach a bit.

If your pet vomits blood, has vomiting and diarrhea, can't keep water down, or has been vomiting more than twenty-four hours, you need to contact your veterinarian. Pets can dehydrate and prolonged vomiting may be a sign of an obstruction. Obviously, if you are quite sure Spot swallowed a ball and he is now vomiting, you should not wait before contacting your veterinarian.

Wounds

Very often, wounds are not quite as bad as they seem. Small cuts on the ear are an example of this. Even a tiny cut seems horrendous since your dog shakes his head and blood goes everywhere. What looks like a full scale bloodbath is probably less than ½ teaspoon of blood total.

For cuts or wounds, apply pressure if there is bleeding. Even your hand will work for a small cut. Squirting blood means an artery has been nicked and these will take more pressure and a longer time to clot off. Use steady, but gentle pressure. Do *not* use a tourniquet unless you are trained in emergency technicques. Tourniquets require skilled, careful application—otherwise they can do even more damage. If the wound has bled, it is probably fairly clean. Cover it lightly with bandage material if needed and take your pet to your veterinarian.

Puncture wounds often need to heal from inside out. You may need to keep the wound slightly open for drainage and to minimize the chances of infection. Lacerations may require suturing.

If the wound is more of a scrape or is highly contaminated with mud or dirt, it will need gentle cleansing. Just using a flushing solution such as saline may be enough. Water will work, if that is what you have available. If the wound goes deep, you should flush the surface area and go to your veterinarian so it can be properly cleaned. Once it is cleaned, you can apply a bandage if needed or simply put on some ointment. Remember that pets will try to lick off anything you put on their skin. If you don't need a bandage, apply the ointment, then feed your pet, take him for a walk, or play with him to distract him from the ointment.

Check your bandages often. A wet bandage can cause skin necrosis. A bandage that is too tight (look for swelling above or below it) can cut off circulation and cause major tissue damage. Also remember that some animals are extremely clever at removing bandages. Birds are some of the most skilled bandage removers! Your veterinarian may give you a neck collar or Elizabethan collar (large plastic collar) for your pet to wear. This prevents your pets from chewing out sutures or removing bandages.

Normal Values

DOGS

Temperature: 100–102.5° F. If your pet goes below 100 or above 103, this is definitely abnormal. Stress can elevate temperatures.

Heart rate: This varies a great deal with the size of the dog. It can range from 60 to 160 beats per minute. Know the normal for your pet! Stress can elevate this factor as well.

Respiratory rate: 10–30 breaths per minute.

CATS

Temperature: 100–102.5° F. If your cat goes below 100 or above 103, this is definitely abnormal. Stress can elevate temperatures.

Heart rate: 100–140 beats per minute. Know the normal for your pet! Stress can elevate this factor as well.

Respiratory rate: 20–30 breaths per minute.

RABBITS

Temperature: 101.5–103° F. Stress can elevate temperatures.

Heart rates: 130–160 beats per minute. Know the normal for your pet! Stress can elevate this factor as well.

Respiratory rate: 30–50 breaths per minute.

How to determine normals:

For temperature, always use a rectal thermometer. You may need someone else to help you gently restrain your pet.

For heart rates, you can place your hand on your pet's chest and feel the heartbeat or you can reach into the inner thigh area (groin) and feel the femoral pulse. Your veterinarian can show you how to do this. Usually we count for fifteen seconds, then multiply by four to get the rate per minute.

For respiratory rates, you can watch the chest movement of your pet or hold your hand close to the nose and count the movement of air out of the lungs. Usually we count for fifteen seconds, then multiply by four to get the rate per minute.

First Aid Kit

Listed below are the basics for a very good home or travel first aid kit. To be honest, all of these items can be used for both pets and people, so you don't really need separate ones. At the end of our basic list I will include some possible "customizing" options.

Artificial tears—to flush out sore or red eyes, to remove any foreign items such as dust or seeds.

Roll of gauze—this will help for bandages and can serve as a quick muzzle.

Gauze or Telfa® pads—to put on a wound.

Vet wrap® or Elastikon®—these are sturdy, elastic wraps which work wonderfully to hold bandages on. *Be careful*—make sure they aren't too tight!

Adhesive tape—this can be used to hold a bandage on as well—always leave a short tab to make it easier to remove.

Antibiotic ointment—there are many good generic ointments.

Cortisone or aloe ointment—there are many good generic ointments.

Saline or ear flush—this can be used to flush out small wounds or infected ears.

Tweezers—to remove thorns or splinters; some may be used for ticks.

Scissors—to cut the bandaging material.

Thermometer

Styptic powder or silver nitrate powder—to stop small bleeding wounds such as a nail cut too short.

Towel—to wrap an injured cat, bird, small dog, or reptile in.

Duct tape—to make temporary booties if you hike with your dog and he gets an injured paw.

Disposable heat and ice packs—small packets that are activated when you crush them.

Antihistamine—to give after a bee sting or other allergic encounter.

Hydrogen peroxide—to cause vomiting (this has gone out of favor as a wound-flushing agent). *Always* consult your veterinarian or the National Poison Control Center before you make your pet vomit—some toxins will cause more trouble if they come back up!

Aspirin—to give for pain and as an anti-inflammatory—*do not* use for your cat.

Diarrhea medication—this can be something like Kaopectate® or Pepto-

Bismol®. I like the Pepto-Bismol® tablets as they are lightweight, take up little space, and are less messy to give.

Activated charcoal—this should be used only for possible poisoning cases and under the guidance of your veterinarian or the National Poison Control Center.

For the "natural pet":

Rescue Remedy—a flower essence recommended for stress and trauma.

Arnica—for trauma and wounds. *Only* use the homeopathic version orally—this can be toxic otherwise!

One sterile needle for acupuncture to restore breathing and treat shock.

Customizing for your pet:

Epileptic pets—get some diazepam from your veterinarian (pills or enema) to have on hand if your pet has bad seizures. Contact your veterinarian if you need to use this.

Allergic pets—for pets who have severe, anaphylactic reactions to things like bee stings, get an epi-pen kit and have your veterinarian show you how to use it.

CHAPTER 19

Medicating Your Pet

———◆———

Currently, medicating your pet tends to refer to getting a pill or liquid medicine into your pet's mouth and safely on its way to his stomach. There are ear, eye, and topical medications, of course, but those tend to be easy compared to the perils of oral treatments. Those days may be slowly fading though as we look at compounding to flavor medications and to reformulate medications so they can be used in gels and patches. In the meantime, we are still faced with "pushing our pills."

Try to remember to stay patient, keep your sense of humor, and remember just how much you do truly love your pet as you endure scratches, nasty glances, and hasty retreats at the sight of you. Of my own pets, my elderly English setter, Toby, held the record for swallowing eleven times while I held his mouth, then casually spitting the soggy pill to one side when I released him. When I had to treat my newly adopted cat, Jenny, for ear mites, I lost more blood than if I had given daily donations to the Red Cross. Persevere and someday you can look back and smile!

It is often said to clients that the easy part of helping their sick pet is diagnosing her—the hard part is when the owner takes the pet home and has to medicate her. The old story about "belling the cat" seems particularly apt when you try to medicate an unhappy feline.

First, you need to be sure you understand the directions for giving the medication. Is it to be given orally or is that liquid to be used as drops in the ears or eyes? Pills are virtually always given orally, but liquids are more versatile. Also make sure you know just how much medication needs to be given at each treatment and how often treatments should occur. This should be clearly marked on the container of the drug.

Be sure to ask your veterinarian if the medication can be given with food (food is often an easy way to trick our pets into taking their pills!). Also, check about drug interactions if your pet is already taking some medications—even monthly flea or heartworm treatments should be noted.

If your pet is difficult to handle or treat, make sure you ask your veterinarian for other treatment methods. Perhaps you could arrange for someone to come out to your house to help you give medications if needed or switch your pet to injections at the hospital. If you get bitten or badly scratched while medicating your pet, contact *your* physician!

Medicating Your Dog

Giving pills or capsules can be easy or a real rodeo. For a dog, if the drug can be given with food, you might just want to make up a couple of little meatballs of canned food. Put the pill or capsule in one. Feed one or two nonmedicated meatballs first, then sneak in the medicated one. Watch carefully to be sure Fido swallows it down. Cats are rarely greedy enough to quickly swallow down medicated offerings.

To give a pill to a dog who is not a true chowhound, or if a pill is to be given without food, you need to actually place the pill or capsule in the back of the mouth. If your dog is aggressive and likely to bite, do *not* attempt this—discuss an alternate way of medicating your dog with the veterinarian. While taking Fido to the clinic for daily injections is a hassle, dealing with a dog bite wound is even worse.

To pill a dog, have the dog sitting quietly beside you. Gently reach over the top of the muzzle and squeeze in right behind the whiskers with your left hand. This will make the jaw drop slightly. Now pull gently down on the lower jaw with your right hand. As the mouth opens, put the pill or capsule as far as you can into the back of Fido's mouth. Then close the mouth and blow into the dog's nose. Blowing into their nose makes them forget about carefully holding that pill in the back of their mouth and they swallow it. Gently stroking the neck can also induce a dog to swallow. Watch your dog to be sure he has swallowed once or twice, then release him. Still keep a careful eye on him for a minute or two to be sure he hasn't tucked that capsule into his cheek and that he doesn't suddenly spit it out at you.

Liquids can be messier to deal with. Very few dogs will cheerfully drink up a medication, though flavored compounded variations may fool some dogs. Most likely you will have to directly give the medication to Spot. Ideally your medication came with a plastic dropper or a plastic syringe.

Have Spot sitting quietly by your side. Draw up the prescribed amount of fluid and open the cheek pouch on the side of the mouth. Gently dribble the medication in aiming for the back of the mouth, but not forcefully spraying it. (You don't want to put any medication into the trachea by accident.) With a plastic dropper you don't have to worry if Spot chews on it a bit, though don't let him actually bite off and swallow a piece of it.

Ear medications are commonly in ointment or liquid form. Check your label carefully to see if both ears are to be treated or just one and if you are to clean the ear or prepare it in any way before putting in the medication. Have Fido sitting quietly at your side and gently pull the ear straight up. The medication should be dropped or squeezed directly down into the ear canal. Then gently massage the ear from the outside (holding it closed). Be prepared that as soon as you finish Fido may shake his head vigorously and spray you and the surrounding area! It is nice to follow up an ear medicating with a treat so that Fido does not come to think of this as a battle. Very sore ears may need extra gentle handling. If Fido will not let you treat his ears, contact your veterinarian and you can work out a different treatment arrangement. Sometimes a veterinary technician from the practice or an experienced pet sitter could come out to help you at home.

Eye medications also usually come in liquid or ointment. These are generally expensive medications and concentrated such that only a drop or two are needed to treat your pet. Have Spot sitting quietly beside you. Check your label carefully to see if you need to treat one or both eyes and if you need to clean or flush the eye before medicating.

Gently tip Spot's head back a little and carefully pull down on the lower lid. Drops can simply be applied from above to drip onto the eye, while ointments should be carefully applied to the inside of the lower lid. When Spot closes his eye, the medication will be spread across the eye.

If you need to put ointments or powders on a wound or sore, have your pet lie quietly while you apply it. Then feed Fido, play with him, or take him for a walk so he is distracted from the medications. Otherwise pets often immediately turn around and lick the medication off. Some topical medications can be dangerous if ingested and certainly if the medication is removed right away, it doesn't have a chance to do its job.

Some medications are now coming in gel form or can be formulated into gel form. Some medications are also available in patches. These medications can be applied topically (on the skin) and will be absorbed. Make sure you get dosage information from your veterinarian and check where to safely place the medications. They may need to be on bare skin or may need to be placed where your pet will not be able to lick or chew.

Some dogs need daily injections—such as diabetics who get insulin once or twice daily. Have your veterinarian or veterinary technician show you exactly how to give these medications and if possible practice a few times using sterile fluids.

Medicating Your Cat

Cats can be a true challenge to medicate. If your cat is feisty and difficult to handle, be sure your veterinarian knows whether you are capable of medicating your pet. If you can't medicate Kitty, perhaps she could come in for daily injections or you could arrange for a veterinary technician or experienced pet sitter to come out to your house to help you. This is no time for false pride!

If your cat is a true chow hound, you can try hiding a pill or capsule in food, but that rarely works. Cats are not often fooled and don't usually gulp their food like a hungry dog will.

This may sound silly, but when you get up in the morning, don't start thinking "Got to medicate the cat!" Cats seem to sense when trouble is coming even better than dogs. They might prepare all weapons or retreat to a hiding place where they are totally invisible (at least to a human bent on finding them to pill them). Do your best to hide your oncoming stress and quietly and calmly approach your cat.

To give a pill or capsule, have Kitty sitting quietly in your lap, which should be covered by a thick towel to prevent scratches. Gently reach over Kitty's head and squeeze the upper muzzle behind the whiskers with your left hand. This causes the lower jaw to drop and the mouth to open slightly. With your right hand, carefully pull the lower jaw down and place the pill as far back in Kitty's mouth as you can. Close the mouth and give a quick blow into Kitty's nose. The blow into the nose startles the cat and makes them often gulp the pill. Cats can be extremely good at holding even very bitter pills in the back of their mouth without swallowing. Rubbing the neck gently may also encourage your cat to swallow.

If your cat strongly objects to being medicated, you can try using the above method but with Kitty firmly wrapped up in a towel with just her head out. That way all four feet are wrapped up and you are safe from scratches.

Liquid medications for cats usually come with plastic droppers or syringes, so you don't have to worry if Puss tries to chomp on the dropper. Your veterinarian may be able to have Puss's medication compounded with a tasty flavor so that she won't spit it all back directly into your face!

Carefully draw up the correct amount of liquid medication. Have Puss sitting quietly in your lap (again, cover your lap with a thick towel). Put the dropper into the cheek pouch and gently dribble the medication in, stopping to let Puss swallow as needed. Do not squirt the medication in quickly or spray it onto the back of Puss's throat or you may get some medication into the trachea.

If your cat needs ear medications, make sure you know if both ears need to be treated or just one. Check if you need to clean the ear before putting in the medications. Again, have Kitty sitting quietly in your lap on a thick towel (wrapped if need be). Gently pull the ear to be medicated straight up. Squeeze the ointment right down into the ear canal or drop the liquid down into the canal. Gently rub the ear after medicating to work the medicine down the canal. Be prepared that Kitty may shake her head vigorously after being medicated and may hold her ears off to the side for a few minutes (airplane ears!).

Eye medications are also usually drops or ointments. Make sure you know if one or both eyes need to be medicated and if you need to clean or flush the eyes before treating. Have Puss sitting quietly in your lap on a thick towel (wrapped if need be). Gently pull the lower lid down. Drops can be applied from above and ointment should be carefully squeezed onto the lower lid. When Puss blinks, the medication will be spread across the eye.

If your cat needs to have an ointment or powder put on a wound, you should do this gently, then feed him or play with him to distract him from the medication. If your cat simply licks it off right away, it certainly won't let the medication do its job. Some topical medications can be dangerous if ingested.

Some medications are now coming in gel form or can be formulated into gel form. Some medications are also available in patches. These medications can be applied topically (on the skin) and will be absorbed. Make sure you get dosage information from your veterinarian and check where to safely place the medications. They may need to be on bare skin or may need to be placed where your pet will not be able to lick or chew. Cats are excellent and flexible athletes and can often reach places that surprise us!

Some cats such as diabetics may need daily injections. Have your veterinarian or a veterinary technician show you exactly how to give these medications. If possible, practice a few times with some sterile fluids.

Medicating Rabbits and Pocket Pets

Rabbits and pocket pets like hamsters and guinea pigs can be tricky to treat. They are rarely fooled by medications hidden in food. If your pet is difficult to treat or handle, let your veterinarian know. Perhaps you can arrange for injections at the veterinary hospital or for a veterinary technician or experienced pet sitter to come out to your home to help you.

The easiest method of medicating these pets at home is usually liquid or crushed pills mixed in with liquid or soft foods like apple sauce. Always check with your veterinarian before crushing any medications or mixing them with food items.

To give liquid medications, hold your pet gently in your lap. Cover your lap with a thick towel in case they eliminate and in the case of rabbits to prevent any scratches. If your pet is very active or resistant, you can try wrapping her in a towel so just her head is out. Most liquid medications come with plastic droppers or syringes so you don't have to worry if Bunny chews on it a little. Try not to let him bite off a piece and swallow it, however!

Carefully draw up the correct amount of medication in the dropper. Then gently put the dropper in the corner of the mouth, by the cheek. Most of these pets have large, long incisors and if you try to open the mouth and medicate from the front it will be very difficult. By coming in from the side, you avoid those incisors. Gently dribble the medication in, allowing your pet to swallow. Your veterinarian may be able to get your medications compounded with tasty flavors, which might help.

For ear medications, be sure you know if one or both ears are to be treated and if you need to clean the ear before medicating. Most ear medications will be ointments or liquids. Gently hold your pet on your lap with a thick towel. Carefully pull the ear straight up and drip or squeeze the medication into the ear. After applying the medication, gently massage the ear to work the medication down in.

Eye medications are also usually drops or ointments. Make sure you know if one or both eyes are to be treated and if you need to clean or flush the eye before treating. Gently hold your pet in your lap on a thick towel. Pull the lower lid down gently. The drops can be applied from above and the ointment can be carefully squeezed onto the lower lid.

Your pet may need topical powders or ointments applied. Do so gently, then try to distract your pet by playing with it or feeding some favorite treats.

Some topical medications can be dangerous if ingested, and if your pet licks the medication off right away, it can't do its job.

Medicating Birds and Reptiles

Medicating birds and reptiles can be a challenge too. You can always try to hide medications in foods—sweet fruits for birds or even push pills into the dead mouse for a snake. Many of the medications for these species are injectables and will be given by your veterinarian. There are special mouth gags (plastic blocks with central holes) through which or around which you can sometimes pass medications. You need to have your veterinarian show you exactly how to medicate these pets.

CHAPTER 20

Warnings—Signs of Illness to Be Aware Of

—————◆—————

While sometimes a pet's illness does sneak up on us, very often there are tell-tale warning signs. I have listed some of them here for you to be aware of. Watch for these signs when you do your weekly hands-on check of your pet. Any change from the "normal" is worth investigating.

- Weight loss. Suddenly you can feel your pet's ribs easily or maybe even see them easily.
- Weight gain. This may be true weight gain (loss of a "waist," can't feel ribs anymore without pushing through padding) or a distended abdomen due to fluid buildup.
- Hair or feather loss. Not your routine shedding, but bare patches or thin hair. Possibly with redness or crusting. Note if your pet is suddenly itching more than usual.
- Eating more or less than usual. Your pet's appetite often reflects their general health. While dogs and cats may eat less on very hot or humid days, if your pet isn't eating well for more than a day or so, you should be concerned. With some diseases, your pet will eat all his food and go looking for more.
- Drinking more or less than usual. Pets, just like people, need fluids daily. If your pet is not drinking or is suddenly licking the water bowl dry, you need to be concerned. Most pets can go a few days without eating, but dehydration sets in quickly. Drinking more than usual can indicate kidney failure or diabetes—both serious problems.
- Less active. A pet whose activity level drops acutely may be in pain, may have a fever, or may have trouble moving. Pets with neurologic problems may stay quiet simply because their balance is off. Obviously a lame pet needs some medical attention.
- Vomiting. While we can all forgive the occasional hairball on the floor,

vomiting is not normal. Unless your pet has coughed up a hairball or gagged a minute then stopped, vomiting has to be considered a sign of something wrong. If your pet vomits more than once or twice, you should contact your veterinarian. This may be cause for a veterinary visit. Small and young pets can dehydrate easily. If there is blood in the vomit, contact your veterinarian right away.

- Diarrhea. Diarrhea is not normal, either. Unless you have abruptly changed diets or you know your pet snuck a treat they shouldn't have gotten, you should contact your veterinarian. Diarrhea for more than one day is cause for a veterinary visit. Small and young pets can dehydrate easily. If there is blood in the diarrhea, contact your veterinarian right away.
- Behavior changes. A friendly pet who suddenly is hiding or acting aggressively may very well have a health problem.
- Changes in the "normals." If your pet is suddenly breathing faster or harder than normal, has an increased heart rate, or a temperature change from normal, you have cause for concern. Hopefully you know your pet's normals, so you can recognize changes. Remember that weather and activity may influence these variables, but your pet should get back to normal fairly quickly.
- Any unusual lumps, bumps, or discharges. While all changes are not necessarily serious, it is important that you note them down and ask your veterinarian about them on your next appointment. A discharge from the eyes, ears, or nose may require a visit. Check growths for any discharges, changes in size or color, or if they become painful.

CHAPTER 21

Pet Health Insurance

———◆———

Many of us would like to be able to just pull out our insurance card and have our pets paid for through our family plan. Unfortunately, even with a dog named Susan, like one of our Corgis, it isn't that simple. Pet health insurance companies have often been long on promises and short on delivery of goods. There are a couple of reputable, long-standing companies but this is clearly not a financially stable area. And despite our personal love of our pets, pet insurance is a business.

If you decide to try pet insurance, look carefully for the financial rating of the company and try to find out their track record on fulfilling their promises. Perhaps someday pet health insurance will be more widespread and provide a wider safety net for people whose pets have serious injuries or illnesses. And remember, your pet's best insurance against major health catastrophes is good preventative care!

In human health, insurance has become an important part of care management. Having good health insurance may mean choices can be made for the best possible care without any concerns about payment. That is also the goal of pet health insurance programs, but most are not at that point yet.

Just as with human health insurance, there are many different plans and options in pet insurance, as well as many different companies. Plans range from including basic care such as vaccinations to strictly emergency coverage for large bills such as orthopedic surgery from trauma or cancer therapies. Whether or not pet health insurance makes sense for you depends on many different factors. Your veterinarian may not be set up to deal with insurance plans and you need to verify that with their office. You may have to file all the paperwork yourself. If you have no trouble covering routine veterinary care for your pets, you may just want an "emergency policy" to cover unusual accidents or severe chronic problems such as cancer therapies.

Different plans vary in cost as well and most require either a deductible or a copayment. Preexisting illnesses in older pets may not be covered, and costs for even basic plans can vary with the age and breed of your pet. Where you live, how many pets you are insuring and the current health of your pet(s) are all factors that may influence the cost of your coverage. This is definitely a time to read all the "fine print" and be sure you understand exactly what benefits you receive for what cost.

Some veterinary health plans cover a certain percentage of your bill (such as 70 percent of any surgery, including anesthesia costs). Other plans may have a benefit schedule just like many human insurance plans. Under these plans, it is determined that a certain price is "standard" for certain care and the plan pays all or part of that "standard" price. So, if the benefit schedule says it generally costs $500 to repair a certain type of fracture and your bill comes to $750, your plan only covers you up to $500.

The cost of a plan also varies quite a bit with the coverage. If you want routine care such as vaccinations covered, you will generally pay more. For a higher incident limit or annual limit, you will pay more. When a plan stipulates an "incident," that means one injury or illness. So if your plan has an incident limit of $1,000 and your dog is hit by a car and veterinary bills come to $1,200, your plan will cover you up to the $1,000 limit. An annual limit covers all of your claims for one calendar year. Normally you cannot carry over unused amounts to the next year's limit.

Virtually all the plans seem to cover spaying or neutering (a real plus for responsible pet ownership!), surgery and anesthesia, diagnostics including radiographs (x-rays), hospitalization for care, dental injuries, drugs prescribed by a veterinarian, and euthanasia. Some plans will cover alternative therapies such as acupuncture or chiropractics, but only if administered by a licensed veterinarian.

Most pet health insurance plans will not cover routine care such as vaccinations and dental cleanings unless you purchase an extra rider policy. Special diets, health problems related to breeding such as C-sections, boarding, congenital defects, and many preexisting conditions are not usually covered. Behavior counseling and training are not usually covered, and unless grooming is prescribed by a veterinarian for health reasons, it is not covered by most plans. Cosmetic surgery such as tail docking or ear cropping is not covered by any plans at this time. Commercial enterprises such as breeding kennels and training kennels are often exempt.

Some insurance plans have developed arrangements with online pharmacies and travel agencies to offer you further possible discounts on care. They cannot limit you to using only their "associated" companies, however.

Pet health insurance has not taken over in a big way in veterinary medicine at this time. Whether it is the added paperwork hassle, the limits people perceive on care, or the hope that your pet won't need major veterinary care is not clear. Pet health insurance companies are often short lived. Check out the financial stability of the companies you are investigating and find out how long they have been in existence. Check if your normal insurance company offers any pet health coverage.

If you wish to investigate pet health insurance, some websites are included below. There are new companies being developed all the time (as of this writing the American Kennel Club is interested in developing a program), and this listing is not meant to be inclusive or exclusive:

Veterinary Pet Insurance at www.petinsurance.com or 1-800-872-7387.

Premier Pet Insurance at www.ppins.com or 1-877-774-2273.

Pet Care Insurance at www.petcareinsurance.com or 1-866-275-7387.

CHAPTER 22

Poisonings

———◆———

Poisonings can be very frightening experiences. When we see our pet showing serious signs of toxicity, it is difficult to remain calm and collect the information that might save Kitty's life. I have included Poison Control contact numbers here, but no one can help if you don't have any idea what your pet got into. Keep medications and pesticides in their original labeled containers! Stay calm and be prepared to provide as much information as possible about what and how much of a toxic substance your pet was exposed to.

Almost any substance can be a poison if given in the wrong amount or to a pet with a prior health problem. Some poisons are fatal in very small amounts while other substances would require ingesting huge amounts before toxic signs appear. While medications and other drugs automatically come to mind when we think of poisons, many household items can be dangerous too. And contrary to popular belief, just because something is natural or organic does not necessarily mean it is not poisonous. Plants and herbs can be some of our most toxic household items. Recently grapes and raisins have been implicated in kidney failure in some dogs.

If you know your pet has swallowed a toxic item or gotten a toxic item on its skin, you need to contact your veterinarian right away. A call should also be put in to the National Animal Poison Control Center (phone numbers at the end of this chapter). While your local hospital may be willing to give you some advice, remember that they don't know animal physiology. People safely take acetaminophen all the time, but one pill could kill your cat.

When you make the call, if possible, you should be able to clearly state what signs your pet is showing (vomiting, staggering when it walks, salivating, etc.) and how much of what substance it got into. This is where having clear labels on medications with the exact dose, strength, and number of pills is important. Keeping pesticides, medications, and yard chemicals in their original labeled containers is important. Obviously this won't always be possible, but if you have that information, it can make helping your pet much more efficient. The Poison Center may even be able to tell you that four pills of such and such in a fifty-pound dog is not a problem and simply to let Fido sleep it off. Knowing the ingredients in a pesticide can help determine how serious it is that Kitty just walked through a puddle and licked her feet off.

Treatment for certain poisons may be very specific with a certain antidote or may require supportive care while trying to bind as much poison as possible into harmless forms. If you don't know what caused your pet's signs, treatment will have to be supportive and general, but may still be effective.

One of the best ways to deal with poisonings is to prevent them. Thinking of it as "babyproofing" your house will help you with ideas to keep everyone safe—including baby locks on cupboards and outlet covers to prevent electrical injuries.

Know which of your plants in your house or yard can be toxic and make sure your pets can't chew on them. Easter lilies can be quite dangerous for cats, for example, while eating rhododendron clippings could cause fatal cardiac signs. Ideally remove any very dangerous plants or keep them in areas of your yard that aren't accessible to pets.

Cleaning agents can cause caustic burns or mild stomach upsets depending on the exact chemicals they contain. All of these agents should be safely stored away from pets. This also applies to pesticides—even flea control products that are safe to use on a pet may not be safe if consumed.

Rodenticide baits are often attractive to our dogs and cats as well as the rodents they are designed for. Some are so powerful that if your cat or dog eats a mouse poisoned by one of these chemicals, your pet can be poisoned too. Some of the newer products may require weeks or more of treatment to totally cure your pet.

Keep all medications—both prescription and over-the-counter—safely stored in their original labeled containers out of reach of pets. Never use any medication on your pet without checking with your veterinarian first!

Don't count out your own medications and leave the pills on the table, even for a minute. And if you drop any pills, make sure you find all of them! For example, a small young dog was brought into our clinic comatose. We could find nothing wrong, heart rate was steady, breathing fine, but the dog was nonresponsive. The owner could not come up with any exposures to anything toxic. While we had the dog under supportive care, the owner went home and found out that her visiting parent had dropped blood pressure pills that morning. A careful count of the bottle, knowing how many pills had been in the prescription and how many had been consumed, led to the realization that Spot had taken one pill. As soon as we knew the exact medication, we were able to contact the National Poison Control Center and customize our treatment of this dog for the specific problem. This case had a happy ending: Spot was out like a light for almost forty-eight hours, but awoke with no problems!

Remember that some food items can be dangerous as well. Chocolate (particularly the rich baker's chocolate), onions, alcohol, and tobacco can be poisonous to our pets. Grapes and raisins are currently under investigation for some associated illnesses.

Chewing on a battery or swallowing pennies can lead to toxicities. Antifreeze is a common poison and should be stored very carefully and spills thoroughly cleaned up. The sweet taste attracts pets and even ingesting a small amount can do fatal kidney damage.

Treatment for poisonings can vary greatly. It may be recommended that your pet vomit up as much as possible or you may need to give medications to try to neutralize or absorb it. Activated charcoal is often an important part of the treatment regimen as are intravenous fluids. Specific antidotes are used where possible. Always check with your veterinarian before you try any treatments at home (including inducing vomiting as there are some poisons where that is *not* indicated).

RESOURCES

Animal Poison Control Center at 1-888-4ANIHELP [426-4435]. The fee is $45.00 per case with follow-up calls at no charge. (This can be paid by credit card.) Treatment protocols and literature citations can be provided. The second number is 1-900-443-0000 (still $45.00 per case). Many products are covered by the Animal Product Safety Service. In these cases the product manufacturer absorbs the cost of the call. You can always call and check if the item you are concerned about is covered by this program. The Animal Poison Control Center is under the auspices of the ASPCA. You can get some information off the website at www.aspca.org.

American Veterinary Medical Association has a nice section on their website devoted to small animal poisonings. This can be reached at www.avma.org/ pubhlth/poisgde.asp.

American Animal Hospital Association has an excellent section on poisons for pet owners at their website as well. This can be reached at www. healthypet.com.

Your local Cooperative Extension Office has pamphlets on poisonous plants. And remember, the very best way to deal with poisonings is to avoid them in the first place!

Treating Poisoning Cases

The treatments for different poisonings vary greatly depending on the poison. You should *always* contact your veterinarian and/or the National Poison Control Center before doing *any* treatments yourself! If you use an inappropriate treatment, you could actually worsen your pet's condition.

First and foremost, if you can identify the poison, that makes treatment dramatically simpler and more effective. Look around for the pill bottle or container. Grab the chewed-up box or wrapper. Any identifying information you can relay will help your pet. Important information would include both the substance involved and, if possible, the amount.

Treating a poisoned pet starts with the very basics. You need to be sure your pet is breathing and her heart is working. (See "CPR," page 76, if needed.) If your pet is seizuring, try to keep her quiet and calm. Most seizures last less than a minute. If the seizures go much longer than that, you need to get Fido to the veterinarian right away. Nonstop seizures, known as status epilepticus, are the only time you should try to move a seizuring pet. Make sure you do not get bitten!

If your pet is not seizuring, move him away from the area you found him, just in case the poison is in the environment. If your pet obviously has a toxic substance on the coat (such as some plant and yard sprays), immediately try to wash this off. Cats, dogs, and rabbits are notorious for licking themselves clean and you don't want them ingesting anything toxic. You may need a degreasing soap such as dishwashing liquid for greasy substances.

For poisons that your pet has ingested, you will need some guidance. Activated charcoal can be given for almost anything toxic. This substance tends to absorb poisons to itself, minimizing the amount of dangerous material that Kitty will absorb into her system. It is not an antidote, though, and won't reverse any signs of toxicity you already see.

Making your pet vomit the toxin back up is often a good idea, but *always* check first with your veterinarian or the National Poison Control Center. Caustic agents like bleach may do more damage if they are vomited back up. Ingested oils are more likely to be aspirated (inhaled into the lungs) if you make your pet vomit and this can lead to deadly pneumonias. Swallowed pills can usually be vomited up without problems.

Depending on the substance your pet has gotten into, your veterinarian may suggest giving Spot something to neutralize the pH (adding something alkaline like baking soda if it is an acid or adding an acidic material if it is alkaline). Again, *always* check with your veterinarian before giving anything to a pet you feel may be poisoned. That includes the things your mother always said like giving milk—though the protein and calcium in milk can be helpful in binding up some substances.

Once your pet reaches the veterinary hospital, some additional techniques may be used. Gastric lavage entails passing a stomach tube into you pet's stomach and trying to dilute and flush back out any toxins. Enemas can be useful for some problems. Almost all pets will be put on intravenous fluids to dilute toxins and keep the kidneys in prime shape. Diuretics may be used as well to increase urine output. Other medications may be used to adjust urine pH up or down. In some cases a pet may even be referred to a veterinary college teaching hospital or other facility that offers short-term peritoneal dialysis for pets.

Depending on the exact poison ingested, there may be a specific antidote. Antidotes are used only when we are sure what the poison was as some antidotes could make your pet even more ill if she is being treated for the wrong poison.

Many, if not most, poisonings could be prevented. Not letting your pet run loose, keeping household items that are poisonous safely locked away, storing medications and dangerous yard and lawn products in safe areas will all reduce the chances of your pet accidentally being poisoned.

CHAPTER 23

Planning for Disasters

———◆———

Clearly we all hope to avoid hurricane evacuations, tornados, and ice storms, but it doesn't always work out that way. The weather waits for no man or animal and we need to be prepared, especially if we live in areas with frequent rough weather.

One of the cardinal rules of disaster planning is to take your pets with you if at all possible in the face of an evacuation. If it isn't safe for you to stay at home, it probably isn't safe for your pet(s) either. Not only that, but if you do get evacuated, you may not be allowed to return home for days. Think of the pet owners kept out of the area around the World Trade Center or near wildfire burns.

So, you need to make arrangements to bring the whole family with you. It is always nice if you have some warning and can make arrangements ahead of time. Most emergency shelters will not allow pets due to space limitations, people with allergies, etc. Try to find hotels, boarding kennels, or veterinary offices in a "safe" area that might take in pets. See if you can leave standing reservations for your animals. Perhaps you have friends or relatives out of the immediate area who could help.

Hopefully your pets are well socialized and trained. Pets who are trained, used to tolerating some confinement, and comfortable in new surroundings will handle evacuations much better than a pet who never leaves home. Disasters remind us how valuable crate and leash training our dogs can be!

Realize that you need to consider all of your pet's needs. You should have food, medications, bottled water, litter bags—litter as in cat litter or baggies for poop scooping, bowls, and bedding material with you. Everything should be in waterproof containers to keep it dry. You can't count on electricity, so add a can opener if your pet eats canned food and try to figure out ways to keep reptiles and birds warm.

Ideally your pets will have leashes, harnesses, carriers, or cages so that there is no chance they might escape in all the hustle and bustle. Towels over cages will hold in warmth and the disposable hand and foot warmers ice fishermen use might be packed into corners. A first aid kit is a good idea for the whole family and most items are interchangeable for people and pets.

Dogs, cats, and rabbits can all wear collars or harnesses with tags, even if they are also in carriers. Keep pets leashed at all times or confined. In a strange place they might panic, run off, and get lost. Have a copy of important health papers like rabies certificates with you in a waterproof plastic container. Ideally you will also have identification photos and any important medical records with you. If your pet needs refrigerated medications, pack a small cooler with freezer packs.

Do not put water bowls in cages or carriers to travel. The spill and wet mess may just make your pets more uncomfortable. A few ice cubes will hold a dog or cat for quite a while. For your bird, rabbit, pocket pet, turtle, or lizard, you can put some juicy fruit in the cage. Birds and some reptiles can also be misted to keep them hydrated. Your snake may need a bowl to soak in.

Some of my friends live in either earthquake areas or hurricane areas. They have "disaster kits" packed and ready to go at a moment's notice. If they need to evacuate, they can put the kit in the car, grab their pets, and be off. They know they have everything they need already set. The kits need to be checked at least twice a year to replace items and update forms, but can truly save you time and hassle in an emergency.

DISASTER KIT

Food in waterproof containers and a can opener if you use canned foods—this is especially important if your pet is on a prescription diet. Possibly some chew items for dogs who might get bored sitting in shelters.

Bottled water.

Bowls—you can get great collapsible fabric ones at camping stores or many pet stores.

Medications—any medications your pet needs or is on—well labeled and in waterproof containers.

Important paperwork—rabies certificates, vaccination records, any important health information along with identification photos, possibly even copies of registration papers—all of this in a waterproof container (could be something as simple as a locking plastic gallon size freezer bag).

Leash, harness, collar, tags, carrier, or cage—whatever you need to safely confine or control your pet.

Bedding or towels.

Flashlight.

First aid kit.

"Space blankets"—coated to reflect heat or hold heat in depending on which side you use.

WEBSITES FOR FURTHER INFORMATION

The Humane Society of the United States at www.hsus.org

The Federal Emergency Management Agency at www.fema.gov

CHAPTER 24

Endings: Hospice and Euthanasia

◆

Unfortunately, even with the best of care, the newest medications and wonderful diet, our beloved pets will age and eventually die. Modern veterinary medicine has prolonged our pets' lives, but we still can't make them immortal (cloning aside—and that is a topic beyond this book!).

When our pets are clearly failing, we need to make some decisions. Ideally we steel ourselves and decide on burial or cremation, where to bury if we go that route, etc. Then we need to look at making the last days of our dear companions as comfortable as possible.

Veterinary medicine is taking a cue from human medicine here. Hospice care is becoming much more common. In the case of our pets, we ourselves are doing virtually all of the nursing care, but we are using pain medications more extensively and delving into alternatives that might keep Fido comfortable.

There are a number of excellent books and videotapes on pet massage available, including the more specific Tellington Touch®. These techniques can ease sore muscles, calm an anxious pet, and simply convey our love. Along with daily massages, you may want to investigate some of the therapeutic beds or even just add extra cushions to your pet's favorite resting spot. A ramp to replace steep steps or a stool to help an aged feline hop up to her favorite windowsill all make life easier for our aged companions.

Acupuncture has almost gone mainstream with its capability of relieving pain in many cases. This can be a real boon for older pets with liver or kidney problems who can't handle many medications safely. Make sure you are dealing with a veterinary acupuncturist, as there are some differences between pets and people.

Prescription diets can help reduce the stress of the body by providing the simplest, best nutrients for an ill pet. Most of the companies who make prescription diets will also provide home diet recipes for certain illnesses if your pet becomes increasingly finicky with age. Encourage your older pets to drink plenty of fresh water. Check with your veterinarian to see if your pet needs some extra vitamins or any added supplements to her usual diet.

If you feel your pet needs some pain medications, discuss the many options with your veterinarian. Transdermal patches may work or you may need to give oral liquids or pills. Make sure your veterinarian is aware of any and all medications and supplements your pet may be taking so you can avoid bad drug interactions.

How do you know when the time for euthanasia has arrived? I tell people to try and look at their pets objectively (obviously not easy to do, but try). Is your pet in pain that we can't relieve? Is your pet having more "bad" days than "good" days? Can your pet still do some of his favorite things? Sometimes pets develop such mental stress from not being able to fetch or walk that they are chronically upset. You know your pet better than anyone else. It is hard to know when it is time to let go—probably one of the most unselfish decisions you will ever make. When that decision is made out of love, it is the "right" time.

Your veterinarian will try to make this time as easy for you as possible. Some clinics offer house calls for euthanasia. Most clinics try to schedule euthanasias at quiet times for the clinic so you don't have to sit around in a crowded waiting room. Often the necessary paperwork can be done ahead of time to minimize waiting as well.

If your pet is very anxious or known to be aggressive, a sedative may be given ahead of time.

Your pet will receive an injection in the vein for euthanasia. The euthanasia compounds are usually combination drugs. Most have a muscle relaxant, a local anesthetic, and then an overdose of a barbiturate. Different companies have slightly different formulas.

If your pet has good circulation, she will usually have passed on even before the needle is removed from the vein. The brain goes first and you can tell that by the loss of the "blink reflex"—you touch near the eye and your pet no longer blinks. Unlike the dramatic scenes in the movies, the eyes don't normally close by themselves. Your pet's heart will gradually slow and stop as will the breathing rate. Sometimes a pet will have a reflex "gasp," but that is just the air leaving the body. Many times your pet will leak urine or pass stool as the bladder and intestinal muscles relax and die.

This is always a difficult time for everyone concerned. You can feel relieved though that your pet is no longer in any discomfort. Many people choose to make donations to an animal charity or toward research for animal health problems in their pet's memory. Local animal shelters, breed rescue groups, veterinary colleges, and the Morris Animal Foundation are all worthy causes.

PART IV

Individual Drugs and Medications

Acepromazine

Acepromazine is a tranquilizer of the phenothiazine family. As such it has a calming effect on pets, while lowering blood pressure and possibly affecting motor skills (pets may walk with a wobble). Acepromazine does interfere with temperature regulation. It is metabolized by the liver and excreted in the urine.

Acepromazine is primarily used to calm anxious animals down, to help with motion sickness, and as a preanesthetic. It is not a pain medication. Used as a preanesthetic, it reduces the amount of anesthetic drug needed.

Acepromazine comes with a number of cautions. It should be used very cautiously in older pets or very young pets as it does lower blood pressure and interfere with temperature regulation. It lowers seizure thresholds, so it should not be used in pets with epilepsy. It is often prescribed to help with traveling pets, but the temperature regulation failure should be kept in mind. Occasionally a pet will become hyperexcitable, not tranquil, when given acepromazine. For that reason, a trial dose should be tried at home before a trip.

Acepromazine is used both as an injectable (primarily by your veterinarian as a preanesthetic and often in combination with atropine) and as a pill. The pill form is the form commonly dispensed.

ROUTINE DOSAGES: This is another drug with many caveats. The dosage may need to be adjusted carefully for your individual pet. Giant breeds and greyhounds may need a lower dose, while terriers may be somewhat resistant and require a higher dose. Brachycephalic dogs (dogs with short, pushed-in faces) may be more susceptible to the side effects. This drug should be used only under the direction of your veterinarian, and you should consult your veterinarian for the proper dose for your pet.

Acepromazine should be used only with extreme care in older pets and very young pets due to the cardiac and temperature regulation effects. It should never be used in pets with epilepsy or a history of having had a seizure. It has been safely used as a tranquilizer for rabbits.

If you feel your pet has overdosed on acepromazine, you should contact your veterinarian and the National Poison Control Center.

COMMON BRAND NAME: Promace

Acetaminophen

Acetaminophen is a synthetic nonopiate analgesic which influences normal body functions to relieve pain and lower fevers. It is not an anti-inflammatory medication. Acetaminophen should be used cautiously due to the potential for liver or kidney problems and *never* used in cats! Acetaminophen can be fatal to cats even in small doses. It should not be used postoperatively after halothane anesthesia.

Acetaminophen is available as tablets or elixirs—both to be given orally.

ROUTINE DOSAGES: Acetaminophen is not an FDA-approved medication for pets, and even though it is widely available over-the-counter, it should be used only under the guidance of your veterinarian.

For dogs: 5 mg/lb given orally twice daily.

For cats: *Do not use!!!*

For rabbits: No longer recommended.

Side effects include liver problems, and overdoses (which is virtually any amount in cats) may lead to death. If you feel your pet has overdosed on acetaminophen, you should contact your veterinarian and the National Poison Control Center.

COMMON BRAND NAME: Tylenol

Acetylcysteine

Acetylcysteine is an N-acetyl derivative of L-cysteine (an amino acid or protein building block). This medication influences normal body functions by reducing the viscosity (thickness) of pulmonary secretions and some eye discharges. This is its mucolytic action, but it is also used as an antidote for acetaminophen poisoning in cats. Acetylcysteine is used topically for eye problems such as KCS (keratoconjunctivits sicca), as an inhalant for pulmonary secretions, and intravenously for acetaminophen toxicity.

The normal formulations of acetylcysteine are inhalants, topical versions, and oral solutions. It is given by intravenous injection for cases of poisoning. This medication tastes quite bad and oral preparations may need to be disguised in food.

ROUTINE DOSAGES: Acetylcysteine is not FDA approved for use in pets and should be used only under the guidance of your veterinarian.

For dogs: Dosages vary with the condition being treated (respiratory or antidote for toxicity).

For cats: Dosages vary with the condition being treated (respiratory or antidote for toxicity).

Side effects, particularly of the oral preparations, may include gastrointestinal signs and hives. Overdosages may show severe gastrointestinal problems. If you feel your pet has overdosed on acetylcysteine, contact your veterinarian and the National Poison Control Center.

COMMON BRAND NAMES: Mucomyst; Mucosil

Albuterol

Albuterol is a sympathomimetic amine drug which works as a bronchodilator (opening airways and making it easier to breathe). This is a drug which affects a normal body function, not fighting infection.

Albuterol is most commonly used for problems such as feline asthma and chronic canine bronchitis—both of which can be affected by secondhand smoke. It is sometimes used in combination with steroids to relieve inflammation as well.

Albuterol is metabolized in the liver, so it should be used with caution in pets with liver disease. Pets with diabetes, seizures, cardiac problems, or suffering from hyperthyroidism, should also be very carefully monitored if albuterol is used. Potassium levels can be changed by albuterol and should be checked by periodic blood tests, but serious problems with this primarily occur with overdosaging.

Care needs to be taken when using albuterol with some other drugs as well. Phenylephrine, ephedrine, and some gas anesthetics can increase its effect while albuterol may lower the effectiveness of digoxin. Digoxin is a fairly common medication used in pets with heart problems so a different choice of medications would be better for pets with cardiac disease.

Albuterol is mainly used in pets as an oral medication, though inhalers do exist. The use of inhalers may become more prevalent in the future.

ROUTINE DOSAGES: Albuterol is not FDA approved, so this should be used only under the direct supervision of your veterinarian.

For dogs: 0.01–0.03 mg/lb one to three times daily.

For cats: 0.01–0.03 mg/lb one to three times daily.

Side effects that can be seen with albuterol are related to its direct function. Pets may have increased heart rates, develop tremors, and act very nervous or hyperactive.

Overdosing in pets may lead to an abnormally low level of potassium, heart problems, and excitement. If you suspect your pet is overdosed, contact your veterinarian and call the National Poison Control Center.

Albuterol can cross the placenta, so it should not be used unless necessary in pregnant animals or in very young pets.

COMMON BRAND NAMES: Proventil; Ventolin

Allopurinol

Allopurinol is a medication that adjusts normal body functions. In this case it is an inhibitor of the enzyme xanthine oxidase. It helps to prevent the transition of purines (DNA protein building blocks) to uric acid and urates.

This drug is primarily used in Dalmatians to treat dogs with urate urinary/bladder stone problems. Dalmatians have a unique defect in their liver and kidney enzymes that contributes to the formation of urate stones. Birds and tortoises with gout are also sometimes treated with this medication.

Allopurinol should not be used in any pets which have shown allergic reactions to it. Pets with underlying liver or kidney problems should use this medication only if clearly needed and under close supervision. Mixing allopurinol with diuretics or urinary acidifiers will reduce its effectiveness. Caution should also be used if allopurinol is given with anticoagulants such as warfarin or bronchodilators such as aminophylline, as the effect of those drugs may be increased. Combining allopurinol with many antibiotics has been associated with skin rashes in people.

Allopurinol is normally given with food and the food should be low in purines (such as eggs and cheese) to assist with treatment.

ROUTINE DOSAGES: Note this drug is not FDA approved for pets, so it should be used only under the direct supervision of your veterinarian.

For dogs: 5 mg/lb three times daily with the dose reduced over time to 10mg/kg once daily.

For cats: 3 mg/lb per day.

For birds: Crush one 100 mg tablet into 10 ml of water. Add 20 drops to 1 ounce drinking water.

For tortoises: 10 mg/kg given orally once daily.

A side effect sometimes seen with allopurinol is skin hypersensitivity reactions. Overdosing with allopurinol is not common but it can occur if the high dose level is given over long periods of time. This can result in the formation of xanthine bladder stones. For acute overdosing, you should contact your veterinarian and the National Poison Control Center.

Ideally this medication would not be given to breeding animals or very young puppies or kittens.

COMMON BRAND NAMES: Zyloprim; Purinol

Amikacin

Amikacin is a semisynthetic aminoglycoside antibiotic. This is a medication that acts against outside infections. Amikacin is a bactericidal antibiotic, meaning it kills bacteria outright. It is effective against aerobic gram-positive and gram-negative bacteria including *E. coli, Pseudomonas,* and *Salmonella.* It is often used for respiratory infections in birds and reptiles or shell disease in turtles.

While amikacin is good for bacteria that have gentamicin resistance, it is not great for central nervous system infections. This bacteria can greatly influence gastrointestinal bacteria and should *not* be used in rabbits.

Extreme care should be taken if amikacin has to be used in a pet with kidney problems. It should not be combined with other nephrotoxic (kidney-damaging) medications. Pets on diuretics need to be carefully monitored or switched to a different antibiotic.

Due to the potential for ototoxicity (damage to the ears and hearing), amikacin should not be used unless necessary in working dogs.

Amikacin is an injectable antibiotic and will most likely be given by your veterinarian at their clinic.

ROUTINE DOSAGES: Amikacin is only FDA approved for use in dogs. If it is used in other species, it should be under the guidance of your veterinarian.

For dogs: 2.5–5 mg/lb given by intramuscular or subcutaneous injection two or three times daily.

For cats: 2.5–5 mg/lb given by intramuscular or subcutaneous injection two or three times daily.

For birds: 40 mg/kg given by intramuscular injection once or twice daily—primarily used for sinusitis problems in macaws.

For reptiles: Care must be taken to ensure adequate hydration.

Snakes: 5 mg/kg given intramuscularly once, then 2.5 mg/kg given intramuscularly every 3 days—used for respiratory infections.

Water turtles: 10 mg/kg given by intramuscular injection daily for shell disease.

Tortoises: 10 mg/kg given by intramuscular injection daily for shell disease.

Side effects may include kidney problems or hearing losses. Overdosing can exacerbate those side effects. If you feel your pet has overdosed on amikacin, you should contact your pet's veterinarian and the National Poison Control Center.

Amikacin has been shown to cause kidney and hearing loss problems even in fetuses so it should not be used in pregnant pets unless absolutely necessary.

Aminopentamide

Aminopentamide is an antispasmodic and smooth muscle relaxant. It also helps to reduce stomach secretions (primarily gastric acids). It is mainly used to treat vomiting and/or diarrhea. It should be kept in mind that by slowing the rate of intestinal transit, it can also increase the absorption of toxins present in the gut. Often a pet will receive just one dose of this medication while treatment is getting under way for gastrointestinal problems. Aminopentamide does interact with some other medications. Certain tranquilizers may increase its effect, and aminopentamide itself can increase the effect of diuretics. Aminopentamide is also felt to antagonize the action of metaclopramide.

This medication should *not* be used in pets with glaucoma, pets with certain cardiac problems, or if there is a chance of gastrointestinal or urinary obstruction.

Aminopentamide is available both as a tablet and an injection.

ROUTINE DOSAGES (Note that many veterinarians will use only one dose of this, then switch medications.):

For dogs: 10 pounds and under: 0.1 mg two or three times daily.

11–20 pounds: 0.2 mg two or three times daily.

21–50 pounds: 0.3 mg two or three times daily.

51–100 pounds: 0.4 mg two or three times daily.

Over 100 pounds 0.5 mg two or three times daily.

For cats: 10 pounds and under: 0.1 mg two or three times daily.

Over 10 pounds: 0.2 mg two or three times daily.

Side effects may include vision blurring and dry eyes or dry mouth.

Signs of overdosing can include dryness of the eyes and mouth, retention of urine, unsteadiness, seizures, and erratic heart rates. If you suspect your pet is overdosed, contact your veterinarian and the National Poison Control Center.

COMMON BRAND NAME: Centrine

Aminophylline/Theophylline

These two drugs are closely related and most of the discussion will apply to both medications. Where there are differences, it will be noted.

Aminophylline and theophylline are xanthine bronchodilators. These medications open airways and make it easier for pets to breath so they influence normal body activities.

Aminophylline and theophylline are often used to treat feline asthma and chronic canine bronchitis. (Note: Secondhand smoke is just as dangerous for pets as it is for people and may be a contributing factor to those two syndromes in pets.) These drugs may be combined with steroids to ease serious breathing difficulties.

Aminophylline and theophylline should not be used in pets with reactions to xanthine drugs, including theobromine (from chocolate) and caffeine. Pets with liver or kidney problems should use these medications only with care, as they are metabolized in the liver. Cardiac patients will need careful monitoring as will patients with hyperthyroid conditions.

Drug interactions need to be avoided with these medications as well. They should not be used with pets receiving ketamine or ephedrine and not if a pet will be anesthetized with halothane. Aminophylline and theophylline may decrease the effect of some seizure medications and increase the effect of allopurinol, cimetidine, and some antibiotics. Be sure to let your veterinarian know if your pet is taking any other medications so she can make sure your pet won't have any adverse reactions. Information on drug interactions is continually being upgraded and new information added.

Ideally these medications are given orally and on an empty stomach.

ROUTINE DOSAGES: Note, these medications are not FDA approved for use in pets. Be sure you know if your theophylline is the long-duration form!

For dogs: Aminophylline 3-6 mg/lb two or three times daily.

Theophylline 5 mg/lb three or four times daily or the long-duration form 10 mg/lb twice daily.

For cats: Aminophylline 2-3 mg/lb two or three times daily.

Theophylline 2mg/lb two or three times daily or the long-duration form 12 mg/lb once daily.

Side effects of aminophylline and theophylline can be central nervous system excitement or gastrointestinal upsets with vomiting or diarrhea.

Overdosage of these two medications can manifest itself as central nervous system signs or cardiac signs. If you think your pet has been overdosed, contact your veterinarian immediately and the National Poison Control Center.

These medications can cross the placenta so they are not routinely used in pregnant pets or in very young or old pets. Pets with liver, kidney, or cardiac problems should only use these medications under carefully supervision.

COMMON BRAND NAMES: Theo-Dur; Elixophyllin; many generics available

Amitraz

Amitraz is an enzyme inhibitor (specifically of monoamine oxidase) and also inhibits the release of insulin. It influences normal body functions, but most importantly in veterinary medicine, it functions as a topical parasiticide.

Amitraz is used as a topical dip for cases of generalized demodicosis (red mange) and as a collar preparation for use against ticks.

It is *not* recommended for use in cats or rabbits. Puppies under four months should not be treated with amitraz, and great care should be used with this medication on the toy breeds of dogs and any dogs with diabetes (due to the insulin effect). Pets receiving amitraz dips should not be stressed for at least twenty-four hours following treatment.

When giving the dip, owners should wear gloves and diabetic owners should be especially careful not to come into contact with this medication.

ROUTINE DOSAGES: The dose for the dips will be adjusted by your veterinarian for your pet (exactly what dilution they feel you should use for you dog).

The collars should be carefully fitted with the excess cut off and discarded according to package directions.

This should *not* be used on cats or rabbits.

The most common side effect seen with amitraz is sedation and this can be profound in some pets.

Overdosings occur most often from pets chewing on the collars and/or swallowing pieces of the collar. Pets may show an increase in blood glucose, a decrease in body temperature and profound sedation. If you feel your dog is overdosed, contact your veterinarian and the National Poison Control Center.

Amitraz is not recommended for breeding animals, but dogs with generalized demodex should be neutered or spayed anyway.

COMMON BRAND NAMES: Mitaban (dip); Preventic (collar)

Amitriptyline

Amitriptyline is a tricyclic antidepressant medication. As such, it is a drug that influences a normal body function. The primary uses of amitriptyline in pets are separation anxiety in dogs and urine spraying in cats. It may take weeks before the effect of this medication is apparent in your pet's behavior. Behavior-influencing medications should always be combined with behavior-modifying training.

Amitriptyline should not be used with other antidepressant medications or with cimetidine. Always make sure your veterinarian is aware of any other medications your pet may be taking before you add this drug.

Amitriptyline is normally given orally to pets.

ROUTINE DOSAGES: Amitriptyline is not FDA approved for pets, so it should only be used under the guidance of your veterinarian.

For dogs: 1–2 mg/lb twice daily (increased doses used for some behaviors).
For cats: 5–10 mg/cat once daily.

A wide range of side effects can be seen in pets taking amitriptyline—most of them not serious. These include sedation, conversely, hyperactivity, gastrointestinal upsets, and or more seriously bone marrow depression. Some pets may show a "dry mouth."

Overdosing of amitriptyline can lead to cardiac arrhythmias or cardiorespiratory collapse. If you feel your pet has overdosed on amitriptyline, contact your veterinarian and the National Poison Control Center.

COMMON BRAND NAME: Elavil

Ammonium Chloride

Ammonium chloride is a urinary acidifier. While it influences a normal body function, it is also often used in conjunction with antibiotics to help fight infection. By lowering the pH of the urine, ammonium chloride helps to prevent the formation of some bladder stones and crystals and makes some antibiotics more efficient.

Ammonium chloride is metabolized in the liver and should not be used in patients with liver, kidney, or pancreatic diseases.

Ammonium chloride is primarily used orally and is given with food to minimize the chances of stomach irritation. It should not be used with any of the special acidifying diets as this can cause problems.

ROUTINE DOSAGES:

For dogs: 10–20 mg/lb twice daily to lower urine pH to 5.5–6.5.
For cats: 10 mg/lb twice daily to lower urine pH to 5.5–6.5.

Side effects of ammonium chloride use can include stomach irritation and vomiting. Overdosing ammonium chloride can cause metabolic acidosis. The signs may include vomiting, thirst, an increase in respiratory rate (breathing), an increase in heart rate, and depression. Pets may have a drop in their blood potassium values as well. If you feel your pet is overdosed, you should contact your veterinarian and the National Poison Control Center.

This medication is not recommended for use in pregnant pets.

COMMON BRAND NAMES: Uroeze; MEq-AC

Amoxicillin

Amoxicillin is a synthetic antibiotic of the penicillin family of drugs. This is a bactericidal drug (meaning it kills bacteria as opposed to simply inhibiting bacterial growth). Amoxicillin has a broad spectrum of activity but will not work against bacteria that are resistant due to production of an enzyme called penicillinase. It works quite well against most *Staphyloccus* species and most *Streptococcus* species, but not very well against *Pseudomonas* species. Amoxicillin may be combined with clavulanate potassium to increase its range of effectiveness.

Respiratory infections, bladder infections, and skin and soft tissue infections are common situations where amoxicillin is used. Amoxicillin should not be given in combination with a bacteriostatic antibiotic (one which inhibits bacterial growth), as you reduce the efficacy of both medications. Amoxicillin is excreted via the urine. When combined with clavulanate potassium, it can be quite helpful for periodontal infections.

Amoxicillin is in the penicillin family, so it should not be used for pets with penicillin allergies. Owners with penicillin allergies themselves should use caution when giving this medication to their pets. (The addition of clavulanate potassium means to also beware of any pets allergic to the cephalosporin class of antibiotics.) Amoxicillin may be given with food and is most commonly used orally though there are injectable forms. It comes in both pill form and a dry powder, which is reconstituted to a liquid for dosing. The liquid can be kept refrigerated though that is not required. After two weeks, any unused liquid amoxicillin should be discarded.

ROUTINE DOSAGES (higher dosages may be used for specific infections):
For dogs: 5–10 mg/lb twice daily for at least five to seven days.
For cats: 5–10 mg/lb once daily for at least five to seven days.
For birds: 150–175 mg/kg given orally once or twice daily.
For reptiles: 22 mg/kg given orally once daily (works best in combination with an aminoglycoside antibiotic).

Side effects are rare, but can include diarrhea due to action against intestinal bacteria.

Overdosaging is rare, but signs might include vomiting or diarrhea. Contact the National Poison Control Center or your veterinarian if you have concerns.

Amoxicillin is considered to be quite safe for use in puppies and kittens and in pregnant pets if necessary (though safety for pregnant pets has not been specifically tested).

Older pets with kidney disease may require a slightly lower dose since amoxicillin is excreted via the urine.

Amoxicillin should *not* be used for pets with penicillin allergies or for many pocket pets. Guinea pigs can have a fatal anaphylactic shock reaction and rabbits may develop fatal bacterial changes in their gastrointestinal systems.

COMMON BRAND NAMES: Amoxil; Amoxi-Drop; Amoxi-Tab; Clavamox (with clavulanate potassium added)

Ampicillin

Ampicillin is a semisynthetic antibiotic of the penicillin family of drugs. This is a bactericidal drug (meaning it kills bacteria as opposed to simply inhibiting bacterial growth). Ampicillin has a fairly broad spectrum of activity including both gram-negative and gram-positive bacteria. It is also effective against some anaerobic bacteria such as the *Clostridia*. The usefulness of ampicillin is limited somewhat by any bacteria with resistance due to the production of penicillinase.

Respiratory infections and soft tissue infection can be treated with ampicillin, and it is commonly used for long-term treatment of bladder infections. It should not be combined with any bacteriostatic antibiotics, as you reduce the usefulness of both medications. It is primarily excreted via the urine.

Ampicillin would not be the drug of choice if your pet has penicllin allergies, and owners with penicillin allergies should use caution when administering this drug. Ampicillin should not be given with tranquilizers or some antihistamines, so make sure your veterinarian knows if you are using other medications on your pet. This is a medication that should be given on an empty stomach, an hour before feeding time or two hours after. Due to these recommendations, ampicillin is not used orally very much except for long-term use in treating bladder infections (cystitis). Injectable ampicillin is commonly used during the hospital stay of pets.

ROUTINE DOSAGES:
For dogs: 10 mg/lb three times a day for at least five to seven days.
For cats: 10 mg/lb three times a day for at least five to seven days.

For birds: 100 mg/kg given by intramuscular injection (ampicillin is not well absorbed so not very effective orally in birds).

For reptiles: 3–6 mg/kg given by intramuscular injection once or twice daily.

For rabbits: 10–25 mg/kg given by intramuscular injection once daily—not to be used for more than five days.

Side effects are uncommon but there could be vomiting or diarrhea. If your pet shows these signs, stop the medication and contact your veterinarian.

Overdosaging is not common, but signs could include vomiting or diarrhea, just like the possible side effects. Contact the National Poison Control Center or your veterinarian if you have concerns.

Ampicillin appears to be quite safe, but should *not* be used orally in rabbits or pocket pets. Even the injectable version should be used only by a veterinarian and with care in them. This is another antibiotic that can affect the bacteria in the gastrointestinal tract and cause serious illness or death in these pets.

If your pet is a diabetic, it should be noted that ampicillin has been identified as occasionally causing false positives on urine glucose test strips. Your veterinarian may have you wait on dosing your pet until you have checked a morning urine in these cases.

COMMON BRAND NAMES: Amcill; Polycillin; Polyflex

Apomorphine

Apomorphine is a centrally acting emetic—this means it works on brain receptors to cause vomiting. It is in the morphine family of drugs and it effects a normal body function as opposed to fighting infection. Drugs in the morphine family are not routinely used for cats. Apomorphine is metabolized in the liver and then excreted in the urine.

Apomorphine is used to make pets vomit, so it can be part of the protocol for treating a poisoned dog. It should not be given to dogs that are not aware, are very weak, or with certain toxins and poisons (some poisons do even more damage on the way up if the pet is made to vomit). Whenever a dog vomits, there is concern about aspiration pneumonia (a pet accidentally inhaling some of the vomited material), so the dog should be awake and able to stand if possible before giving this medication.

Apomorphine is in the morphine family, so it should not be combined with any opiates or barbiturates. Apomorphine is most commonly given as a tablet (or part of a tablet) tucked into the lower eyelid of the dog. From there the medication is rapidly absorbed. It can also be given as an intramuscular injection or an intravenous injection.

ROUTINE DOSAGES: Apomorphine is not FDA approved for pets and should be used only under the direct supervision of a veterinarian.

For dogs: 1.5–6 mg in the conjunctival sac of the eye.

Not for use in cats.

Not for use in rabbits or rodents.

The most common side effects are either central nervous system stimulation or depression. Some dogs will experience protracted vomiting.

Apomorphine can be overdosed and present signs of overstimulation or depression as well as protracted vomiting. You should use this medication only under the direct supervision/contact of your veterinarian. If you feel your dog is overdosed, you should contact your veterinarian immediately and call the National Poison Control Center. Apomorphine should *not* be given to rabbits or rodents. These animals do not routinely vomit and the stresses caused by the medication could do serious damage.

COMMON BRAND NAME: Apomorphine

Aspirin

Aspirin's scientific name is acetylsalicyclic acid and this is a drug that influences normal body functions. Aspirin seems to function primarily by decreasing the synthesis of prostaglandins. It acts as an analgesic (painkiller), fever-reducing agent, anti-inflammatory, and to reduce platelet aggregation (interfering with blood clotting).

Aspirin is used in pets for pain and also for its tendency to reduce clotting. Cats with cardiomyopathy who tend to throw clots may be treated with aspirin. Since cats are deficient in the glucuronide enzymes, aspirin should be used as a very low dose and on an infrequent dosing schedule.

Aspirin is metabolized in the liver and excreted via the kidneys. It should not be used in pets with bleeding ulcers, asthma, or any bleeding problems. It should be used with care in pets with kidney problems.

There are a number of drug interactions with aspirin. It is affected by medications that change the blood pH—making blood more acidic or more alkaline. The diuretic furosemide increases its excretion while the seizure medication Phenobarbital increases the metabolism of aspirin. It should not be routinely combined with corticosteroids or other nonsteroidal anti–inflammatories. Some antibiotics interact with aspirin such as tetracycline and perhaps aminoglycosides. Aspirin may affect some urine glocuse tests so it should be used with care in diabetics.

Your veterinarian should be aware of any other medications your pet is receiving if aspirin is added to the treatment regimen. And you should not give your pet aspirin without consulting your veterinarian.

Aspirin comes in tablet or caplet form and may be given with food.

ROUTINE DOSAGES: Aspirin has no formal FDA approval but has been "grandfathered" in, as it has been used reasonably safely for so long. The dosages given vary with the problem being treated. You should always consult your veterinarian before using aspirin.

For dogs: 4–10 mg/lb given twice daily or down to 2–5 mg/lb given once daily.

For cats: 4 mg/lb given every other day or 10 mg/lb given every three or four days. *Note:* Never use aspirin for your cat without consulting your veterinarian!

For rabbits: Start with one 81 mg tablet once daily—use only under veterinary guidance.

The most common side effects of aspirin are gastrointestinal signs such as vomiting and sometimes with blood. This can be minimized by giving the aspirin with some food.

Overdosing with aspirin can lead to depression, vomiting, fevers, and increased breathing rates. Coma and even death may occur. If you feel your pet has overdosed on aspirin, contact your veterinarian and the National Poison Control Center immediately.

Aspirin is not recommended for use in pregnant pets as it may delay parturition (birth). It should not be given shortly before any surgeries either due to the increased bleeding tendencies.

Atropine

Atropine is an amine antimuscarinic. This is a medication which influences many normal body functions. It is often used as a preanesthetic treatment to minimize respiratory secretions and keep heart rates stable. It is also used in ophthalmic preparations to help relieve pain in the eye. Atropine is used as an antidote for some types of toxins and poisonings. It is sometimes combined with other medications to reduce motility in the gastrointestinal tract.

Atropine is metabolized in the liver and excreted in the urine. Atropine should not be used in pets with liver or kidney problems or in hyperthyroid pets. Atropine should never be used in pets with glaucoma and with caution in pets with increased heart rates or the possibility of gastrointestinal or urinary obstructions. Since it slows down motility in the intestinal tract, it could prolong the absorption of any toxins present there.

Certain tranquilizers and antihistamines may increase the activity of atropine, while atropine may itself increase the efficiency of certain diuretics. The action of metaclopramide is felt to be antagonized by atropine.

Atropine is used in veterinary medicine primarily as an injectable or an ophthalmic preparation.

ROUTINE DOSAGES: Atropine is used in dogs, cats, birds, and reptiles. The dosages vary greatly depending on the reason for use of the drug and any other possible drug interactions. The exact dose used in your pet should be determined by your veterinarian and will most likely be given as an injection under her direct supervision.

Side effects which may be seen with the use of atropine are dry eyes and/or mouth, vision problems including blurring, and central nervous system changes.

Overdosing of atropine can lead to an increased heart rate, dryness of the eyes and mouth, stasis of the gastrointestinal tract, and central nervous system signs. If you feel your pet has had an overdose, contact your veterinarian and the National Center for Poison Control.

COMMON BRAND NAMES: Atropine sulfate; various ophthalmic preparations

Benzoyl Peroxide

Benzoyl peroxide is an ingredient in some medicated pet shampoos. While it does have some antibacterial action (particularly against *Staphyloccus*), it is not considered a primary antibiotic. It does work to moderate some natural skin processes gone haywire. Benzoyl peroxide is very effective in degreasing skin, especially the extreme keratinization sometimes seen with seborrhea. It is often included as part of the treatment for seborrhea or pyoderma (skin infections). Shampooing with benzoyl peroxide is sometimes done before using medicated dips like amitraz for demodectic mange or for some of the yeast treatments.

The main side effect of benzoyl peroxide is related to its useful properties. It can dry the skin out too much. A shampooing schedule should be set up with your veterinarian with regular checkups to be sure the skin isn't getting too dry.

This medication should *not* be used internally or in or on the eyes. If your pet consumes any benzoyl peroxide, you should contact your veterinarian and the National Poison Control Center.

It comes in both shampoo and gel formulations.

COMMON BRAND NAMES: Allerderm; Oxydex; Pyoban

Bethanecol

Bethanecol is a medication that influences a normal bodily function. It acts as a smooth muscle stimulant. Smooth muscle is present in the intestinal tract, the respiratory tract, some vascular areas, and along the urinary tract.

Due to its area of action, bethanecol could be used for gastrointestinal problems, respiratory problems, and some cardiac problems. It is used primarily for the treatment of bladder problems in pets. If a pet has had a urinary blockage, the bladder may have stretched and may not contract normally. Bethanecol is used to increase the muscle tone.

Bethanecol should ideally not be used with antihypertensive medications and its action is decreased by atropine (which can be used as an antidote for bethanecol overdosages). It should not be used in pets with epilepsy, asthma, hyperthyroidism, or many gastrointestinal problems. It should *never* be used for a pet who still has a urinary obstruction!!! The pet must have an open urethra or possibly even a catheter in place. Otherwise the bladder could rupture.

Bethanecol is used as an oral medication, best if given on an empty stomach. There are injectable forms of bethanecol, which may be used in the veterinary hospital for subcutaneous injections—not intravenous or intramuscular!

ROUTINE DOSAGES: Bethanecol is not FDA-approved for pets so should be used only under the guidance of your veterinarian.

For dogs: 5–25 mg three times daily.

For cats: 1.25–5 mg three times daily.

For reptiles: 2.5 mg/kg given subcutaneously; check with your vet.

The most common side effects are mild gastrointestinal signs—nausea, vomiting, and diarrhea.

Signs of overdosing with bethanecol can include overstimulation of the gastrointestinal tract, the respiratory sytem, or the cardiovascular system. If you feel you pet has overdosed with bethanecol, you should contact your veterinarian and the National Poison Control Center.

COMMON BRAND NAME: Urecholine

Bismuth Subsalicylate

Bismuth subsalicylate is a mucosal protectant. This is a substance that influences normal body functions but also has minor antibacterial effects. The bismuth part is primarily a mucosal protectant in the gastrointestinal tract and provides some protection against endotoxins (toxic substances made by bacteria—often in the gastrointestinal tract). The subsalicylate part interferes with prostaglandins, providing some anti-inflammatory effect.

Bismuth of subsalicylate is used in cases of diarrhea in dogs. It is not recommended for use in cats.

Care should be taken in using bismuth of subsalicylate in pets with bleeding problems. This medication should not be combined with aspirin or tetracycline antibiotics. Bismuth subsalicylate may interfere with some urine glucose tests so use with care in diabetic pets.

Bismuth of subsalicylate may darken the stool.

Bismuth of subsalicylate comes in both liquid and tablet forms and is available over the counter. The liquid form should be shaken well and not mixed with milk.

ROUTINE DOSAGES: Bismuth of subsalicylate is not an FDA-approved medication for use in pets and should only be used under the guidance of your veterinarian.

For dogs: 0.5 ml/lb (1/2 tsp/5lbs) given orally three to four times daily.

The most common side effect of bismuth subsalicylate is change in stool color—stools may appear quite dark. Overdosing is very unusual with this medication, but if you feel your pet has overdosed, you should contact your veterinarian and the National Poison Control Center.

COMMON BRAND NAMES: Pepto-Bismol®; Bismatrol

Buspirone

Buspirone is an antianxiety medication, therefore a drug which influences normal body functions. It is in a new class of medications called azaspirodecanediones. It is not intended as a sedative.

In pets, buspirone is used as an adjunct to behavior modification. Its most common and successful use is for cats that spray urine in inappropriate places. It has not been as successful for anxiety treatment in dogs as some other medications. It may take weeks before the drug's effects on behavior are seen.

Buspirone should not be used with other behavior-modifying drugs, and care should be used if it is combined with any other medications. Patients with liver problems may need a decreased dose and careful monitoring.

Buspirone is commonly given orally and with food.

ROUTINE DOSAGES: Buspirone is not FDA approved for pets, so it should be used only under the guidance of your veterinarian.

For dogs: 2.5–10 mg two or three times daily.

For cats: 2.5–5 mg two or three times daily.

Side effects are not common with buspirone, though it can be difficult to pick up some side effects of behavior medications in pets. Occasionally a cat will show increased aggression with this medication.

Overdosing is not common with buspirone. In people, signs that are noted include nausea, dizziness, and drowsiness. If you feel your pet is overdosed, contact your veterinarian and the National Poison Control Center.

COMMON BRAND NAME: BuSpar

Butorphanol

Butorphanol is a medication that affects bodily functions—relieving coughing and providing pain relief. It is a narcotic pain medication and potent cough medication. It is also used to reduce nausea seen with some chemotherapy drugs such as cisplatin.

Butorphanol is becoming a commonly used postsurgery pain medication.

Butorphanol is metabolized in the liver with most of the excretion being in the urine, but some going into the bile and passing out in feces. Care should be taken if butorphanol is used in pets with liver or kidney problems. The dose may need to be drastically reduced. Pets who are hypothyroid, debilitated, or have head trauma should be given this medication only if necessary. Caution should also be used when treating dogs with heartworm disease.

Butorphanol is a narcotic, so it should not be used with tranquilizers or anticonvulsants as they may increase their sedative effects.

Butorphanol is used both orally and as an injection. It is FDA approved for injection for pain in both dogs and cats, but only orally for dogs for coughing. It is routinely and safely used orally in cats, however.

ROUTINE DOSAGES: See the note above about FDA approval.
  For dogs: for pain—0.1 mg/lb twice daily.
    for cough—0.25–0.5 mg/lb two to four times daily as needed.
  For cats: for pain—1 mg two to four times daily as needed.
  For rabbits: for pain—0.4mg/kg given by subcutaneous injection every four to six hours as needed.
  For birds: It is questionable at this time if birds do truly get pain relief (analgesia) from butorphanol. Check with your veterinarian.

The most common side effect seen is a mild sedation. This can be a plus in postsurgical pets who need to remain quiet. Some pets may show a decrease in respiration as well.

It is quite rare to see overdosages with butorphanol, but it could cause depression of the central nervous system and lead to coma. If you feel your pet is overdosed, contact your veterinarian and the National Poison Control Center.

Butorphanol does cross the placenta and gets into the milk of nursing pets so it should not be used in pregnant or nursing pets.

COMMON BRAND NAMES: Torbutrol; Torbugesic

Carbenicillin

Carbenicillin is a synthetic penicillin antibiotic. This drug is used to treat outside infections such as those caused by the bacterial group *Pseudomonas*. Carbenicillin is sometimes combined with an aminoglycoside antibiotic or other synthetic penicillins such as ticarcillin for greater efficacy. There is some resistance seen in the bacteria.

Carbenicllin is primarily eliminated through kidneys so it should be used with care in pets with kidney disease. It is most often used to treat pets with urinary or prostate infections.

In snakes, carbenicillin is used for ulcerative stomatitis.

This is a member of the penicillin family so it should ideally not be used in pets with known penicillin allergies.

Carbenicllin comes in oral tablets and has a bitter taste so it is often mixed with food to dose pets.

ROUTINE DOSAGES: Carbenicillin is not FDA approved so this medication should only be used under the guidance of your veterinarian.

For dogs: 6–20 mg/lb given orally three or four times daily.

For cats: 6–20 mg/lb given orally three or four times daily.

For birds: Primarily used in Pscittacines and mixed with fruits or other foods: 100–200 mg/kg given orally twice daily.

For tortoises: 400mg/kg intramuscular injection every two days.

For snakes: 400 mg/kg intramuscular injection once daily.

Side effects to the use of carbenicillin include hypersensitivity reactions and allergic reactions. This drug should be avoided in pets with known penicillin allergies. It is possible that clotting problems may also be noted.

Overdosing would be unusual, but if you feel your pet has overdosed on carbenicillin, you should contact your veterinarian and the National Poison Control Center.

Carbenicillin does pass the placenta and into milk so it should not be used in nursing or pregnant pets unless absolutely necessary.

COMMON BRAND NAME: Geocillin

Carprofen

Carprofen is an nonsteroidal anti-inflammatory drug (NSAID) of the cyclo-oxygenase inhibitory family. This means it is not a steroid like prednisone, but it does work to reduce inflammation and, by so doing, also alleviates pain. These drugs may work on prostaglandins and may affect helpful prostaglandins as well as inflammatory ones. The exact method of action is not totally understood. It is primarily used to relieve pain associated with osteoarthritis in dogs—not for cats! (It is currently approved for use in cats in Europe but at very low and infrequent dosaging.)

This medication is protein bound in circulation and gets metabolized in the liver. Carprofen is about 80 percent eliminated in the feces after liver biotransformation and the remaining 20 percent or so is passed in the urine.

This class of medication should not be given with steroids or in combination with other NSAIDs. Carprofen is not recommended for dogs with known bleeding disorders such as von Willebrand's disease.

Carprofen comes in chewable tablets and caplets and is given orally where it is very well absorbed. It can be taken with or without food.

ROUTINE DOSAGE:

For dogs only: 1 mg/lb twice daily.

Carprofen should not be used in any dog who has previously shown some sensitivity to it or an allergic reaction to other NSAIDs. Due to the possible effect on prostaglandins, dogs taking this medication should be carefully observed for renal (kidney) and gastrointestinal problems. Serious liver problems have also been observed in some dogs, with Labrador retrievers showing up as the breed in one quarter to one third of the time. In most cases, if a dog starts to show signs of side effects, stopping the drug right away and treating if necessary end the complications. Rarely, and without warning, serious side effects and death can occur.

Carprofen overdosage signs are unusual (it is safer than many other NSAIDs when it comes to gastrointestinal signs or renal failure), but ulcers and bloody stools may occur.

If your dog has taken more than the normal dose, you should contact your veterinarian and the National Poison Control Center. If your dog has problems from a normal dose, contact your veterinarian and report the adverse drug reaction.

Carprofen has not been thoroughly tested in breeding animals so it should not be given to pregnant or lactating bitches or to young puppies.

COMMON BRAND NAME: Rimadyl

Cefadroxil

Cefadroxil is a semisynthetic antibiotic of the cephalosporin family. Cefadroxil is a bactericidal antibiotic, meaning that it kills bacteria as opposed to simply stopping or slowing the growth of bacteria. Cefadroxil should not be combined with bacteriostatic drugs (which slow or inhibit bacterial growth), as you would reduce the effectiveness of both drugs. It is capable of killing the penicillin-resistant bacteria such as some *Staphylococci* and is quite effective against many gram-negative organisms. There are, however, some bacteria developing resistances to the cephalosporins.

Cefadroxil is often used for skin and soft tissue infections and sometimes for resistant urinary infections. It is excreted via the kidneys, so dosaging may need to be adjusted in pets with renal disease.

Cephalosporins are not routinely combined with aminoglycoside antibiotics due to concerns about renal toxicity, but may be used together under veterinary supervision in some cases.

Cefadroxil comes in both liquid drops and tablets and may be given with food. Once the powder has been reconstituted to make the drops, the medication is good only for fourteen days, after which it should be discarded. Dosing your pet at mealtime may help with any mild nausea.

ROUTINE DOSAGES:
   For dogs: 10mg/lb twice daily for a minimum of three to seven days.
   For cats: 10 mg/lb once daily for a minimum of three days.
Cefadroxil should not be used for pets with cephalosporin allergies and with caution in pets with known penicillin allergies. Owners with allergies to these classes of medications should exercise extreme care when handling these medications. Rarely are any side effects noted and these consist primarily of mild gastrointestinal upsets.

Overdosages are rare and the primary signs seen are mild gastrointestinal upsets. If you have concerns, you should contact the National Poison Control Center or your veterinarian.

Some of the cephalosporins will give false positive results on certain urine glucose test strips, so if your pet is a diabetic, discuss this with your veterinarian.

Cephalosporins may cross the placenta and be found in milk, so they should be used with caution in pregnant or nursing animals. They do appear to be safe in puppies and kittens, though specific studies have not been done. Older animals with kidney problems should be closely monitored while on any cephalopsorin.

COMMON BRAND NAMES: Cefa-Tabs; Cefa-Drops

Cephalexin

Cephalexin is a seminsynthetic antibiotic of the cephalosporin family. It is a bactericidal antibiotic, meaning that it kills bacteria as opposed to slowing or inhibiting the growth of the bacteria. Cephalexin should not routinely be combined with any bacteriostatic drugs (which slow bacterial growth) as you would reduce the effectiveness of both drugs. There are some resistant bacteria developing to the cephalosporins.

Cephalexin is used for respiratory infections, otitis media, and other soft tissue and skin infections, as well as urinary tract problems. It is primarily excreted via the urine so dosaging may need to be adjusted in pets with renal problems.

Cephalosporins are not routinely combined with aminoglycoside antibiotics due to concerns about renal toxicity, but may be used together under veterinary supervision in some cases.

Cephalexin comes in both tablets and a powder to make an oral liquid formulation, but is primarily used as tablets. It should be noted that at this time it is not an FDA-approved medication for use in animals despite its frequent and safe use. It is important here to use this medication only via the supervision and direction of your veterinarian. Cephalexin can be given with food, and this may be advisable if your pet shows any gastrointestinal upset.

ROUTINE DOSAGES:
For dogs: 10 mg/lb given orally three times a day.
For cats: 10 mg/lb given orally three times a day.
For birds: 35–50 mg/kg given orally 4 times daily.
For reptiles: 20–40 mg/kg given orally twice daily.

Cephalexin should not be used for pets with cephalosporin allergies and with caution in pets with known penicillin allergies. Owners with allergies to these classes of medications should exercise extreme care when handling these medications. Rarely are any side effects noted, and these consist primarily of mild gastrointestinal upsets or rarely a rash.

Overdosages are rare and the primary signs seen are mild gastrointestinal upsets. If you have concerns, you should contact the National Poison Control Center or your veterinarian.

Some of the cephalosporins will give false positive results on certain urine glucose test strips, so if your pet is a diabetic, discuss this with your veterinarian.

Cephalosporins may cross the placenta and be found in milk, so they should be used with caution in pregnant or nursing animals. They do appear to be safe in puppies and kittens though specific studies have not been done. Older animals with kidney problems should be closely monitored while on any cephalopsorin.

COMMON BRAND NAMES: Keflex; Biocef

Chloramphenicol

Chloramphenicol is a bacteriostatic antibiotic (meaning it interferes with bacterial growth) which has a wide range of effectiveness against both gram-positive and gram-negative bacteria. It is very good for some anaerobic infections and against *Rickettsia*. It is not often combined with bactericidal medications as this may lower the effectiveness of both drugs, though it has been historically used with penicillin.

Chloramphenicol is metabolized in the liver though a small amount is excreted unchanged in the urine. This drug can cross the blood-brain barrier and is good for central nervous system infections. It is included in many eye and ear topical ointments.

Due to its metabolism by the liver, chloramphenicol can interfere with a variety of other medications. It can prolong the duration of pentobarbital anesthesia. Many of the seizure-control medications are also metabolized by the liver so care must be used in combining these medications. There is some evidence that chloramphenicol may decrease antibody response to vaccinations, so ideally you would hold off on boosters or primary vaccinations until after the treatment with chloramphenicol is completed.

Chloramphenicol comes in both oral and injectable forms, including a liquid. It should not be given to fasting pets. Currently chloramphenicol is primarily used in topical medications—including both ophthalmic and otic preparations. Due to the potential for human side effects, I recommend wearing gloves and/or washing your hands carefully after treating your pet with this medicine.

ROUTINE DOSAGES: Topical dosages will vary with the problem being treated. Follow your veterinarian's directions.

For dogs: 10–25 mg/lb given orally three times daily.

For cats: 10–25 mg/lb given orally twice daily.

For pocket pets: 50mg/kg given orally three times daily.

For birds: 1 ml/300 g given orally two to four times daily (absorption may be erratic).

For reptiles: 20–50mg/kg given orally.

For rabbits: 50 mg/kg given orally 2 or 3 times daily.

Chloramphenicol has almost disappeared from human medicine due to its effect on bone marrow. Some patients can develop a fatal aplastic anemia. This side effect is rarely seen in animals, though many pets will develop reversible bone marrow suppression if on chloramphenicol for long periods of time. Cats seem to be more susceptible to the bone marrow problems. Gastrointestinal signs are more common.

If a pet consumes a large amount of chloramphenicol, it is recommended to empty the gastrointestinal tract. Depending on the time frame involved, this could mean inducing vomiting, absorbing the medication, or other treatments. Call your veterinarian and contact the National Poison Control Center.

Chloramphenicol is not recommended for use in very young puppies and kittens or pregnant or nursing females. It should be avoided in patients with liver problems and also any pets with anemia. It should never be given to any food animal.

With the concerns for human health, chloramphenicol has lost favor as an antibiotic for pets. It is an excellent medication for pocket pets, however, and very useful in reptiles. Note that it is not approved for use in many of these species and is used as "extra label"—meaning under the direct guidance of your veterinarian.

COMMON BRAND NAMES: Currently seen primarily as generic chloramphenicol or chloromycetin.

Chlorothiazide

Chlorothiazide is one of the thiazide diuretics, so this is a drug that influences a normal body function. Diuretics act to increase the fluid loss, usually by increasing the amount of urine produced. The thiazide diuretics also increase the loss of potassium and have been replaced to a large extent by furosemide.

Chlorothiazide is used for pets with congestive heart failure, hypertension (high blood pressure), and to reduce the risk of calcium oxalate crystals or bladder stones, especially in dogs.

Chlorothiazide may increase the effect of some heart medications such as digitalis and may also influence the amount of insulin needed by diabetic pets. Diuretics should be used with care in pets with kidney problems as well.

It comes in both a powder and tablets and is usually given as tablets to pets.

ROUTINE DOSAGE: Chlorothiazdie is FDA approved for use in dogs only.
For dogs: 5–20 mg/lb given orally twice daily.

Side effects of chlorothiazide include dehydration, low blood potassium levels, and increased blood calcium levels. Pets taking any diuretic should always have plenty of fresh water available.

Overdosages show severe cases of the side effects with possible seizures, coma, and even death. If you feel your pet has overdosed on chlorothiazide, you should contact your veterinarian and the National Poison Control Center.

Chlorothiazide may pass in the milk of nursing mothers so ideally it would not be used in them.

COMMON BRAND NAMES: Oretic; Diuril

Cimetidine (Famotidine, Ranitidine)

These three medications are histamine H_2 receptor antagonists. Their use is to prevent or reduce the production of acid by the stomach so they influence normal body functions. They are commonly used in the treatment of ulcers, mast cell tumors, and for chronic vomiting of unknown cause. Cimetidine, famotidine, and ranitidine can also be used for acetaminophen overdosages, as part of cancer therapy, and to help with the use of replacement enzymes in pancreatic insufficiency. Cimetidine is the least effective but also the least expensive of the three medications, so it is currently used more commonly in veterinary medicine.

These medications are metabolized in the liver and excreted in the urine so they should be used with caution in patients with liver or kidney problems. Cimetidine in particular can also cause a rebound effect in stomach acid production when treatment is stopped.

All three medications may cause interactions with other drugs, but cimetidine seems to be the worst. The effects of aminophylline, some tranquilizers, metronidazole, warfarin, and some narcotic pain medications may all be increased by these drugs. Tetracycline, ketoconazole, digoxin, and antacids may all show a decreased effect if these medications are combined. It is recommended that pets taking digoxin or antacids along with cimetidine, famotidine, or ranitidine should have staggered dosing with medications spread at least two hours apart.

Cimetidine, famotidine, and ranitidine are given orally at home.

ROUTINE DOSAGES: Note these medications are not FDA approved for pets, and in addition, the doses used in pets with renal (kidney) failure may need to be markedly decreased from those listed here.

For dogs: Cimetidine 5 mg/lb three to four times daily.
Famotidine 0.25 mg/lb once or twice daily.
Ranitidine 0.5–1 mg/lb two to three times daily.
For cats: Cimetidine 5 mg/lb three to four times daily.
Famotidine 0.25 mg/lb once daily.
Ranitidine 0.25–2 mg/lb twice daily.
For reptiles: Cimetidine 4 mg/kg two to three times daily. (*Note:* always check with your veterinarian before using this in a reptile.)
For rabbits: Cimetidine 5–10 mg/kg given once or twice daily.

Overdosages can occur with these drugs, though ranitidine is considered very safe and cimetidine is quite safe also, with overdosing signs of increased heart rates and increased respiratory rates. Famotidine can cause vomiting, increased heart rates, and even collapse with massive doses. If you suspect your pet is overdosed, contact your veterinarian and the National Poison Control Center right away.

Obviously these medications should be used with caution in older pets who are more likely to have cardiac, liver, or kidney problems.

COMMON BRAND NAMES: Tagamet (cimetidine); Pepcid (famotidine); Zantac (ranitidine)

Cisapride

Cisapride is a substituted piperidinyl benzamide. This is a medication that influences normal body functions and acts to increase gastric emptying. It must not be used in pets with gastrointestinal obstructions or ruptures.

In pets, cisapride is commonly used to treat chronic constipation or megacolon (an enlarged colon due to fecal buildup) in cats and now for megaesophagus (a dilated esophagus due to delayed emptying) in dogs.

Cisapride should be used with caution in pets with liver problems. Care must be taken if cisapride is being given along with other oral drugs. The increase in emptying times may decrease their absorption.

There are some dangerous drug combinations involving cisapride that must be avoided. Cisapride should not be given with the antifungal medications such as ketoconazole or itraconazole, as the combination may cause serious arrhythmias of the heart. Some antibiotics may do this also. You should always be sure that your veterinarian is aware of any and all medications or supplements you pet is already taking if cisapride is added to her treatment regimen.

Cisapride comes in tablet and liquid suspensions. Ideally cisapride is given thirty minutes before feeding your pet.

ROUTINE DOSAGES: Cisapride is not an FDA-approved drug for use in pets, so it should only be used under the guidance of your veterinarian.

For dogs: 0.2 mg/lb given three times daily.

For cats: 2.5 mg total for cats 10 pounds or under; 5 mg total for cats 11 pounds or over, given two or three times daily.

For reptiles: 0.5–2 mg/kg given once daily.

For rabbits: 0.5 mg/kg given one to three times daily.

Side effects seen with cisapride are rare, but do include gastrointestinal signs. Pain or diarrhea may be noted. Overdosages are unusual, but if you feel your pet has overdosed on cisapride, you should contact your veterinarian and the National Poison Control Center.

Cisapride has been shown to cause problems in developing fetuses in laboratory animals including rabbits, so it should not be used in pregnant pets.

COMMON BRAND NAME: Propulsid

Clindamycin

Clindamycin is a member of the lincosamide family of antibiotics and is a bacteriostatic drug, meaning it inhibits the growth of bacteria, but does not kill them outright. (There are some situations where clindamycin can act as a bactericidal drug, actually killing the bacteria, but it is primarily bacteriostatic.) It is most effective against gram-positive bacteria, including anaerobes, and also works against some protozoa.

Clindamycin is commonly used for skin infections—including deep abscesses and also for prostatitis (though studies on the safety in fertile males have not been completed). It is excreted partly through the kidneys in the urine and also via the liver in bile. For these reasons, it should be used with caution in pets with kidney or liver disease. It should also not be used in pets with allergic skin disease or who have had allergic reactions to it or a related drug, lincosamide.

It should not be combined with erthromycin or chloramphenicol or with any neuromuscular-blocking medications.

While most pet owners would be dealing with liquid or capsules, clindamycin does have an injectable form, which may be used by your veterinarian.

ROUTINE DOSAGES: It should be noted that currently clindamycin is not an FDA-approved drug for use in cats, so it should be used in cats only under the direct supervision/guidance of your veterinarian.

> **For dogs:** 2.5–12.5 mg/lb twice daily, depending on type of infection being treated.
>
> **For cats:** 2.5–12.5 mg/lb twice daily, depending on type of infection being treated.

Clindamycin should not be used in rabbits or rodents due to its effect on intestinal bacteria.

Clindamycin rarely causes side effects, but the ones seen would be gastrointestinal with vomiting and diarrhea.

Overdosing is rare, but gastrointestinal signs such as vomiting and diarrhea (particularly bloody diarrhea) could be seen. If you have concerns, you should contact the National Poison Control Center or your veterinarian.

Safety studies have not been done in reproducing pets, but clindamycin can be passed through the milk of nursing mothers and may cause diarrhea in puppies and kittens. It should be used with caution in pets with liver and kidney problems.

Clindamycin should *not* be used in rabbits, hamsters, guinea pigs, or other pocket pets, due to its ability to interfere with normal gastrointestinal bacteria. These changes can be fatal in these pets.

COMMON BRAND NAMES: Antirobe; Cleocin

Cyclophosphamide

Cyclophosphamide is a cytotoxic (kills cells) agent and an immunosupppressant. As such, it influences normal body functions. Cyclophosphamide is included in many chemotherapy protocols.

Cyclophosphamide is metabolized in the liver and care should be taken using this medication in pets with liver or kidney problems.

Cyclophosphamide has many drug interactions. Care should be taken if used in pets on Phenobarbital (seizure medication) or other barbiturates, with allopurinol, many diuretics, or with digoxin. Always make sure your veterinarian is aware of any other medications your pet may be taking before you start using cyclophosphamide.

ROUTINE DOSAGES: Cyclophosphamide is not FDA approved for pets. Dosages are customized to individual pets based on their size in meters squared (m^2).

Side effects seen with this drug can range from minor, such as hair loss, to serious problems like suppression of the bone marrow. Gastrointestinal upsets may be noted and hemorrhagic (bloody) cystitis is not uncommon. Pets receiving cyclophosphamide should have regular blood work done to check for bone marrow problems.

Overdosing is possible as this is a strong medication with potential for serious side effects. If you feel your pet is overdosed with cyclophosphamide, contact your veterinarian and the National Poison Control Center.

Cyclophosphamide may cause sterility and has been shown to cause birth defects and fetal death. It should not be used in breeding animals. It also passes in the milk, so it should not be used in nursing pets.

COMMON BRAND NAME: Cytoxan

Cyclosporine

Cyclosporine is an immunosuppressant medication. It influences normal body functions and reduces the inflammatory response. It is used in two ways in pets—as an immunosuppressant for things like kidney transplants and autoimmune disease (when your pet's body attacks itself), and also to reduce responses for perianal fistulas and for certain eye problems.

The ophthalmic use of cyclosporine is the most common. Cyclosporine is used to treat "dry eye," also known as keratitis sicca and pannus.

Again, if cyclosporine is used systemically, there are many interactions with other drugs. Always make sure your veterinarian is aware of any other medications your pet might be taking. When used as an ophthalmic ointment, there is much less chance of either side effects or drug interactions.

Cyclosporine is given to pets as an oral medication with a fatty food or in eye ointment preparations.

ROUTINE DOSAGES: Note that cyclosporine is only FDA approved for ophthalmic preparations in pets. Given systemically, it should only be used under the guidance of your veterinarian.

For dogs: 5 mg/lb once daily.

For cats: 5 mg/lb once daily.

For ophthalmic use: 1/4-inch ointment on lower eyelid twice daily.

When cyclosporine is used systemically (given orally to treat problems and absorbed throughout the body), there can be quite a few side effects. These include increased shedding, nausea and other gastrointestinal signs, liver and kidney damage, and increased gum tissue. Rarely seizures have been noted in cats and lameness in dogs.

Overdosing can occur with cyclosporine. It has a narrow safety margin when used systemically and it is important to check blood levels routinely in pets taking this medication for any length of time. Signs can include liver and kidney damage. If you feel your pet has overdosed with cyclosporine, you should contact your veterinarian and the National Poison Control Center.

COMMON BRAND NAMES: Optimune; Sandimmune

Diazepam

Diazepam is a benzodiazepine tranquilizer. As such, it modifies normal body functions and in this case acts directly on the central nervous system (such as the brain). Diazepam is metabolized in the liver and excreted primarily via the urine.

Diazepam will decrease muscle tone, help to control seizures (though dogs can become refractory to this if it is used routinely), reduce anxiety, and cause sedation. Less commonly, diazepam is used for urine spraying by cats, for thunderstorm phobias, and for motion sickness. It can work quite well as an appetite stimulant for ill cats. Diazepam is sometimes combined with other medications for minor surgical procedures. Diazepam has been used for aggression in dogs, but may actually cause an increase in aggression in some dogs.

Diazepam does interact with some other drugs. It should not be routinely used in combination with other tranquilizers, sedatives, or barbiturates. It may increase the effects of the digitalis glycosides such as digoxin. Diazepam is a controlled substance under the jurisdiction of the Drug Enforcement Agency and is considered to be addicting—at least in people.

Diazepam can be used as an injectable (most often to break up seizures) or orally in tablet form. An enema version is currently available to help with seizure control. Ideally, diazepam tablets should be given on an empty stomach unless your pet shows gastrointestinal upset. Antacids should not be given at the same time as they decrease the rate of absorption.

ROUTINE DOSAGES: This is not an FDA-approved drug for pets so should be used only under the guidance of your veterinarian.

For dogs: Dosages vary greatly depending on the problem being treated— consult your veterinarian.

For cats: Dosages vary greatly depending on the problem being treated— consult your veterinarian.

For rabbits: Diazepam has been used as a tranquilizer. Consult your veterinarian for dosages.

For birds: 0.6 mg/kg given by intramuscular injection.

Side effects in dogs can include depression and sedation or even a paradoxical excitement! In some cats, a fatal liver problem can develop. This is not caused by an overdose, but can occur even with the standard dosages. The exact cause is unknown and there is no way to screen for this sensitivity at this time. Care should be taken using diazepam in any pet with liver or kidney problems.

Overdosing with diazepam can cause sleepiness, depression, and even lead to a fatal coma. If you feel your pet has overdosed on diazepam, contact your veterinarian and the National Poison Control Center.

Diazepam has been associated with birth defects and does pass into milk, so it should not be used in breeding animals or nursing mothers. Dosages may need to be reduced in older pets or pets with liver or kidney problems. Care should be taken if this drug is used in working animals such as guide dogs or police dogs. Their working abilities may be affected.

COMMON BRAND NAMES: Valium; Dizac

Dichlorophene

Dichlorophene is a phenol derivative used as a tapeworm medication. Combined with toluene, it is also effective against roundworms and hookworms. This is a poorly absorbed medication which often dissolves or aids in the digestion of parasites. Segments of the tapeworms are not commonly seen post-deworming with this medication.

Dichlorophene is an over-the-counter medication, but there are many other safer dewormers currently available.

Dichlorophene is given as oral tablets and it is recommended that your pet fast for twelve hours before treating and four hours after treatment.

ROUTINE DOSAGES:

For dogs: Follow package instructions (approximately 100 mg/lb).

For cats: Follow package instructions (approximately 100 mg/lb).

Side effects are commonly seen including increased salivation, vomiting, and diarrhea.

Some pets will show incoordination and neurologic signs. Rarely a pet may seizure and even die.

Overdosing with dichlorophene is easy to do as there is a narrow margin of safety, though death is rare. Overdosed pets may show neurologic signs or gastrointestinal signs. If you feel your pet is overdosed with dichlorophene, contact your veterinarian and the National Poison Control Center. There are currently many other safer tapeworm medications available.

You need to be especially careful using this medication on puppies, kittens, or senior pets.

COMMON BRAND NAME: Happy Jack Tapeworm Tablets

Diethylcarbamazine

Diethylcarbamazine is a parasiticide that paralyzes the parasites, leading to their death. It is best known as a preventive medication for heartworm disease, though it can be used to prevent roundworms at the same dose level, or to treat roundworms at a higher dose level. There are more effective roundworm medications available. It is excreted in the urine.

Diethylcarbamazine is a very effective heartworm preventive medication, but must be used daily and pets must be free of the microfilarial stage of heartworm when given this medication. Pets with microfilaria present in their blood when given diethlycarbamazine can go into fatal anaphylactoid shock. Diethylcarbamazine is given as an oral tablet with some chewable versions available. A liquid version is also available. It is may be given with food.

ROUTINE DOSAGES:
> **For dogs:** 3 mg/lb daily from the start of mosquito season until two months past as a heartworm preventive; 55–110 mg/lb once for the treatment of roundworms.
> **For cats:** 25–50 mg/lb once for the treatment of roundworms.
> **For ferrets:** 5.5 mg/kg.

It is quite safe otherwise, with minimal side effects. Rarely a pet will show some mild gastrointestinal upset. Remember to test for microfilaria before using this medication!

Overdosages with diethylcarbamazine are not common but pets could show vomiting or depression. If you feel your pet is overdosed with diethylcarbamazine, you should contact your veterinarian and the National Poison Control Center.

Diethylcarbamazine is considered to be safe to use in pregnant pets. There have been questions about reduced fertility in male dogs on diethylcarbamazine, but more studies need to be done.

COMMON BRAND NAMES: Difil; Filaribits; Carbam; Decacide

Digoxin/Digitoxin

Digoxin and digitoxin are similar digitalis glycosides, which are used to treat various cardiac ailments. These medications influence normal body functions. Digoxin is considered to be slightly safer in pets with liver disease while digitoxin is considered to be slightly safer in pets with renal disease, due to differences in metabolism. Digoxin is the more commonly used form in pets.

These are drugs which are used for pets with congestive heart failure, dilated cardiomyopathy, and some cardiac arrhythmias. They cause the heart to beat with increased strength and lower the heart rate so the heart becomes more efficient. Digoxin or digitoxin should be considered part of a cardiac management medication regimen.

These drugs have a fairly low toxicity threshold, so blood levels should be monitored on a regular basis. Potassium levels need to be checked as well. Patients with low thyroid levels should be watched with extra care, and as mentioned above, liver and kidney disease patients may need special supervision.

There are many drug interactions with the digitalis glycosides, and your veterinarian should always be aware of all the medications your pet may be taking. Diuretics, which are often part of a cardiac disease regimen, can influence the levels of these drugs. The cardiac glycosides come in both tablets and elixirs and should be given on an empty stomach.

ROUTINE DOSAGES: Note, digoxin is FDA approved for use in dogs only. Use in any pet should be under only the guidance of your veterinarian as these are powerful medications. There seems to be differences in bioavailability between brands of digoxin. Do not change brands without consulting your veterinarian and monitoring your pet closely.

For dogs: 0.0025–0.005 mg/lb given twice daily (this dose may need to be individually adjusted for your pet).

For cats: 0.0015–0.002 mg/lb given twice daily (this dose may need to be individually adjusted for your pet).

For birds: Digoxin has been used in birds—consult your veterinarian for dosages.

Side effects can include decreased appetite, gastrointestinal signs, weakness, and depression. If mismanaged, death is a possibility. Doberman pinschers seem to be quite sensitive to these drugs.

Overdosing is common with digoxin and careful monitoring is needed. Signs may include gastrointestinal upsets, depression, and weakness or cardiac problems—even fatal ones.

If you feel your pet is overdosed with digoxin, contact your veterinarian and the National Poison Control Center.

COMMON BRAND NAMES: Cardoxin; Lanoxin

Diltiazem

Diltiazem is a calcium channel blocker—one of the newer class of cardiac medications. It influences normal body functions, by relaxing smooth muscles and decreasing the speed by which calcium is absorbed by muscles. Diltiazem is used to treat some cases of heart failure, certain heart arrhythmias, and is helpful in hypertrophic cardiomyopathy—most often seen in cats.

Diltiazem should be used in care with pets who have liver or kidney disease or any ailment that lowers the heart rate.

Diltiazem should not be used in combination with ACE inhibitors (like enalapril), and extreme care should be taken if it is used with digoxin. Many drugs may influence its activity, so be sure your veterinarian is aware of any other medications your pet may be taking.

Diltiazem comes in regular and sustained-release tablets. Most pets are treated with the regular tablets.

ROUTINE DOSAGES: Diltiazem is not FDA approved for animals, so it should be used only under the guidance of your veterinarian.

For dogs: 0.25–0.75 mg/lb given three times daily (dose for regular tablets).

For cats: 0.9–1.2 mg/lb given two or three times daily (dose for regular tablets).

Side effects, which are rare, may include abnormal rhythms of the heart, low blood pressure, and collapse.

Overdosing with diltiazem can lead to decreased blood pressure, a very low heart rate, and even collapse, with possible death. If you feel your pet has overdosed with diltiazem, contact your veterinarian and the National Poison Control Center.

Diltiazem does cross the placenta and pass into the milk, so it should not be used in pregnant pets or in nursing pets.

COMMON BRAND NAMES: Cardizem; Dilocor

Diphenhydramine

Diphenhydramine is an antihistamine—meaning it is a medication to relieve histamine effects, such as allergies and pruritus (itching). It is a mild sedative and may help in cases of motion sickness. Diphenhydramine is also used in treating some cases of organophosphate or carbamate poisonings.

Diphenhydramine is metabolized in the liver and then mostly excreted via the urine. It should not be used in patients who are hypersensitive to it or other similar antihistamines.

Due to some of its actions, it should also not be used in pets with glaucoma, bladder obstructions, hyperthyroidism, or cardiac problems. Obviously you would not want to combine diphenhydramine with any other central nervous system depressants.

Diphenhydramine can be used as an injectable, but is most commonly dosed orally. This is an extra-label use of this medication so it should be used only under the supervision and direction of your veterinarian.

ROUTINE DOSAGES:
   For dogs: 1–2 mg/lb three times daily (this may be adjusted to the individual case).
   For cats: 1–2 mg/lb three times daily.
Side effects that can be seen are depression (though you may want the drug to sedate your pet a bit), occasionally gastrointestinal signs, or a dry mouth and urine retention. Some pets seem to become resistant to the sedative effect over time.

Overdosing diphenhydramine can lead to excitement, seizures, coma, and even death. If you suspect your pet is overdosed with diphenhydramine, contact your veterinarian immediately and also the National Poison Control Center.

Diphenhydramine should not be used in pregnant pets or very young pets as very little data is known.

COMMON BRAND NAMES: Benadryl; Histacalm

Enalapril

Enalapril is an angiotensin converting enzyme (ACE) inhibitor. As such it is a medication that is used to help treat cardiac problems and effects normal body functions. Enalapril relaxes blood vessel walls, making it easier for the heart to pump blood, and therefore oxygen, to the body.

Enalapril is used in our pets as part of the treatments for heart failure, dilated cardiomyopathy, and hypertension (increased blood pressure). It can slow down the heart rate, decrease pulmonary edema (fluid in the lungs), and reduce coughing.

Since enalapril is converted in the liver, it should be used with care in patients with liver problems. Renal failure pets may need a reduced dosage schedule if they take enalapril. It is recommended that any pet being put on enalapril have a complete cardiac and renal function evaluation first. Blood levels of this medication and potassium blood levels should be routinely checked.

Enalapril comes in both tablets and injectable forms. Pets primarily take the tablets and best if taken on an empty stomach.

ROUTINE DOSAGES: Enalapril is FDA approved for use in dogs only. In both dogs and cats, this medication should be used only under the guidance of your veterinarian. The dosage may need to be reduced in pets with any renal problems.

For dogs: 0.25 mg/lb given once or twice daily (start with once).

For cats: 0.1–.25 mg/lb given once or twice daily (start with once)

Side effects of enalapril may include gastrointestinal signs, kidney failure signs, or low blood pressure. If enalapril is used with diuretics or nonsteroidal anti-inflammatories, pets will need careful monitoring for side effects.

Overdosing can occur with enalapril. Pets can show severe low blood pressure or develop renal failure. If you feel your pet has overdosed with enalapril, contact your veterinarian and the National Poison Control Center.

Enalapril has been shown to cause problems in pregnant laboratory animals, so it is not recommended for use in pregnant pets. It also passes in the milk, so should not be used in nursing pets.

COMMON BRAND NAMES: Enacard; Vasotec

Enrofloxacin (Similar to Ciprofloxacin)

Enrofloxacin is an antibiotic of the flouroquinolone group (which happens to include ciprofloxacin of anthrax treatment fame, but which is not commonly used for animals). These drugs are bactericidal (meaning they kill bacteria as opposed to simply inhibiting bacterial growth). It should not be combined with any bacteriostatic drugs as the usefulness of both medications will be reduced. The flouroquinolones have a wide range of activity against both gram-negative and gram-positive bacteria, but due to extensive use, some resistances are now appearing. This will limit their use in the future.

Enrofloxacin is used for infections in many tissues, but is not good for penetrating the central nervous system.

Enrofloxacin should also be given with care in combination with antacids or theophylline (a bronchodilator).

Enroxfloxacin comes in both pill form and injectable. It is considered to be very bitter so pills should go down cleanly! There are now some human cherry-flavored liquids, which tends to be the bunny's version of choice! Ideally enrofloxacin should be given two hours before or after meals to enhance absorption. Enrofloxacin is now being included in some ear medications as well—follow your veterinarian's directions for its use this way.

ROUTINE DOSAGES:

For dogs: 2.5-5 mg/lb twice daily for at least five to seven days.

For cats: 2 mg/lb per day (see cautions below).

For pocket pets: 5–15 mg/kg twice daily.

For rabbits: 5–15 mg/kg given orally twice daily.

For reptiles: Consult your veterinarian for the appropriate dosage.

Side effects and overdosages are rare, but pets can present with vomiting or anorexia. There is some concern about seizures being exacerbated in pets receiving this medication. Contact the National Poison Control Center or your veterinarian if you have concerns.

There are some serious limitations on the use of enrofloxacin. It should not be used in young growing dogs (and possibly cats) as it does interfere with the proper development of bone and cartilage. For this same reason, it is not used in pregnant animals very often, as it is felt the developing fetuses could be affected.

More recently it has come to the attention of veterinarians that, if enrofloxacin is used at a dosage greater than 5 mg/kg per day in cats, an acute, usually irreversible blindness can occur. There is some feeling that even this dosage is too high.

COMMON BRAND NAME: Baytril

Erythromycin

Erthromycin is an antibiotic of the macrolide family of drugs. As such, it is a medication that fights infections. While erythromycin is primarily a bacteriostatic antibiotic (inhibiting the growth of bacteria as opposed to killing them), it can be bacteriocidal in some cases.

Erythromycin is considered to be the drug of choice at this time for *Campylobacter* problems and is used for skin infections. It is a decent antibiotic for prostate infections as well. Erythromycin is excreted in the liver and should be used with care in patients with liver problems.

Erythromycin does interact with many other medications. It should not be combined with many other antibiotics such as penicillin, chloramphenicol, or clindamycin. It may increase the levels of digoxin in the blood, necessitating a decrease in digoxin dose when on this antibiotic. It may also decrease the rate of theophylline clearance and even lead to toxic levels if not carefully monitored. Make sure your veterinarian is aware of any other medications your pet is taking when your pet goes on erythromycin—there are other drug interactions as well as those noted here.

Erythromycin does come in both oral and injectable forms, but is generally used orally in pets. It is commonly given with food.

ROUTINE DOSAGES:
  For dogs: 5–11 mg/lb given two or three times daily.
  For cats: 5–11 mg/lb given two or three times daily.
  For birds: 60 mg/kg given twice daily (check with your veterinarian as this can vary with bird species).
  Erythromycin should not be given orally to rabbits or rodents.

This is considered a very safe antibiotic, but vomiting is sometimes seen as a side effect. Ideally it is given on an empty stomach, but giving with food may reduce side effects.

Overdosing is unusual with erythromycin, but it can cause vomiting. If you feel your pet is overdosed with erythromycin, contact your veterinarian and the National Poison Control Center.

Erythromycin does cross the placenta and gets into milk. It is used in children, but care should be taken if this medication is needed for pregnant or nursing pets.

COMMON BRAND NAMES: EryPed; E-Mycin; Erythro-100

Erythropoietin

Erythropoietin is a hormone that increases red blood cell production. This is a medication that affects a normal body function. Eyrthropoietin is normally manufactured in the kidneys, so pets with renal failure may develop severe anemias (PCVs or packed cell volumes of 25 percent or less).

Erythropoietin is a genetically engineered recombinant human version of this hormone. Some pets, up to 25 to 30 percent, may eventually develop antibodies against the erythropoietin so it will no longer be effective.

This medication should not be used in pets with hypertension (high blood pressure) or iron deficiency. In fact, iron supplements are commonly given while pets are taking erythropoietin. Erythropoietin is primarily given as injections and would be given at the veterinary hospital.

ROUTINE DOSAGES: This is not FDA approved for use in pets, so should be used only under the guidance of your veterinarian.

For dogs: 100–200 units/lb given three times weekly (adjust over time).

For cats: 100–200 units/lb given three times weekly (adjust over time).

Side effects are rare, but may include seizures or increased blood pressure.

Overdosing is not common, but if you feel your pet has overdosed with erythropoietin, you should contact your veterinarian and the National Poison Control Center.

COMMON BRAND NAMES: Epogen; Marogen

Estrogen (Diethylstilbesterol and Estradiol Cypionate)

Estrogens are steroid hormones, normally manufactured by the ovaries (and in small amounts by other tissues). These are medications that affect normal body functions.

Diethylstilbesterol is a pill which is currently off the market due to concerns in human usage, but may become available again. Estradiol cypionate is an injectable form of estrogen.

Estrogens are used in pets to help with urinary incontinence in spayed females, mostly dogs, as a mismate precaution, again, mostly in dogs, and for help in treating certain hormone-responsive tumors such as prostate cancers in dogs.

The most common usage has been for urinary incontinence in spayed female dogs. The diethylstilbesterol increases urethral tone, stopping urine leakage. It should not be used in intact females, due to potential for serious side effects.

Estrogens are metabolized in the liver and should be used with caution in pets with liver problems. Care should be taken if estrogens are used at the same time as any anticoagulants, or other drugs which might stimulate liver enzymes such as phenobarbital. Your veterinarian should be aware of any other medications your pet is taking if your pet is prescribed estrogen.

ROUTINE DOSAGES: These medications are not FDA approved for use in pets and should be used only under the guidance of your veterinarian. Dosages are quite variable and will be customized to your pet.

Side effects of these medications are primarily seen long term and some can be quite serious. Pets may show gastrointestinal signs such as vomiting or diarrhea, increased eating and urinating, and the serious effects of pyometra (infected uterus in an intact female) or fatal aplastic anemias. Cats can develop liver or cardiac lesions. Male dogs taking estrogens (such as for prostate problems) can develop feminine characteristics with long-term usage.

Overdosing of estrogens can most seriously lead to fatal anemias. If you feel your pet has overdosed on estrogen medications, you should contact your veterinarian and the National Poison Control Center.

COMMON BRAND NAMES: Premarin; ECP; DES

Febendazole

Febendazole is a benzimidazole deworming medication. As an anthelmintic, this is a medication that fights parasites in the body.

Febendazole is effective against a wide range of parasites—roundworms, hookworms, lungworms, lung flukes, and even one type of tapeworm (*Taenia*). Febendazole comes in a variety of forms—paste, granules, and liquid. The granule form is most commonly used in pets. This form is mixed in with your pet's meals so it can be given with food.

ROUTINE DOSAGES: Febendazole is FDA approved for use in dogs and many wild cats, though not in domestic cats. It is routinely used in cats, but should only be given under the guidance of your veterinarian.

For dogs: 23 mg/lb given once daily for three days (dosage may vary for some parasites).

For cats: 23 mg/lb given once daily for three days (dosage may vary for some parasites).

For birds: 10–50 mg/kg once (if not molting or nesting). For certain parasites, birds may need to be dosed for three or five days—consult your veterinarian.

For reptiles: 50–100 mg/kg once—may need to be repeated.

For rabbits: 20 mg/kg given once—may need to be repeated.

Side effects are rare, but include vomiting. Febendazole is considered to be a very safe deworming medication.

Overdosing is uncommon, but if you feel your pet is overdosed on febendazole, contact your veterinarian and the National Poison Control Center.

Febendazole is a very safe medication and can be used in pregnant and nursing pets as well as young puppies and kittens.

COMMON BRAND NAME: Panacur

Fentanyl

Fentanyl is an opioid (narcotic) painkiller. This is a very powerful analgesic and can be addictive due to its narcotic nature. It is a Drug Enforcement Administration (DEA)–controlled medication.

Fentanyl is commonly used in pets for postoperative or chronic pain management. It should be used with care in pets with liver, kidney, or cardiac problems. Amylase and lipase values (blood test used to check pancreatic function) may be increased by fentanyl use.

Fentanyl should not be combined with any other depressants—including most tranquilizers, antihistamines, or dips like amitraz. It is sometimes combined with droperidol to make an anesthetic.

Fentanyl can be injectable or in transdermal patches (patches to put on the skin so the drug is slowly absorbed over time). Patches are the most common form used in veterinary medicine. Patches are applied to areas with shaved hair or minimal hair growth (such as the groin). The patch should be lightly bandaged over so your pet can't remove it or ingest it and the patch should be kept dry. If people come in contact with the gel, it is suggested that they thoroughly wash their hands.

ROUTINE DOSAGES: Fentanyl is not FDA approved for use in pets, so it should be used only under the guidance of your veterinarian. The patch should be applied by your veterinarian and may last for three or more days. Your veterinarian may adjust the dose by covering part of the patch. The patch should be removed by your veterinarian and disposed of carefully.

Side effects are rare, but may include respiratory depression or a slowing of the heart rate.

Overdosing with fentanyl is unusual, but can cause severe respiratory depression or lowered heart rates. If you feel your pet has overdosed on fentanyl, contact your veterinarian and the National Poison Control Center.

Fentanyl has caused damage to fetuses of laboratory animals, so it is not recommended for use in pregnant or nursing pets.

COMMON BRAND NAMES: Duragesic; Sublimaze

Fipronil

Fipronil is a gamma-aminobutyric acid (GABA) inhibitor. This drug attacks the central nervous system of parasites such as fleas, ticks, and mites, so it is a drug that fights infestations. While mammals also possess GABA, ours is limited to our brains and fipronil cannot pass the blood-brain barrier, making this a very safe medication.

Fipronil is used to treat flea and tick infestations in dogs and cats, and also to act as a preventive to keep these parasites from becoming established on your pet. The medication is most commonly applied as an oil-soluble drop, which gets into the sebaceous glands and hair follicles. From there it works for thirty days or more and is even active for a time on hairs that are shed out.

This is not an oral medication, but comes in spray and spot-on formulations. Ideally pets should not be bathed for forty-eight hours before or after application of fipronil. Owners should wear gloves and wash after application despite the safety of the drug as this is standard procedure for using parasiticides.

ROUTINE DOSAGES: This medication is FDA approved for dogs and cats for flea and tick control. It should be used as directed on the package information sheets, following the once-a-month guidance.

The only side effects seen are greasy spots where the spot-on version is applied and rarely a mild irritation at that spot. It should not be combined with other parasiticides without discussion with your veterinarian.

Overdosing with fipronil is extremely rare, but if you feel your pet has overdosed with fipronil, you should contact your veterinarian and the National Poison Control Center.

Fipronil is considered safe for puppies over eight weeks, kittens over twelve weeks, and in pregnant and nursing pets, as well as senior pets.

COMMON BRAND NAME: Frontline

Fluconazole

Fluconazole is a triazole antifungal medication. As such, it is a medication that attacks infestations of the body. This is a potent antifungal medication with activity against both superficial problems such as ringworm and yeasts, and even more activity against deep or systemic fungal infections such as *Histoplasmosis* and *Cryptococcosis*. It is considered by some to be the drug of choice for *Cryptococcosis* in cats.

This drug should be used with care in patients with liver or kidney problems due to its metabolism and excretion. There are many drug interactions with fluconazole and your veterinarian should be aware of any other medications your pet may be taking. Some of the drugs fluconazole interacts with include cimetadine, terfenadine, digoxin, and phenobarbital.

Fluconazole is given in tablet form and with meals.

ROUTINE DOSAGES: This is not an FDA-approved medication for pets, so it should be used only under the guidance of your veterinarian. It may take one to two weeks for results of treatment to be noticed, and pets may need to be on this medication for two to four months for serious infections.

For dogs: 1.75–2.5 mg/lb given once daily.

For cats: 1.75–5 mg/lb given twice daily.

For birds: 5–10 mg/kg once daily as an adjunct to *aspergillosis* treatment.

Side effects can include decreased appetite and rarely liver damage or anaphylactic reactions. This is one of the safest antifungal medications, though quite expensive.

Overdosing with fluconazole can show up as decreased respiratory rate, salivation, gastrointestinal upsets, and cyanosis (blue or purple mucous membranes from lack of oxygen). If you feel your pet has overdosed on fluconazole, contact your veterinarian and the National Poison Control Center.

Fluconazole is not recommended for use in pregnant pets.

COMMON BRAND NAME: Diflucan

Fludrocortisone

Fludrocortisone is a synthetic adrenal mineralocorticoid and corticosteroid. It is used to replace cortisol and aldosterone normally manufactured by the adrenal glands, and as such influences normal body functions. This medication is used primarily for pets who develop Addison's disease or hypoadrenocorticism. It helps to regulate metabolism and salt and mineral balance. Sometimes it is combined with prednisone.

Fludrocortisone is a medication that requires healthy kidneys to be effective. Pets on fludrocortisone should have their kidney function evaluated and may require potassium supplements.

Pets need to be carefully observed for sudden changes in weight—either increases or decreases, as well as checking for edema (swelling) in the legs. Regular blood work to evaluate the electrolytes is considered to be an important part of treatment.

There are numerous drug interactions with fludrocortisone. These include digitalis and diuretics. Insulin dosages may also be influenced by fludrocortisone. It is important that your veterinarian be aware of any other medications your pet may be taking.

Fludrocortisone comes as tablets.

ROUTINE DOSAGES: This is not an FDA-approved medication for pets so should be used only under the guidance of your veterinarian.

For dogs: 0.1–1 mg given once daily (adjust dose based on blood work).

For cats: 0.1 mg given once daily (adjust dose based on blood work).

Side effects can include increased drinking and urination.

Overdosing with fludrocortisone may show up as weakness with low potassium levels, cardiac signs including edema, and increased drinking and urinating. If you feel your pet has overdosed with fludrocortisone, contact your veterinarian and the National Poison Control Center.

Fludrocortisone may affect fetuses and is passed into the milk. It is not recommended for use in breeding animals or very young animals. Senior pets with renal problems will need very close monitoring if they must take fludrocortisone.

COMMON BRAND NAME: Florinef

Furosemide

Furosemide is a loop diuretic (meaning it works directly at the level of the kidneys). As such, it is a drug that affects a normal body function. It should not be used in pets with renal failure (or only under careful monitoring), as this limits its action. This is a potent diuretic.

Furosemide is best known for its inclusion as part of the standard treatment regimen for heart problems. It is excellent for reducing pulmonary edema (fluid in the lungs), assisting in congestive heart failure care, and for cardiomyopathy cases, especially in cats. Furosemide can also be used to reduce abdominal fluid buildups due to liver failure. As mentioned, care should be taken if furosemide is used in pets with renal problems. It should also not be used in pets that are dehydrated or having electrolyte problems.

Furosemide does interact with a fair number of other drugs. Your veterinarian should always be aware of any other medications you pet is taking when you add furosemide. The chances of ototoxicity (hearing damage) and renal damage are increased if furosemide is given with any of the aminoglycoside antibiotics. It can increase the likelihood of digitalis toxicity and may influence the dose of insulin needed for diabetic pets.

Furosemide comes in many forms—oral tablets and liquids, as well as injectables for use by your veterinarian.

ROUTINE DOSAGES:
   For dogs: 1–2 mg/lb given two or three times daily.
   For cats: 1–2 mg/lb given two or three times daily.
   For birds: 0.05 mg/300 g intramuscular injection twice daily. (Lories are very sensitive to this medication—use caution!)

For reptiles: 5 mg/kg given intravenous or intramuscular injection as needed—make sure the pet is not dehydrated.

For rabbits: 2–5 mg/kg given twice daily.

Side effects can include causing dehydration and reducing electrolyte concentrations, particularly potassium. Pets taking furosemide should have potassium levels checked periodically. Less common side effects include allergic reactions, anemia, and damage to hearing (especially if combined with certain antibiotics).

Overdosing with furosemide can cause acute signs of increased heart rate, lethargy leading to collapse and coma, or even seizures. Many of these signs may be related to low potassium levels. On a chronic scale, furosemide has been associated with some renal damage. If you feel your pet is overdosed with furosemide, contact your veterinarian and the National Poison Control Center.

Ideally, furosemide would not be given to pregnant or nursing pets.

COMMON BRAND NAMES: Lasix; Disal; Diuride

Gentamicin

Gentamicin is a member of the aminoglycoside family of antibiotics. As such, it is most effective against gram-negative organisms, but will work against some gram-positives. Resistance to the older aminoglycosides such as gentamicin are showing up, and amikacin is becoming more popular. Gentamicin is a bactericidal antibiotic, meaning that it kills bacteria as opposed to simply inhibiting their growth. It is sometimes combined with other antibiotics to increase the range of effectiveness, but not usually with bacteriostatic antibiotics, as that reduces the efficacy of both medications.

Gentamicin is not absorbed well from the intestines, so for a systemic (whole-body) effect, injections are commonly used. It is excreted mainly via the kidneys. Gentamicin tends to be reserved for sepsis cases, cases needing a decrease in intestinal bacteria, and in topical medications for eyes, ears, and skin.

Gentamicin should be used very cautiously in pets on diuretics or with any other medications that can cause kidney problems or ototoxicity.

As mentioned, gentamicin is primarily used in veterinary medicine in topical preparations or via injection in hospitalized pets. The hospitalized pets can receive extra fluids and careful monitoring to minimize any effects on the kidneys.

ROUTINE DOSAGES: These are only guidelines on dosing gentamicin. Many factors must be considered to use this medication in an individual animal. The age, state of the kidneys, state of hydration, etc., are all factors that may affect the amount of the dose or the dosing interval.

For dogs: 1.1–2.2 mg/lb two or three times daily by injection.

For cats: 1.1–2.2 mg/lb two or three times daily by injection.

For birds: Consult with your veterinarian—doses can vary with species, though 10 mg/kg given by injection two times daily is usually well tolerated.

For reptiles: Consult with your veterinarian—these pets have a very low dosage rate and may need fluids given concurrently.

For rabbits: 6.5 mg/kg given once daily by injection.

Gentamicin should be avoided in any pet with aminoglycoside allergies. It has some serious side effects. It is associated with irreversible ototoxicity in some pets leading to deafness and can also cause renal failure. While topical versions are less likely to cause these side effects, gentamicin can be absorbed systemically through inflamed skin or in the ear via ruptured eardrums.

Overdosing can lead to kidney failure and/or ototoxicity. Call your veterinarian and the National Pet Poison Control Center immediately if your pet is overdosed.

Gentamicin is not routinely used in pregnant pets or very old or very young pets. It is virtually never used in rabbits and the pocket pets (or only under close supervision), owing to its effect on gastrointestinal bacteria.

COMMON BRAND NAMES: Gentocin; Garamycin; Otomax; Gentocin Otic

Glipzide

Glipzide is a sulfonylurea antidiabetic medication that influences normal body functions. It is not an insulin substitute, but is useful in some cases of diabetes mellitus that lack insulin or are nonresponsive to insulin. It is primarily used in cats with non-insulin-dependent diabetes mellitus or Type II diabetes. It will help to lower blood glucose and get glucose into the cells, where it can be used.

Glipzide should be used carefully in cats with liver, kidney, or thyroid problems. Glipzide does have quite a few drug interactions. It is important that your veterinarian is aware of any other medications your pet may be taking if you add glipzide. Certain antibiotics, cimetidine, and phenobarbital are some of the drugs the glipzide interacts with. Glipzide should be given with food.

ROUTINE DOSAGES: This is not an FDA-approved drug for pets, so it should be used only under the guidance of your veterinarian.

For cats: 0.25 mg/lb twice daily, but adjust to individual as needed. Cats may need a trial period to determine if this medication works for them and to adjust the dose. Blood glucose samples should be taken frequently.

Side effects are rare but may include vomiting or, even more rarely, liver damage.

Overdosing with glipzide could lead to dangerously low blood glucose. Such pets are weak and uncoordinated and may go on to seizures, shock, and even death. If you feel your pet is overdosed with glipzide, contact your veterinarian and the National Poison Control Center.

Glipzide should not be used in pregnant or nursing pets or very young pets.

COMMON BRAND NAME: Glucotrol

Griseofulvin

Griseofulvin is an antibiotic (produced by a bacteria) that works only against ringworm fungae. This is a medication that is used to treat infestations. As an antifungal, griseofulvin works only against the skin fungae of the ringworm group, not systemic fungal infections.

Griseofulvin is given orally, but then concentrates in new skin, hair, and claws to destroy the fungal elements. It is commonly combined with topical treatment such as baths and dips.

Griseofulvin should not be used in pets with liver problems and it can cause bone marrow suppression in cats, particularly kittens. Phenobarbital seems to interfere with the absorption of griseofulvin. The dose of griseofulvin may need to be increased in pets also taking phenobarbital.

Griseofulvin comes in tablets and should be given with a fatty meal for best absorption. There are two formats—microsize and ultramicrosize. The ultramicrosize is better absorbed and the dosage will be less.

ROUTINE DOSAGES: This is not an FDA-approved medication for pets, so it should be used only under the guidance of your veterinarian.

For dogs: 25 mg/lb given once daily—can be divided—of the microsize; 15 mg/lb given once daily—can be divided—of the ultramicrosize.

For cats: 25 mg/lb given once daily—can be divided—of the microsize; 15 mg/lb given once daily—can be divided—of the ultramicrosize.

Treatment may require weeks to months of dosing for complete results.

The most common side effects are gastrointestinal upsets, but rarely anemia, depression, a weak gait, or liver damage can be seen.

Overdosing with griseofulvin is rarely seen, but if you feel your pet is overdosed with griseofulvin, contact your veterinarian and the National Poison Control Center.

Griseofulvin does cause birth defects in kittens and should not be used in pregnant or nursing pets and only with care in young kittens.

COMMON BRAND NAMES: Fulvicin (microsize); Grifulvin (microsize); Gris PEG (ultramicrosize); Fulvicin P/G (ultramicrosize)

Halothane

Halothane is an inhalant general anesthetic which influences normal body functions by disrupting consciousness. Halothan is both an anesthetic and an analgesic (has painkilling properties).

Halothane is primarily breathed out with expired air, but some is metabolized by the liver. This anesthetic should be used with caution in pets with liver disease, malignant hyperthermia in their history, or cardiac arrhythmias.

Caution should be taken in combining halothane with drugs that influence the myocardium (heart muscle), any neuromuscular-blocking agents, and some of the aminoglycoside antibiotics. It is not routinely combined with ketamine (another general anesthetic) either.

ROUTINE DOSAGES: Halothane is FDA approved for use in pets, but these general anesthetics need to be used in anesthesia machines and should be used only by your veterinarian. Halothane has been used on dogs, cats, and pocket pets.

Side effects of halothane can include cardiac depression, liver problems, and decreased blood pressure. Overdoses can show any of those signs and even lead to death.

Halothane should not be used in pregnant pets if possible or in nursing pets as it can pass into the milk.

COMMON BRAND NAMES: Halothane; Fluothane

Heparin

Heparin is an anticoagulant, so it helps to prevent and dissolve clots. This is a drug that influences normal body functions. Clearly, heparin will be used in cases where there is excessive or unnecessary clotting. These include DIC (disseminated intravascular coagulation—a serious, often fatal syndrome), thromboembolism such as can be seen with feline cardiomyopathy, and pulmonary embolisms. Some veterinarians advocate the use of heparin for AIHA (autoimmune hemolytic anemia, where the pet's body attacks its own red blood cells) and for pancreatitis.

Heparin is a natural medication and is derived from either pig intestine or cow lung tissues. This can lead to hypersensitivity reactions in some pets.

Obviously heparin should be used with care in any pet that has a coagulation defect or a severe bleeding disorder. Platelets must be present for this drug to work. Ideally, pets should have clotting function tests before treatment and to monitor treatment.

Heparin should be used with care if your pet is taking other medications. Make sure your veterinarian is aware of any other medications your pet might be taking before giving it heparin. Other anticoagulants may increase the possibility of bleeding problems, the actions of insulin and corticosteroids may be decreased, and the action of diazepam may be increased. Heparin is itself affected by some antihistamines and digoxin. Heparin is basically used as an injection in pets, either intravenous (in the vein) or subcutaneous (under the skin). These injections would be given by your veterinarian.

ROUTINE DOSAGES: This drug should only be used under the guidance of your veterinarian.

> **For dogs:** 30–40 units/lb given two or three times daily (may vary with the problem being treated).
>
> **For cats:** 75–100 units/lb given three times daily for thromboembolism.

Side effects that can be seen with heparin treatment are hematomas, bleeding, and pain at injection sites.

Overdosing with heparin can lead to serious bleeding problems. Early warning signs include bloody urine or tarry stools. If you feel your pet is overdosed on heparin, contact your veterinarian and the National Poison Control Center.

Ideally, this medication would not be used in pregnant or nursing pets or very young pets.

Hydrochlorothiazide

Hydrochlorothiazide is one of the thiazide diuretics and as such it influences normal body functions. Any of the diuretic drugs increase fluid loss from the body—usually as urine. The thiazide diuretics tend to drain potassium from the body as well and have been replaced for many uses by the diuretic furosemide. Hydrochlorothiazide can be used for congestive heart failure, hypertension (high blood pressure), and most commonly to reduce the risk of calcium oxalate crystals or stones in the bladder or urine.

Hydrochlorothiazide may increase the effect of some heart medications such as digitalis and may also influence the amount of insulin that diabetic pets need. Use care in either of these situations. Diuretics should always be used with care in pets with kidney problems as well.

Hydrochlorothiazide comes in both solutions and tablets, but is most commonly used in the tablet form for pets.

ROUTINE DOSAGES: Hydrochlorothiazide is not FDA approved for use in pets so it should be used only under the guidance of your veterinarian.
  For dogs: 1 mg/lb given orally twice daily for calcium oxalate risk reduction in dogs.
  For cats: 5–10 mg/cat given orally once or twice daily for heart problems; 1–2 mg/lb given orally once or twice daily for hypertension.
Side effects of hydrochlorothiazide can include dehydration, lowered blood levels of potassium, and increased blood levels of calcium. Any pet taking a diuretic should always have plenty of fresh water readily available.

Overdosing with hydrochlorothiazide usually shows up with severe versions of the side effects, leading to possible seizures, coma, and even death. If you feel your pet has overdosed with hydrochlorothiazide, you should contact your veterinarian and the National Poison Control Center.

COMMON BRAND NAME: Hydrozide

Hydrocodone

Hydrocodone is a narcotic cough suppressant. It is a medication that influences normal body functions. This is a very potent cough medication that acts via the brain. It should be used only for dry coughs and not if the pet has a moist cough or a cough with secretions. It is primarily used for dogs with kennel cough or collapsing tracheas. As a narcotic, hydrocodone is a controlled drug under the direction of the Drug Enforcement Agency (DEA).

Hydrocodone should be used cautiously in pets with hypothryoidism, kidney disease, Addison's disease (hypoadrenocorticism), or head trauma. It may interact with other medication, including other narcotics, and should not be combined with acetaminophen.

Hydrocodone is used in pets in an oral form—either liquid syrup or tablets.

ROUTINE DOSAGE: This drug is not FDA approved for use in pets so it should only be used under the guidance of your veterinarian. Narcotics are rarely used in cats.

For dogs: 0.12 mg/lb given two to four times daily.

Side effects seen with hydrocodone include sedation, constipation, or vomiting.

Overdosing with hydrocodone can lead to deep sedation, central nervous system depression, and coma. This is a potent medication.

Ideally hydrocodone would not be used in pregnant or nursing pets or very young or very old pets.

COMMON BRAND NAME: Hycodan

Hydrogen Peroxide

Hydrogen peroxide is not a drug per se, but is used for medical purposes. This is a topical antiseptic used for cleaning superficial wounds and is also used as an emetic (to induce vomiting).

It is very important to talk to your veterinarian before you induce vomiting for any reason in your pet. It is also recommended that you contact the National Poison Control Center if you feel your pet has ingested a poison or toxin. Some substances are very caustic or corrosive, and making your pet vomit them back up could cause even more damage. Other substances such as petroleum distillates have a high risk of aspiration pneumonia if they are vomited back up.

Hydrogen peroxide comes as a liquid and is used either topically or to induce vomiting.

ROUTINE DOSAGES: This is not an FDA-approved treatment for pets and should be used only under the guidance of your veterinarian.

For dogs: 5–10 ml/10 lb with total dose not more than 30 ml.

For cats: 5–10 ml/10 lb with total dose not more than 30 ml.

Rodents and rabbits should not be induced to vomit.

The most dangerous side effect of hydrogen peroxide is aspiration pneumonia if you make your pet vomit. Aspiration pneumonia can be fatal and is caused by foreign substances getting inhaled into the lungs. Hydrogen peroxide is quite safe topically.

Overdosing is not common, but if you feel your pet is overdosed with hydrogen peroxide, you should contact your veterinarian and the National Poison Control Center.

Hydroxyzine

Hydroxyzine is an antihistamine—a medication used to control the symptoms of allergies. This is a medication that influences a normal body function.

Hydroxyzine is used in the treatment of itching, and to provide itch and some pain relief for pets suffering from atopy (seasonal allergies). It can help to decrease signs of nausea and to open up airways for easier breathing. It may provide a low level of sedation.

Hydroxyzine should be used with care in pets with enlarged prostates, certain heart failure problems, and gastrointestinal or urinary obstructions. Pets with glaucoma should not receive hydroxyzine. While it is often combined with corticosteroids (resulting in a lower steroid dosage), it should not be combined with other central nervous system depressants.

Hydroxyzine comes in both liquid and tablet forms, with the tablets being used most commonly in veterinary medicine. This is an oral medication.

ROUTINE DOSAGES: This is not an FDA-approved medication for pets and should be used only under the guidance of your veterinarian. It is not commonly used in cats.

For dogs: 1 mg/lb given three to four times daily.

For birds: 2 mg/kg given three times daily or 1.5–2 mg/4 oz of drinking water. Hydroxyzine has been used in birds for allergies, feather picking, and self mutilation. Birds should be carefully observed for drowsiness.

Side effects seen with hydroxyzine can include sedation or a paradoxical hyperexcitability. Overdosing with hydroxyzine can show up as sedation or a sharp drop in blood pressure. If you feel your pet has overdosed on hydroxyzine, you should contact your veterinarian and the National Poison Control Center.

Hydroxyzine has been associated with birth defects in laboratory animals so it should not be used in pregnant or nursing pets.

COMMON BRAND NAMES: Atarax; Vistaril

Imidacloprid

Imidacloprid is an insecticide/parasiticide that works on nicotinic receptors in parasites. This is a drug that attacks outside infections or infestations. This medication causes fleas to show central nervous system signs of paralysis and then death. Only fleas are affected—no ticks, mites, or internal parasites. Very often the fleas will die before they even get the chance to bite the pet!

Imidacloprid is one of the newer, safer flea medications and has few cautions or warnings. It is not intended for internal use—only external use as a spot-on. It tastes quite bitter, and it should not get into your pet's eyes. Some pets show irritation at the area of application.

Imidacloprid is available only as a topical spot-on preparation.

ROUTINE DOSAGES:
For dogs: 10 mg/lb as a spot-on—use as directed once monthly.
For cats: 10 mg/lb as a spot-on—use as directed once monthly.

Owners should wash their hands carefully after applying this medication and not touch the spot-on areas for at least a couple of hours. These precautions are routine for any insecticides.

Imidacloprid may cause some localized irritation where it is applied. If a pet should eat the tubes, this could cause an overdose. Signs of overdosing with imidacloprid include twitching and muscle weakness. If you feel your pet has overdosed with imidacloprid, contact your veterinarian and the National Poison Control Center.

Imidacloprid should not be used on kittens less than eight weeks old or puppies less than seven weeks old.

COMMON BRAND NAME: Advantage

Insect Growth Regulators/Methoprene

Insect growth regulators (IGRs) including methoprene are synthetic hormones intended to influence the growth of parasites such as fleas. These are medications designed to fight outside infections or infestations.

The insect growth regulators represent a novel way of attacking flea infestations. They mimic normal insect growth regulators which would inhibit metamorphosis. So flea eggs and larvae are prevented from developing into adults. Since these are insect hormones, they are considered to be very safe for mammals, such as our pet dogs and cats.

Insect growth regulators may be combined with adulticides to provide a wider spectrum of flea protection. They are available in collars, sprays, and dips.

ROUTINE DOSAGES:
For dogs: use as directed.
For cats: use as directed.

Insect growth regulators are considered to be safe for pets from very young puppies and kittens to seniors.

COMMON BRAND NAMES: Precor; Ovitrol; Siphotrol

Insulin

Insulin is a normal hormone present to help regulate blood glucose. As such, it is a drug that influences a normal body function. In pets with diabetes mellitus, either there is not enough insulin produced or the body is resistant to the insulin produced. Without enough insulin, blood glucose increases while cells are starving, pets show increased drinking and urinating, and there are many severe metabolic problems. Rarely, insulin may also be used to lower potassium levels that are dangerously high.

Insulin is perhaps the most important part of managing a diabetic, but overall care must be adjusted with special foods, regulated feeding times, etc. There are *many* different drug interactions, and your veterinarian should always be aware of any other medications your pet is taking when insulin treatment is initiated. Pets need customizing of their dosage and dosage schedule, as well as their feeding schedule and exercise routines. Even certain illnesses may influence the insulin dose your pet requires.

There are a variety of types of insulin—all of which are given by injection. These all vary at least a little from dog insulin genetically. Pork insulin is closest, but beef and human versions may be used. Pets may develop resistance due to the different species. Some types of insulin are longer acting and may need to be given only once daily; others require multiple doses.

ROUTINE DOSAGES: There are currently no insulin types that are FDA approved for use in pets. This is a medication with powerful effects and should be used only under the careful guidance of your veterinarian. Pets often require hospitalization to regulate their dosage properly and will need frequent blood tests to monitor their care. Dosages must be customized to the individual pet. Insulin has been used in birds as well as dogs and cats and these same precautions apply.

Side effects seen with insulin can include very low blood glucose, or high blood glucose due to antibodies and resistance. Cats in particular seem to become resistant to the human insulin products after time.

Overdosing with insulin can lead to very low blood glucose (hypoglycemia) with associated weakness, incoordination, and seizures. Shock may follow, leading to coma and even death. If you feel your pet has overdosed on insulin, put some honey or Karo syrup on her gums and contact your veterinarian and the National Poison Control Center immediately.

Rarely, puppies will develop "juvenile diabetes." They will need insulin and are notoriously hard to regulate.

COMMON BRAND NAMES: Humulin; Lente; Iletin; NPH

Interferon

Interferon is a natural substance that is antiviral, anticancer, a cytokine (substance helping to communicate between cells), and an immune modulator. As such, it is a medication that fights outside infections and infestations as well as influencing normal body functions. In pets, interferon is most commonly used to treat some cancers and for FELV (feline leukemia) and FIV (feline immunodeficiency virus) cases in cats.

Interferon is often combined with other medications or included as part of a cancer fighting regimen.

The form available is recombinant human interferon alpha. Since it is a human-based substance, pets could develop antibodies and resistance.

Interferon is available both as an injection or an oral medication. It is primarily given orally in pets and not with food.

ROUTINE DOSAGES:

For cats: 30–40 IU in 1 ml of saline given once daily.

Side effects are not common in pets though people sometimes report flu-like symptoms. An overdosage could cause the flu-like symptoms or in rare cases, bone marrow depression. It you feel your pet has overdosed on interferon, you should contact your veterinarian and the National Poison Control Center.

While interferon is considered to be quite safe, it has caused abortion in monkeys, so it should not be used in pregnant pets.

COMMON BRAND NAMES: Intron A; Roferon A

Iodine

Iodine is a trace mineral that has multiple uses for our pets. It is an important part of the thyroid hormones and is also used as a disinfectant. Iodine both influences normal body functions and acts against outside infections and infestations.

Iodine in the povidone version is a disinfectant that is antiviral, antibacterial, and antifungal. It is used topically as a treatment for skin problems including ringworm. The povidone version is less likely to cause skin irritation. Potassium iodine is sometimes used to treat chronic coughs.

As a radioactive element, iodine is used to treat cats suffering from hyperthyroidism. Iodine is present in many common foods and rarely needs to be added to a pet's diet. Care needs to be taken with the topical forms of iodine when treating large open wounds. In those cases, excess iodine may be absorbed and could cause thyroid problems.

COMMON BRAND NAMES FOR TOPICALS: Xenodine; Betadine

Ipecac

Ipecac is an emetic used to induce vomiting. As such, it is a medication that influences a normal body function. Ipecac acts both locally by irritating the stomach lining and also centrally on the brain.

It should be noted that you should always contact your veterinarian before inducing your pet to vomit. Some substances can cause more damage by being brought back up such as caustic liquids, which could do more tissue damage. Petroleum distillates are another group that are dangerous to vomit—often leading to aspiration pneumonia when some of the foreign substance is inhaled into the lungs.

Pets who are in shock, seizuring, or very weak should not be induced to vomit, as they also have a high risk of aspiration pneumonia.

Ipecac is given orally and ideally with water following. It should not be given with dairy products. If treatment will include the use of activated charcoal, it is recommended that the ipecac be given first.

ROUTINE DOSAGES: This is not an FDA-approved medication for pets so it should only be used under the guidance of your veterinarian.

    For dogs: 0.5–1.25 ml/lb with some water (repeat only after consultation with your veterinarian).

    For cats: 1.5 ml/lb with some water (repeat only after consultation with your veterinarian).

Ipecac should not be used to induce vomiting in rabbits or rodents.

Side effects seen with ipecac can include salivation, tearing, and prolonged vomiting.

Overdosing may lead to toxic cardiac effects. If you feel your pet has overdosed with ipecac, you should contact your veterinarian and the National Poison Control Center.

COMMON BRAND NAME: Ipecac

Isoflurane

Isoflurane is an inhalant general anesthetic that influences normal body functions by disrupting the central nervous system to affect consciousness. Most of the isoflurane is breathed out with the air from the lungs, so it is considered to be one of the safest anesthetics. It is relatively safe to use in pets with liver or kidney problems, but it is quite expensive. There is less myocardial depression (less effect on heart muscle) than most other general anesthetics.

Isoflurane should not be used in pets with any history of malignant hyperthermia (potentially fatal high fevers). It should be used with caution in combination with any drugs that effect the myocardium (heart muscle) or neuromuscular blocking agents.

ROUTINE DOSAGES: Isoflurane is FDA approved for use in pets but must be used in an anesthetic machine and should only be used by your veterinarian. It has been used successfully in dogs, cats, birds, reptiles and pocket pets.

Side effects of isoflurane may include hypotension (low blood pressure) from vasodilation, respiratory depression (decreased breathing rate and/or depth), and gastrointestinal signs.

Overdosing can cause severe cases of the above and even death, but isoflurane is extremely safe and problems are less common than with some of the other general anesthetics.

COMMON BRAND NAMES: Iso Flo; Aerrane; Isovet

Itraconazole

Itraconazole is an antifungal medication. It is a member of the triazole drug family and acts to fight both superficial and deep fungal infections by slowing or inhibiting growth. As such, it is a drug designed to fight outside infections of infestations. It is considered to be safer than many of the older fungal fighting medications and is quite good for central nervous system infections.

It is often used in treating *Aspergillosis* and may be combined with topical treatments to treat skin infections such as *Malassezia*. Long term treatment regimens are often required to deal with fungal infections and it may be two weeks before any response at all is noticed.

Itraconazole has many drug interactions—including with seizure medications such as phenobarbital, digoxin, and cimetidine. Your veterinarian should always be aware of any other medications your pet is taking before you start itraconazole. It can also decrease blood glucose—this effect seems to be enhanced in pets taking glipzide for diabetic control.

Itraconazole is found as both capsules and liquid. It is recommended that it be given with food.

ROUTINE DOSAGES: This is not an FDA-approved drug for use in pets and should only be used under the guidance of your veterinarian.

For dogs: 2.5 mg/lb given twice daily.

For cats: 2.5 mg/lb given twice daily.

Side effects of itraconazole include a decreased appetite and liver damage. Pets who are prone to liver damage usually show some anorexia (decreased appetite) first. Rarely, pets may show vasculitis and skin ulcers.

Overdosing with itraconazole can lead to serious liver problems. If you feel your pet is overdosed with itraconazole, you should contact your veterinarian and the National Poison Control Center.

Itraconazole, like many other fungal fighting medications, has been shown to cause some fetal damage and also does pass in the milk. It should not be used in pregnant or nursing pets.

COMMON BRAND NAME: Sporomox

Ivermectin

Ivermectin is a macolide made by soil living bacteria, but acts as a parasiticide, not an antibiotic. It acts on outside infections/infestations and does not directly influence normal body function.

Ivermectin acts via the GABA (gamma amino butyric acid) nerve centers. These are peripheral in insects and parasites as well as in the central nervous system. In mammals, most of these medications are screened out by our blood-brain barrier. That makes these extremely safe medications with a few exceptions. (See note about collies below.)

Ivermectin is used in pets for a heartworm preventative, to remove some intestinal worms, as a microfilaricide, and as a miticide. Pets should be checked for the presence of microfilaria before being given invermectin as a preventative. Ivermectin can be used for mites in snakes.

Ivermectin comes in a variety of forms—oral tablets and paste, liquid oral, liquid injectable, and chewable tablets.

ROUTINE DOSAGES: While ivermectin is FDA approved for use in pets, it is approved only as a heartworm preventative. For its other uses, such as microfilaricide, miticide, and intestinal parasiticide, the dose is increased and should be used only under the direct guidance of your veterinarian.

For dogs: 0.0003–0.0066 mg/lb given orally once monthly.

For cats: 0.011–0.033 mg/lb given orally once monthly.

For reptiles: *Do not use in turtles or tortoises.*

    For lizards, snakes, and alligators: 0.1 mg/lb given by injection or orally and repeat in two weeks for treating ectoparasites (skin parasites) and nematodes (intestinal parasites). *Do not use in indigo snakes,* and use with caution in skinks!

For birds: Used to treat roundworms, capillaria (intestinal and lung parasites), and *Knemedocoptes* (scaly leg mites). Dosage here varies greatly with the species of bird and type of parasite being treated—diluted versions of the standard ivermectin are often required.

For rabbits: Check with your veterinarian. This can be used as an injection or topical for ear mites (both extra-label usages).

Ivermectin is considered safe to use in pregnant or nursing pets with a few exceptions. Side effects are rare due to the blood-brain barrier protective effect, but can include incoordination and dilated pupils.

Cats given an overdose might show blindness and neurologic signs, but generally recover in two to four weeks. If you feel your pet has overdosed on ivermectin, contact your veterinarian and the National Poison Control Center.

Note: Many *collies* have been shown to possess a mutant genetic allele called MDR 1. This mutation opens up the blood-brain barrier (making it leaky, so to speak), and can lead to neurologic signs and even death with ivermectin treatment. While many collies have no problem with ivermectin at the dosages used in heartworm preventatives, many collie owners and breeders choose to use other medications. If you use an ivermectin heartworm preventative, observe your collie carefully for about eight hours after treatment. It is felt that some of the other "collie-like" breeds such as Shetland sheepdogs and Border collies may also have the same or a similar genetic mutation. Loperamide is another drug that is affected by this mutation.

COMMON BRAND NAMES: Heartgard; Eqvalan; Ivomec

Ketamine

Ketamine is a congener of phencyclidine and influences normal body functions by acting as a general anesthetic with analgesic (painkiller) activity. Ketamine accomplishes this by disrupting the central nervous system.

A strength of ketamine is that it has minimal depressant effects on the heart or will increase heart rate. There is either no effect on muscle tone or a slight increase in muscle tone. Ketamine is often used in combination with xylazine for increased muscle relaxation.

Ketamine should ideally not be used in pets with heart problems or a history of seizures. It should be used with caution in pets with liver or kidney problems. Pets should have their eyes lubricated while under the effects of ketamine to prevent their corneas (outermost layer of the eyes) from drying out.

Care should be taken to avoid combining ketamine with any central nervous system depressants, the antibiotic chloramphenicol, or the anesthetic gas halothane, if possible. Ketamine is used as an injectable medication and can be partially antagonized by the use of yohimbine.

ROUTINE DOSAGES: Ketamine is FDA approved for use in cats and subhuman primates. This is a controlled substance and would be used only by your veterinarian. Increasing the dosages will increase the duration of the effects, not the intensity, which increases the safety of this medication. Ketamine has been used in many animals, including rabbits, rodents, pocket pets, reptiles, and birds. It is often combined with xylazine for cats and rabbits.

Side effects of ketamine can include respiratory depression, vomiting, and convulsions.

Overdosages are not common, but signs may include any of the above side effects, particularly respiratory depression. If you feel your pet has overdosed on ketamine, you should contact your veterinarian and the National Poison Control Center.

COMMON BRAND NAMES: Ketaset; Vetalar; Vetaket

Ketoconazole

Ketoconazole is one of the older imidazole antifungal medications. This is a drug that acts against outside infestations. Ketoconazole is used against some deep fungal infections such as *Cryptococcus,* as well as superficial problems such as the yeast *Malassezia.* It is not the best antifungal for central nervous system infections or for use in cats. There is some resistance among fungae to this medication.

Ketoconazole is primarily a fungistatic drug (inhibiting fungal growth as opposed to directly killing fungae), but it can be fungicidal at higher dosages or over long-term usage. It may take two weeks or more for response to treatment to be seen. It is often used for long-term treatment of skin yeast infections in White West Highland terriers.

Ketoconazole also inhibits steroid hormone production and so is used for some cases of hyperadrenocorticism (Cushing's disease) in dogs. It should not be combined with mitotane in this treatment regimen. Pets on long-term ketoconazole treatment may need glucocorticoid supplementation.

Care should be taken in using ketoconazole in pets with liver problems or with low platelet counts. It should be given separately from antacid medications such as cimetidine. It may interact with sedatives and hypoglycemic drugs. Ketoconazole should *not* be given to a pet receiving cisapride as it may lead to fatal heart arrhythmias.

Ketoconazole comes in oral tablets and in shampoo form for skin problems. Ideally, it should be given with food.

ROUTINE DOSAGES: This is not an FDA-approved medication for use in pets, so it should be used only under the guidance of your veterinarian.

For dogs: 2.5–7.5 mg/lb given twice daily for three to six weeks.

For cats: 2.5–5 mg/lb given twice daily.

For birds: The dosage varies with the method of treating the bird. It can be force-fed, added to the water, or added into the food. If added into the food, the standard dose is 10–20 mg/kg given orally once daily.

For turtles: 25 mg/kg given orally once daily (may need to be treated for two to four weeks).

For tortoises: 15 mg/kg given orally once daily.

Side effects of ketoconazole are primarily liver associated, but vomiting or a decreased appetite may be seen. Cats seem to be more sensitive to the liver damage than dogs.

Overdosing can cause liver damage or platelet problems. If you feel your pet has overdosed on ketoconazole, you should contact your veterinarian and the National Poison Control Center.

Ketoconazole may cause damage to fetuses and does pass into milk, so ideally it would not be used in pregnant or nursing pets. It has also been associated with sterility in male dogs.

COMMON BRAND NAME: Nizoral

Lactulose

Lactulose is an osmotic laxative. This is a drug that influences a normal body function—in this case, increasing the amount of fluid in the intestines. The increased fluid softens stools and helps with constipation. Lactulose achieves this because it is a synthetic disaccharide. It is not absorbed and will pull water and ammonia into the intestines from the blood, particularly in the colon. It also helps to acidify the intestinal contents, which then move ammonia.

Lactulose is used in pets as part of the treatment for constipation, for megacolon (where the colon becomes stretched and loses muscle and often nerve tone), and for hepatic encephalopathy. Hepatic encephalopathy is seen in pets with liver disease who build up significant amounts of ammonia in the blood. This high level of ammonia can cause neurologic signs including seizures, coma, and death. Lactulose is a powerful medication and should always be used under veterinary supervision.

Sometimes lactulose is combined with antibiotics—especially in treating hepatic encephalopathy. It should never be used in pets who are dehydrated or who have an obstruction. Special care should be taken if lactulose is used in diabetic pets as it can influence the effects of insulin.

Lactulose does come in an oral liquid form as well as enemas. Most pets take it in the liquid form.

ROUTINE DOSAGES: This is not an FDA-approved drug, so it should be used only under the guidance of your veterinarian.

For dogs: 0.23 ml/lb given three or four times daily for hepatic encephalopathy; 1 ml/10 lb given three times daily for constipation.

For cats: 0.25–5 ml/cat given three or four times daily for hepatic encephalopathy; 1 ml/10 lb given three times daily for constipation.

For birds (for hepatic encephalopathy):

Cockatiel: 0.03 ml given two or three times daily.

Amazon: 0.1 ml given two or three times daily.

Side effects seen with lactulose can include gas, intestinal cramping, and possibly diarrhea.

If a pet is overdosed with lactulose there may be gas, dehydration, pain, and diarrhea. If you feel your pet has overdosed, with lactulose you should contact your veterinarian and the National Poison Control Center.

COMMON BRAND NAMES: Constilac; Cephulac; Dysphalac

Loperamide

Loperamide is a narcotic antidiarrheal, a drug which influences normal body functions. To act as an antidiarrheal, loperamide has a variety of actions. It affects motility, decreases secretions, increases fluid absorption, and even increases anal tone.

Loperamide should not be used in pets with hypothyroidism, or liver or kidney problems. Ideally it would also not be used in pets with Addison's disease (hyperadrenocorticism). One drawback to an antidiarrheal like this one is that it may keep intestinal toxins in the system longer, with more chance for absorption. Care should be taken when using loperamide in a pet taking any central nervous system depressants or any head trauma since it is a narcotic medication. (Also, see note about collies following.)

Loperamide is used to treat some cases of incontinence as well as inflammatory bowel disease patients.

Loperamide is given orally to pets, using either capsules or a solution.

ROUTINE DOSAGES: This is not an FDA-approved medication for use in pets, so it should be used only under the guidance of your veterinarian. Care should always be taken with any narcotic use in cats. Care must also be taken to ensure the accuracy of the dose for cats or small dogs.

For dogs: 0.05–0.1 mg/lb given three or four times daily.

For cats: 0.005–0.05 mg/lb given twice daily.

Ideally, loperamide should not be used in kittens and rarely in puppies.

Side effects that may be seen with loperamide can include sedation or bloating. Some cats may show excitement as the narcotic response. Rarely pets may show pancreatitis.

Pets who are overdosed with loperamide may show constipation, central nervous system depression, and a decreased heart rate. If you feel your pet is overdosed with loperamide, you should contact your veterinarian and the National Poison Control Center.

Note: Many *collies* have been shown to possess a mutant genetic allele called MDR 1. This mutation opens up the blood-brain barrier (making it leaky, so to speak) and can lead to neurologic signs and even death with loperamide treatment. Many collie owners and breeders choose to use other medications. It is felt that some of the other "collie-like" breeds such as Shetland sheepdogs and Border collies may also have the same or a similar genetic mutation. Ivermectin is another drug which is affected by this mutation in collies.

COMMON BRAND NAME: Immodium AD

Lufeneron

Lufeneron is one of the new parasite medications that are quite effective for fleas. It is a drug that acts on outside infestations with minimal effect on normal body functions. Lufeneron does not kill adult fleas.

Basically lufeneron is a form of "flea birth control"—interfering with the production of chitin (the outer layers of fleas). This makes lufeneron a very safe product, since mammals such as our pets don't produce chitin. The drawback is that the fleas must bite the pet for this drug to be effective, so pets with flea allergies will still suffer. Lufeneron will be stored in the body in fatty tissues for a time so it does not require frequent dosing.

Lufeneron is often combined for use with other flea products or other medications for skin problems. Always check with your veterinarian before you add lufeneron products to a treatment regimen to be sure it is safe.

Lufeneron is used orally in our pets though there is an injectable form. Most pets receive liquid or tablets orally and this medication should be given with food.

ROUTINE DOSAGES:
   For dogs: 4.5 mg/lb given once monthly.
   For cats: 13.6 mg/lb given once monthly.

Lufeneron may rarely cause some side effects such as vomiting, mild depression, or a decreased appetite. Giving it with food minimizes the likelihood of these effects.

Overdosing is quite rare also, but if you feel your pet has overdosed with lufeneron, you should contact your veterinarian and the National Poison Control Center.

Lufeneron passes into the milk of nursing pets, but is considered safe to use in pregnant or nursing pets.

COMMON BRAND NAME: Program

Melarsomine

Melarsomine is an arsenic compound which is used to treat heartworm disease in dogs. This is a medication that attacks outside infestations, but it is powerful enough to possibly influence normal body functions and needs to be used with care. This is definitely a medication where care has to be taken to poison the parasite and not the pet!

In heartworm disease, adult parasites may live in the lungs and the heart chambers themselves. Dogs can have varying degrees of heartworm disease—ranging from Class I, which is mild and with few adult heartworms, to Class IV, where there are heartworms right in the portacava. Class IV dogs do best with surgery and have a very grave prognosis. Melarsomine is recommended primarily for Class I and Class II dogs, but can also be used at a reduced dose in Class III dogs who already have some cardiac and pulmonary effects from the heartworm infestation. So dogs who need their heartworm disease treated should be medically stable first. There is always a risk of pulmonary embolism with heartworm disease treatment, and pets need to have restricted exercise for weeks posttreatment to minimize this risk.

Melarsomine is given as a deep intramuscular injection in the lumbar muscles (muscles along the spinal column in the back). Dogs may show some pain and swelling at these areas but this usually clears with time. Most pets are hospitalized for the treatments and the first few days posttreatment.

ROUTINE DOSAGES: Melarsomine is FDA approved for use in dogs, but not cats.

For dogs: 1.1 mg/lb given intramuscularly for two doses, twenty-four hours apart (this may need to be repeated in four months). This dose schedule may be adjusted for dogs with Class III heartworm disease. Restricted exercise for six to eight weeks is recommended.

Melarsomine is considered to be safer than the earlier arsenic treatment—

thiacetarsamide—but still can have side effects. Pets may show gastrointestinal signs such as vomiting directly from the medication, but can also show many problems due to the death of the adult heartworms. Some dogs will have coughing, gagging, loss of appetite, and could even die, due to clots being thrown from the dying worms. Liver damage is not as common with melarsomine as it is with thiacetarsamide.

While melarsomine is considered to be the "safer" heartworm treatment, it does have a very small margin of safety and can easily be overdosed. Signs of overdosing include vomiting, depression, coughing, and even death—some of which are the same as routine side effects. If you feel your dog has overdosed with melarsomine, you should contact your veterinarian and the National Poison Control Center immediately.

COMMON BRAND NAME: Immiticide

Methimazole

Methimazole is in the class of drugs called thionamides, which are antithyroid medications. These are drugs that influence a normal body function.

Methimazole is primarily used to treat cats with hyperthyroidism. It may be used for the life of your cat or it may be used short term to evaluate your cat's kidney and thyroid function prior to surgery or radiation.

Cats receiving methimazole should have regular blood work to evaluate their thyroid hormone levels and to check their platelet and white blood cell levels. Kidney function should always be monitored carefully in cats undergoing treatment for hyperthyroidism.

Methimazole comes in tablet form and is ideally given with food. Many pet owners elect to try special compounded flavored liquid versions of methimazole. Currently there is research ongoing to see if transdermal application of methimazole (the drug being applied with skin gels or patches) will work. This could be a great boon to people with difficult-to-pill cats!

ROUTINE DOSAGES: This is not an FDA-approved drug for pets and should be used only under the direct guidance of your veterinarian.

   For cats: 2.5–7.5. mg given twice daily—note that some cats can be well maintained on once-a-day treatments.

Side effects can be seen with methimazole and most commonly show up in the first three months of treatment. Cats may show a decrease in appetite, some vomiting, lethargy, or in rare cases, scratching around the head and face. Rarely cats will show liver problems, but this is reversible if the medication is stopped. Overdosing long term can lead to anemia or low white blood cells, making the cat open to infections. Acute overdosages may show weakness, a decreased heart rate, and a decreased temperature. If you feel your cat has overdosed with methimazole, you should contact your veterinarian and the National Poison Control Center.

Ideally methimazole should not be used in pregnant or nursing cats.

COMMON BRAND NAME: Tapazole

Methionine

Methionine is an essential amino acid (building block of protein) and a urinary acidifier. As such, this is a medication that influences normal body functions.

Methionine is primarily used to treat bladder problems—cystitis, alkaline urinary stones, and feline urologic syndrome. It is FDA approved for urinary acidification in pets. It should not be combined with the special veterinary prescription urinary diets without careful supervision by your veterinarian.

Methionine should be used with care in pets with kidney failure or pancreatitis. Pets with liver disease should also not receive methionine, as it can increase the chances of developing hepatic encephalopathy.

Methionine comes in many forms—including tablets, chewable tablets, and a flavored gel. Ideally, it would be given at mealtimes.

ROUTINE DOSAGES:
For dogs: 0.2–1.0 g three times daily.
For cats: 0.2–1.5 g once daily.
Side effects seen with methionine are primarily gastrointestinal upsets. Overdosages can lead to gastrointestinal problems, increased respirations, decreased heart rates, weakness, and depression. If you feel your pet has overdosed with methionine, you should contact your veterinarian and the National Poison Control Center.

This medication should not be used in young puppies or in kittens, who have a higher incidence of side effects.

COMMON BRAND NAMES: Methioform; Ammonil; Odor-Trol; Methigel

Methocarbamol

Methocarbamol is a centrally acting muscle relaxant. That means this drug acts on the brain to reduce muscle spasms—as such, it is a medication that affects a normal body function.

Methocarbamol is FDA approved to use in dogs and cats to reduce muscle spasms and inflammation from trauma. It is also sometimes used in the treatment of strychnine poisoning.

Methocarbamol comes in both oral and injectable forms. The injectable form should be used with care in patients with kidney problems and in patients with seizures.

ROUTINE DOSAGES:
   For dogs: 20 mg/lb three times daily to start, then reduce to 10–20 mg/lb three times daily.
   For cats: 20 mg /lb three times daily to start, then reduce to 10–20 mg/lb three times daily.

The most common side effect seen with methocarbamol is sedation. Rarely pets may have gastrointestinal signs, weakness, or ataxia.

Overdosing with methocarbamol shows up with sedation and depression or sometimes vomiting and diarrhea—especially if given in the intravenous form. If you feel your pet has overdosed on methocarbamol, you should contact your veterinarian and the National Poison Control Center.

COMMON BRAND NAME: Robaxin-V

Methoxyflurane

Methoxyflurane is an inhalant general anesthetic and influences normal body functions by disrupting the central nervous system and affecting consciousness. Methoxyflurane has gone out of favor due to the nephrotoxic (kidney-damaging) effects it can cause, along with the prolonged recovery times compared to some of the newer, safer general anesthetics.

Ideally, methoxyflurane would not be used on pets with liver or kidney problems. It should not be combined with any other medications that might damage the kidneys, such as many of the aminoglycoside antibiotics. Care should be taken if methoxyflurane is used with any drugs that influence the myocardium (heart muscle), such as dopamine or epinephrine or any neuromuscular-blocking agents.

ROUTINE DOSAGES: Methoxyflurane is FDA approved for use in pets but should be used only in anesthetic machines and by your veterinarian. As mentioned above, this general anesthetic has fallen out of favor since safer medications are available.

Side effects of methoxyflurane are primarily kidney damage.

Overdoses may show kidney damage, malignant hyperthermia (the development of high fevers), and cardiac signs. Death may result.

Methoxyflurane should not be used in pregnant pets.

COMMON BRAND NAME: Metofane

Metoclopramide

Metoclopramide is both an antiemetic and a gastrointestinal tract stimulant. It acts on the brain for some of its effects and directly on the muscle of the stomach and the esophagus, as well. This is a medication that influences normal body functions.

Metoclopramide is often used with care in patients with kidney failure to control their nausea and vomiting, as well in pets on chemotherapy that may make them nauseous. It should not be used in pets with obstructions or perforations (holes in the stomach or intestines). Pets who have seizures or adrenal tumors should also not take metoclopramide.

There are many drug interactions with metoclopramide, including some antibiotics and sedatives, so you should be sure your veterinarian is aware of any other medications your pet may be taking. Use this medication only under the guidance of your veterinarian. Metoclopramide comes in multiple forms—tablets, syrup, and injectable. Ideally, it is given to your pet about thirty minutes before a meal.

ROUTINE DOSAGES: This is not an FDA-approved medication for pets, so it should be used only under the direct guidance of your veterinarian.

For dogs: 0.1–0.2 mg/lb orally three or four times daily (this dose may be reduced in pets with kidney failure).

For cats: 0.1–0.2 mg/lb orally three or four times daily (this dose may be reduced in pets with kidney failure).

For rabbits: 0.5 mg/kg by injection three times daily.

Side effects seen with metoclopramide include sedation and behavior changes.

This is considered to be a very safe medication but overdosing can lead to sedation, nausea, vomiting, or constipation. If you feel your pet has overdosed with metoclopramide, you should contact your veterinarian and the National Poison Control Center.

COMMON BRAND NAME: Reglan

Metronidazole

Metronidazole is a medication that is best known as an antiprotozoal medication to treat *Giardia,* but is also an effective antibacterial. It is bactericidal (meaning it kills bacteria as opposed to inhibiting the growth) and is effective against some gram-positive bacteria and many gram-negative bacteria. It has excellent action against anaerobic bacteria.

Metronidazole is primarily used for gastrointestinal infections and sometimes to aid in periodontal infections. It has been used successfully with other medications to treat bacterial overgrowths and lymphacytic/plasmacytic colitis. Metronidazole may be combined with other antibiotics to expand the range of action to include aerobic bacteria as well.

Metronidazole is primarily metabolized by the liver. It should be used with caution in pets on seizure medications or taking cimetidine.

Metronidazole should be used very cautiously in pets with liver problems or pets showing any neurologic signs. Any pets sensitive to nitroimidazole drugs should avoid metronidazole. Side effects are most commonly seen after prolonged use of metronidazole and often include neurologic signs. Acute overdoses can cause neurologic signs as well as gastrointestinal problems.

Metronidazole is mainly used in pill or capsule form and is quite bitter tasting. Any gastrointestinal side effects may be minimized by giving metronidazole with food.

ROUTINE DOSAGES: Metronidazole is not FDA approved for use in pets, so all usage is "extra-label"—meaning under the supervision of your veterinarian.

> **For dogs:** Dosages range widely depending on the specific problem being treated, from 10 to 50 mg/kg and from once daily to two or three times daily.
>
> **For cats:** Anywhere from 10 to 25 mg/lb once or twice daily.
>
> **For birds:** 50mg/lb once daily.
>
> **For reptiles:** 150 mg/kg once, then repeat in a week.
>
> **For rabbits:** 20 mg/kg given twice daily.

Overdosages could cause gastrointestinal or neurologic signs. Contact your veterinarian and the National Poison Control Center immediately.

Metronidazole is not considered to be totally safe in pregnant or nursing pets.

COMMON BRAND NAMES: Flagyl; Protostat

Milbenmycin Oxime

Milbenmycin oxime is a macrolide medication derived from soil-living bacteria. It acts against mites, intestinal parasites, and heartworms by attacking their nerve function. Milbenmycin is a medication that works against outside infections and does not influence normal body functions. This is the GABA (gamma-aminobutryic acid) system, which is also present in mammals. In mammals, the GABA system is mostly protected by the blood–brain barrier, so this is a very safe medication—much deadlier to parasites than to the mammalian hosts. Parasites show paralysis and then death.

Milbenmycin oxime is effective against the immature stage of heartworms, called microfilaria, as well as the adults living in the heart and lungs. For this reason, pets being treated with milbenmycin oxime as a heartworm preventative should be tested clear of heartworm disease first. Milbenmycin does work well against many intestinal parasites as well, including whipworms.

This medication has also shown efficacy against mites such as *Demodex* though it is not currently approved for the treatment of demodicosis.

Milbenmycin oxime is sometimes combined with lufeneron to make it a flea control product as well. This medication is given as an oral tablet or chewable.

ROUTINE DOSAGES: Milbenmycin oxime is FDA approved for heartworm prevention and for the prevention and treatment of intestinal parasites in dogs. While it is used for other treatments, the dosages may be different.

For dogs: 0.23–0.45 mg/lb given once monthly.

For cats: 0.23–0.45 mg/lb given once monthly.

Side effects are quite rare with milbenmycin but may include depression and a loss of coordination.

Overdosages may show gastrointestinal signs, loss of coordination, and convulsions though serious signs are rare. If you feel your pet has overdosed with milbenmycin, you should contact your veterinarian and the National Poison Control Center.

Note: Collies have a "leaky" blood-brain barrier, but even they demonstrated only weakness and fever at twelve times the recommended dose.

Milbenmycin is considered to be safe for use in pregnant and nursing pets as well as puppies. It is toxic to fish and care should be used in disposal.

COMMON BRAND NAME: Interceptor

Moxidectin

Moxidectin is a macrolide medication derived from soil-living bacteria. This medication works against outside infections such as heartworm and does not influence normal body functions.

Moxidectin acts via the GABA (gamma-aminobutyric acid) system which is present in insect and parasite nervous systems, but is present in mammals in the brain—safely guarded by the blood-brain barrier. This is a very safe medication for that reason. It is recommended that pets being treated with moxidectin have a negative test for heartworms before starting the preventative.

This medication is given as an oral tablet or chewable.

ROUTINE DOSAGES: Moxidectin is only FDA approved for use in dogs to prevent heartworm disease.

For dogs: 01.36 mcg/lb given once monthly.

Side effects are quite rare with moxidectin but could include gastrointestinal signs, weakness, or itching. Signs of overdosages would be similar. If you feel your pet has overdosed with moxidectin, you should contact your veterinarian and the National Poison Control Center.

Note: Collies have a "leaky" blood-brain barrier, but moxidectin appears to be quite safe for them. Doses up to thirty times the recommended amount have not caused significant problems in collies.

Moxidectin is considered to be safe for pregnant and nursing pets as well as puppies.

COMMON BRAND NAME: Pro Heart

Nitrofurantoin

Nitrofurantoin is an antibacterial medication that is effective against such bacteria as *E. coli, Staphylococcus,* and *Salmonella.* It is a bacteriostatic medication, meaning it slows or inhibits the growth of bacteria as opposed to initially killing them. It is used primarily to treat urinary infections.

This medication is not used extensively. People may be hypersensitive, so we assume some pets might be too. It needs to be used cautiously in pets with liver or kidney problems. It should not be combined with any of the fluoroquinolone antibiotics. Nitrofurantoin may cause false positive urinary glucose tests, so it should be used with caution in diabetic pets as well.

Nitrofurantoin is given orally with food as a capsule or suspension, but another form of this drug, called nitrofurazone, is used topically in ointments, powders, and gels.

ROUTINE DOSAGES: These are not FDA-approved medications and should be used only under the guidance of your veterinarian (nitrofurazone is in some approved topicals).

For dogs: 2 mg/lb given three times daily.

For cats: 2 mg/lb given three times daily.

For birds: soluble powder 9.3 percent, use 1/2 teaspoon per gallon of drinking water and observe for any neurologic signs.

Side effects seen with nitrofurantoin include allergic reactions, gastrointestinal signs, and rarely, hemolytic anemia.

Overdosages may lead to gastrointestinal signs such as vomiting and diarrhea, loss of appetite, and liver problems. If you feel your pet has overdosed on nitrofurantoin, you should contact your veterinarian and the National Poison Control Center.

Cancers have shown up after long-term usage in laboratory animals and there may be an association with infertility in male dogs. There have been cases of fetal damage as well, so these medications should not be used in pregnant pets.

COMMON BRAND NAMES: Furadantin; Macrodantin

Nystatin

Nystatin is an antifungal medication produced by bacteria which is used to treat topical infections of superficial yeasts and can be given orally to treat yeasts such as *Candida.* This is a medication that does not influence normal body functions, but rather, acts to fight outside infections.

Nystatin is not safe to give by injection, as it can cause severe kidney problems, but orally it is not well absorbed, so it is safe to use for the *Candida* problems. When used topically for yeast infections, you should try to prevent your pet from licking it off. Distract them to give the medication time to soak into the skin.

Nystatin comes in a variety of forms—solutions and tablets as well as in combinations with other topical medications in ointments, creams, and powders.

ROUTINE DOSAGES:
   For dogs: 100,000 units orally every six hours.
   For cats: 100,000 units orally every six hours.
   For birds: 300,000 units/kg orally twice daily (for crop problems and other *Candida* infections).
   For reptiles (primarily turtles): 100,000 units/kg orally once daily.
Used topically there are few side effects from the use of nystatin. It is quite harmful to the kidneys, though, if used orally, and an overdose could lead to kidney failure. If you feel your pet has overdosed on nystatin, you should contact your veterinarian and the National Poison Control Center.

Omeprazole

Omeprazole is a substituted benzimidazole which is a new class of drugs that work as gastric acid pump inhibitors. This medication reduces the amount of acid in the stomach and so influences a normal body function.

Omeprazole is primarily used in pets to treat ulcerative diseases of the gastrointestinal tract and to help prevent gastric erosions from certain other medications. It is felt that it might help in treating *Helicobacter* infections. There is some concern as to whether omeprazole is totally safe to use in cats, so caution should be used in treating felines. Omeprazole should also be used with caution in pets that have liver problems.

Since the absorption of many drugs is influenced by the acidity of the stomach, always check with your veterinarian about any other medications your pet is taking if omeprazole is added to their treatment. This is an expensive medication. Omeprazole is usually given as a tablet before meals, ideally in the morning.

ROUTINE DOSAGES: This is not an FDA approved medication, so omeprazole should be used only under the guidance of your veterinarian.

For dogs: 0.1–.4 mg/lb once daily.

For cats: 0.3 mg/lb once daily (see caution above).

Side effects that can be seen with omeprazole include many gastrointestinal signs such as nausea, vomiting, and diarrhea. Rarely, pets will develop blood problems. In people it is suggested that omeprazole not be used for longer than eight weeks at a time. If you feel your pet has overdosed on omeprazole, you should contact your veterinarian and the National Poison Control Center.

COMMON BRAND NAME: Prilosec

Organophosphates

Organophosphates are chemicals that inhibit acetylcholinesterases (important enzymes for muscle and nerve ending interactions). They can influence normal body functions but are used to treat or prevent infestations of fleas, ticks, and mites. Common types of organophosphates are chlorpyrifos, diazinon, and fenthion. While each chemical has a slightly different chemical makeup and slight differences in action, they are all similar enough to be grouped together here.

By acting on the muscle and nerve endings, organophosphates cause paralysis and death of the parasites. The acetylcholinesterases are important for mammals too, however, so we see more problems than with some of the newer, safer pesticides.

These organophosphates are approved for topical use only, and as pesticides, they do come under EPA (Environmental Protection Agency) guidelines. They should not be used on pets that are ill or have heartworm, liver or heart disease, or gastrointestinal problems. Great care should be taken in combining organophosphates with any other medication, especially tranquilizers. There are numerous drug interactions. Check with your veterinarian before you use any organophosphate product.

The dosage depends on the exact form and parasite you are attempting to treat. Read package instructions carefully!!! *Always* check with your veterinarian before using any organophosphate on your pet. Often there are safer alternatives.

Side effects of organophosphates can include gastrointestinal signs such as diarrhea, labored respiration, and rarely, muscle twitching. Signs of overdoses include increased urination and defecation, drooling, vomiting or diarrhea, dilated pupils, muscle tremors, a drop in heart rate, and even seizures and death. If you feel your pet has overdosed on an organophosphate, contact your veterinarian and the National Poison Control Center *immediately*.

There are many forms and brand names of parasite control products which might include organophosphates. These are not recommended for use during pregnancy. Always read the labels carefully and use as directed!

Oxymetazoline

Oxymetazoline is a nasal decongestant. As such, it is a medication that influences normal body functions. This is an over-the-counter medication but should be used only with veterinary guidance.

Oxymetazoline is primarily used for feline upper respiratory infections. It helps the cats to breathe more easily and to eat better. It has also been used in dogs with upper respiratory problems.

ROUTINE DOSAGES: This is not an FDA-approved drug for pets and should be used only under the direct guidance of your veterinarian. This medication can easily be overdosed and directions for dilution should be carefully followed. The standard 0.05 percent solution needs to be diluted in water 1 to 1.

For dogs: 1 drop of the 0.025 percent medication in the nose twice daily.

For cats: Touch the nose with a finger moistened with the 0.025 percent medication once or twice daily. Not to be used more than twice daily.

If oxymetazoline is used for more than three days, pets often show a "rebound" nasal decongestant effect. Pets who overdose with oxymetazoline may show central nervous system depression and even go into shock. If you feel your pet has overdosed on oxymetazoline, contact your veterinarian and the National Poison Control Center.

COMMON BRAND NAMES: Afrin; Neo Synephrine 12 hr.

Oxytocin

Oxytocin (commonly referred to as "pit") is a hormone that is produced by the hypothalamus (part of the brain) and stored in the pituitary gland (near the brain). This is a medication that influences normal body functions. Oxytocin is normally put into use for uterine contractions during delivery and to stimulate milk letdown for nursing.

As a medication, oxytocin is used to move labor along and to help expel retained placentas (the afterbirth). In order for oxytocin to work, your pet will need to have a dilated cervix and the fetus must not be too large for the pelvic opening. This hormone causes powerful contractions in a very strong set of muscles (the uterus) and could cause uterine rupture if not used properly. It is not commonly recommended to use oxytocin for treatment of pyometras (uterine infections).

Oxytocin is sometimes used in egg-bound birds and to help reptiles with egg-laying problems as well.

Oxytocin can work only if your pet's body is basically healthy. Calcium levels and glucose levels need to be checked before giving oxytocin. If your dog has low calcium, even the use of oxytocin may not increase her contractions.

Oxytocin is used as an injectable medication—usually intramuscular but sometimes intravenous.

ROUTINE DOSAGES: This is an FDA-approved medication for dogs and cats, but it is a powerful medication which should be used only under the direct guidance of your veterinarian. Never give oxytocin without consulting your veterinarian.

For dogs: 5–20 units by injection—do not repeat without veterinary guidance.

For cats: 0.5–3 units by injection—do not repeat without veterinary guidance.

For birds: 0.01–0.1 ml (*Note:* mls, not units) given once by intramuscular injection—usually given in conjunction with vitamin A and calcium.

For reptiles: 1–10 units/kg given once by injection, often with calcium. This is not especially effective in most lizards.

Pets who are given too much oxytocin can retain fluids and could even develop water toxicity if this continues long term. Uterine rupture is a possibility if used incorrectly. If you feel your pet has overdosed on oxytocin, contact your veterinarian and the National Poison Control Center immediately.

COMMON BRAND NAME: Pitocin

Penicillin G

Penicillin G is one of the first penicillins developed. It is a natural beta lactam antibiotic from *Penicillium chrysogenum*. This is a medication that acts against outside infestations. Penicillin G is a bactericidal antiobiotic, meaning that it kills bacteria and should not be combined with a bacteriostatic antibiotic, as that reduces the efficacy of both medications. It is not very good for gram-negative bacteria, but is quite good for group A beta hemolytic streptococcus. There are bacteria that have developed resistances to penicillin G.

Penicillin G may have benzathine or procaine added to prolong its activity, requiring less frequent dosing.

The penicillins in general are known for causing hypsersensitivities and should not be used in pets with known penicillin reactions. Caution should be used if your pet has parents or siblings with penicillin reactions.

Care should be used in treating pets with kidney problems with penicillin G. The dose and/or the dosing frequency may need to be reduced.

Penicillin G comes in tablet, injectable, and liquid forms and can be given orally or via injection. If given orally, try to medicate on an empty stomach.

ROUTINE DOSAGES:

For dogs: 10,000 IU/lb given four times daily.

For cats: 10,000 IU/lb given four times daily.

For birds: Very difficult to get the dosages appropriate for small birds due to size.

For reptiles: 10,000 IU/kg given by intramuscular injection daily or every three days, depending on the species and problem being treated. *Note:* Warnings have been reported on the use of penicillin in turtles.

For rabbits: 60,000 IU/kg given by intramusuclar or subcutaneous injection once daily for no more than five days—watch carefully for any signs of diarrhea! *Do not give orally!!*

Do not use in guinea pigs or chinchillas!

Side effects of penicillin can include gastrointestinal signs, such as vomiting or diarrhea. Since penicillin does influence normal gastrointestinal bacteria, it should not be used orally in rabbits or pocket pets. Remember to beware of any hypersensitivity reactions!

Overdosing can cause liver problems, gastrointestinal problems, or neurotoxicity with incoordination (seen in dogs). If you feel your pet has overdosed with penicillin, you should contact your veterinarian and the National Poison Control Center.

COMMON BRAND NAMES: Flocillin; Cual Pen; Pen G (potassium and sodium salts)

Phenobarbital

Phenobarbital is a barbiturate medication that influences normal body functions. As a barbiturate, it comes under special federal regulations due to abuse potential.

Phenobarbital is used for seizure control in our pets—sometimes alone and sometimes in combination with other medications. Many feel it is the drug of first choice for seizure control. It acts by depressing the central nervous system. In a few pets, it may cause a paradoxical excitement—cats seem prone to that problem.

Phenobarbital is not a cure for seizures. It simply attempts to prevent seizures and to decrease the frequency and severity of seizures in a pet.

There are numerous drug interactions with phenobarbital. You should be sure your veterinarian is aware of any other medications or supplements your pet is taking if your pet needs phenobarbital treatment.

Ideally, phenobarbital would not be used or used only with caution in pets with kidney problems, respiratory problems, or liver problems.

Phenobarbital is given orally as a tablet or an elixir.

ROUTINE DOSAGES: This is not an FDA-approved drug for use in pets so it should be used only under the direct guidance of your veterinarian.

> **For dogs:** 0.5–4 mg/lb given orally twice daily (this dose will be customized to your pet).

> **For cats:** 0.5–1 mg/lb given orally twice daily (this dose will be customized to your pet).

If your pet is to go off phenobarbital for a different medication, it is recommended that the dose be gradually reduced. An abrupt decrease could lead to increased seizure activity. Pets on phenobarbital should have periodic blood work to check the level of the medication in their blood and to monitor liver activity. Phenobarbital stimulates liver enzymes and can cause some liver damage long term.

Common side effects of phenobarbital are increased weight and increased thirst. Some pets will develop liver damage over long-term usage.

Overdosages can lead to death. If you feel your pet has overdosed on phenobarbital, contact your veterinarian and the National Poison Control Center.

Phenobarbital should not be used in pregnant or nursing pets.

COMMON BRAND NAME: Solfoton

Phenylbutazone

Phenylbutazone, or "bute" as it is commonly called, is a nonsteroidal anti-inflammatory drug of the pyrazolone class. It is a medication that influences normal body function by providing pain relief, decreasing fever, and acting as an anti-inflammatory. The pain and fever actions occur quickly but the full anti-inflammatory effect may take weeks to occur.

This is a medication with a narrow safety range, especially for pets on diuretics. It should be used with caution in pets with liver, kidney, or heart problems as well. Pets with any type of bleeding disorder or anemia should use other medications.

Phenylbutazone is another drug with many drug interactions. These include some antibiotics, antihistamines, and cardiac and seizure medications. If your pet is to take phenylbutazone, make sure your veterinarian is aware of any other medications or supplements your pet receives.

Phenylbutazone comes in both oral tablets and injectable forms, but the injectable form is rarely used and has some extra side effects. The oral medication form should be given with some food.

ROUTINE DOSAGES: Phenylbutazone is FDA approved for use in dogs only. It should not be used in cats.

For dogs: 1.5–7 mg/lb given three times daily. This dose may be reduced over time. Dogs should not receive more than 800 mg total per day.

Phenylbutazone has quite a narrow safety range. Side effects include ulcers in the gastrointestinal tract and kidney problems. Low blood cell counts have also been reported. Overdosing can lead to kidney failure, anemia, or ulcers (this is usually a chronic effect). If you feel your pet has overdosed on phenylbutazone, you should contact your veterinarian and the National Poison Control Center.

Pheylbutazone has been shown to cause problems with the fetuses in laboratory rodents, so it should not be used in pregnant dogs.

COMMON BRAND NAMES: Bizolin-200; Butatabs D; Butazolidin

Phenylpropanolamine

Phenylpropanolamine is a sympathomimetic amine, meaning it mimics some of the natural substances in the body that control muscle responses, among other things. This is a drug that affects normal body functions. Phenylpropanolamine is primarily used in pets to treat cases of urinary incontinence caused by a decreased sphincter tone (so it increases the tone of some muscles).

This drug should be used with caution in pets with glaucoma, enlarged prostates, hyperthyroidism, diabetes mellitus, or heart problems. Phenylpropanolamine does interact with some other drugs, including aspirin, so your veterinarian should be aware of any medications or supplements your pet is taking if you add phenylpropanolamine to your pet's treatments.

Phenylpropanolamine is available in oral capsules.

ROUTINE DOSAGES: This is not an FDA-approved drug for use in pets, so it should be used only under the guidance of your veterinarian.

For dogs: 0.5–1 mg/lb given two or three times daily.

For cats: 0.5–1 mg/lb given two or three times daily.

Side effects with phenylpropanolamine include not eating and restlessness.

Overdosing can lead to a wide range of cardiac and central nervous system effects. If you feel your pet has overdosed with phenylpropanolamine, you should contact your veterinarian and the National Poison Control Center.

COMMON BRAND NAMES: Propagest; Dexatrim

Phenytoin

Phenytoin is a medication to help control seizures. It is a centrally acting drug (so it acts on the brain) which influences a normal body function. Along with seizure control, phenytoin is sometimes used to help stabilize the heart in digitalis toxicity.

Phenytoin has fallen out of favor, as it has a high potential for causing liver damage and there are now safer alternatives. Pets receiving phenytoin should have regular blood testing done for phenytoin levels and to check liver function.

The liver damage risk is increased if phenytoin is combined with phenobarbital. There are many other drug interactions with phenytoin, including some antibiotics, sedatives, and steroids. It is important that your veterinarian be aware of any other medications and supplements your pet is taking if phenytoin is prescribed for your pet.

Phenytoin is given as an oral capsule and is usually given with food.

ROUTINE DOSAGES: This medication is only FDA approved for dogs and use in cats is not recommended. There are currently no veterinary products available.

For dogs: 9–16 mg/lb given orally three times daily.

For cats: Not recommended.

Side effects of phenytoin include decreased appetite, loss of coordination, and increased gum growth. Chronic overdosing can lead to liver damage, while an acute overdose may cause a coma or even death. If you feel your pet has overdosed on phenytoin, contact your veterinarian and the National Poison Control Center.

COMMON BRAND NAME: Dilantin

Piperazine

Piperazine is an over-the-counter parasiticide used to treat ascarids (round-worms) in pets. This is a medication that acts against outside infestations and has minimal effect on normal body functions. Piperazine acts by paralyzing the worms, which then pass outside the body. Roundworms do have zoonotic potential and stools and parasites should be disposed of carefully and kept away from small children. It should not be used with laxatives as they may remove it from the intestinal tract before it has time to act on the parasites.

Piperazine should not be used in pets with liver or kidney problems or pets who have had seizures. It is quite safe for puppies and kittens and is FDA approved for use in dogs and cats for the treatment of ascarids.

Piperazine comes in a number of different forms—solutions, capsules, pastes, and powders. It is formulated as a wide variety of salts and the dose used may be dependent on the formulation.

ROUTINE DOSAGES: Due to the variety of salt formulations, you must check the dose and use as directed on the package or follow your veterinarian's guidance. Treatment should be repeated in two to three weeks.

Piperazine is also used to treat parasites in birds and reptiles with ascarids (roundworms). Again, due to many formulations, you need to rely on your veterinarian for exact dosing.

Side effects with piperazine are uncommon, but some pets will have diarrhea.

Overdosing with this medication can lead to paralysis and death. Cats who have overdosed may show toxic signs of neurologic problems within twenty-four hours of treatment. If you feel your pet has overdosed with piperazine, you should contact your veterinarian and the National Poison Control Center.

Piperazine is considered to be safe in pregnant animals and healthy puppies and kittens—though caution should be used in cats.

COMMON BRAND NAMES: Happy Jack Kennel Wormer; Pipfuge; Pipa Tabs

Polysulfonated Glycosaminoglycan

Polysulfonated glycosaminoglycan is a substance that acts to protect cartilage and modify the progress of arthritis. As such, it is a medication that influences normal body functions. Polysulfonated glycosaminoglycan is a building block of cartilage and joint fluid. This medication attacks arthritis by inhibiting inflammation that could damage cartilage and stimulating cartilage growth and repair, as well as joint fluid production. Polysulfonated glycosaminoglycan should not be used in pets with infected joints or bleeding disorders (it can act similar to heparin). Caution should be taken when using this in pets with liver or kidney problems.

This medication comes in injectable form. It is normally given intramuscular but your veterinarian may choose to give it directly into the joint (intra-articular).

ROUTINE DOSAGES: This medication is FDA approved for use in dogs, not in cats. It should be used only under the guidance of your veterinarian.

For dogs: 2 mg/lb given intramuscularly twice weekly for four weeks.

For cats: 1 mg/lb given intramuscularly every three to five days for four weeks.

Side effects of polysulfonated glycosaminoglycan include pain from the injection (so sore muscles at the injection site).

Overdosing is not common, but you could see diarrhea or bleeding problems. If you feel your pet has overdosed with polysulfonated glycosaminoglycan, you should contact your veterinarian and the National Poison Control Center.

COMMON BRAND NAME: Adequan

Praziquantel

Praziquantel is a prazinoisoquinolone derivative that acts as a parasiticide against cestodes (tapeworms). This is a medication that acts against outside infestations and has minimal effect on normal body functions. The parasites end up digested, so they may not be seen in passed stool. This is FDA approved for use in dogs and cats.

No fasting is required to use praziquantel and it comes in oral pills and injectable liquid.

ROUTINE DOSAGES: The dosages used for dogs and cats will vary with the exact type of parasite you are treating for. It is important to bring in a stool sample and/or a sample of a tapeworm segment for identification.

For birds: 1/4 of a 23 mg tablet (given orally and repeated in two weeks) has been used in many species. Check with your veterinarian. The injectable form should not be used in finches.

For reptiles: Check with your veterinarian for exact dosages for your pet.

For rabbits: 7.5 mg/kg given orally—repeat in ten days.

Praziquantel is considered to be very safe. Minor side effects include some gastrointestinal upsets. This side effect is increased with the use of the injectable versions.

Overdosing is rare, but if you feel your pet has overdosed with praziquantel, you should contact your veterinarian and the National Poison Control Center.

COMMON BRAND NAMES: Droncit; Drontal

Prednisone/Prednisolone

Prednisone and prednisolone are used interchangeably here since prednisone is converted by the liver to prednisolone to act. These are synthetic glucocorticoids or steroids that influence normal body functions. While steroids have been much maligned, they can be miracle drugs when used properly—especially in pets with autoimmune or immune-mediated diseases.

Slightly different versions of these drugs are used to treat pets in shock, including birds and reptiles. In the above version, steroids have been used as part of the treatment of liver problems, skin problems, autoimmune problems, and heartworm. Prednisone has many actions including anti-inflammatory actions and stimulating hormones.

Steroids can lower the seizure threshold for pets, cause muscle weakness, and increase blood pressure. Along with affecting hormone levels they may increase gastric acid and the deposit of fat and glycogen in the liver. They reduce immune responses and may increase ocular pressure (so use with care in pets with glaucoma). Steroids may cause falsely elevated blood glucose test results and influence thyroid test results as well.

Steroids come in a wide variety of forms including topical ointments, oral pills, and injectable forms. Prednisone/prednisolone is almost always given as an oral pill in our pets.

ROUTINE DOSAGES: The dosages given are for prednisone or prednisolone and are very rough estimates. Your veterinarian will customize the dose for your pet and your pet's individual problem. Ideally steroids should be used at the lowest efficacious dose and for the shortest time necessary. Pets should be gradually tapered off steroid use.

For dogs: .22–5 mg/lb once or twice daily.

For cats: 1 mg/lb once or twice daily.

For birds: 0.2 mg/30 g given orally twice daily.

Short-term side effects may include an increase in drinking, eating, and urinating along with weight gain. Over long term, pets may develop signs of Cushing's disease—an overabundant supply of adrenal glucocorticoids (this time caused by the medication you are giving, not by the body itself making too many steroids). Signs here include gastrointestinal upsets, muscle wasting, and skin problems. The body functions mentioned above such as liver damage and a lowered immune response will also be seen. Cats are more resistant to both long- and short-term side effects than dogs.

Acute overdosing is not common, but overdoses may give any of the signs mentioned above. If you feel your pet has overdosed on steroids, you should contact your veterinarian and the National Poison Control Center.

Steroids should be used only under veterinary supervision in young pets as growth may be affected.

COMMON BRAND NAME: Solu Delta Cortef (an injectable steroid)

Most pills are generic.

Psyllium

Psyllium is derived from the *Plantago* plant. It is the nondigestible fiber of the seed coating. This is a medication that influences normal body function.

Psyllium is considered to be a "bulk" laxative. It is virtually nondigestible by our pets and while in the intestinal tract will absorb extra water. The extra water makes it swell and the increased bulk helps to relieve constipation, megacolon (primarily seen in cats), and large bowel diarrhea.

While psyllium is used in many cases of constipation, its most frequent use in pets is as a long-term additive for cats suffering from megacolon. It make take as long as seventy-two hours from the initial dose to see results due to the action in the intestines. Psyllium should not be used in pets who have actual intestinal obstructions. It is FDA approved for treatment of constipation.

Psyllium may bind digoxin, nitrofuantoin, and salicins (aspirin) if given at the same time. You should wait three hours between dosing with these medications and psyllium. Pets should be encouraged to drink and have water freely available when receiving psyllium.

Psyllium is usually in powdered form.

ROUTINE DOSAGES:

For dogs: 2–10 g given once or twice daily.

For cats: 1–4 g given once or twice daily.

Side effects seen with psyllium include flatulence (gas production), and very rarely, obstruction, if the pet is not drinking well when this medication is used.

Overdosing can lead to fluid stools, but that is uncommon. If you feel your pet has overdosed with psyllium, contact your veterinarian and the National Poison Control Center.

Psyllium is considered safe to use in pregnant and nursing pets if needed.

COMMON BRAND NAMES: Vetasyl; Metamucil

Pyrantel

Pyrantel is a pyrimidine-derived dewormer. This is a medication that works on outside infestations with minimal effect on normal body functions. Pyrantel is used to treat roundworm (ascarid) and hookworm parasites in dogs and cats and is FDA approved for this use. Pyrantel acts by paralyzing the parasites, which may pass out whole in the stools.

While pyrantel is quite safe, it should not be given to severely debilitated pets and it should not be combined with other dewormers or any organophosphates without veterinary guidance.

Pyrantel comes as a tablet, liquid, or paste, though the liquid is used most commonly for small animals. It may be given with food.

ROUTINE DOSAGES:

For dogs: 2.3 mg/lb given orally, then repeat in two to three weeks.

For cats: 9 mg/lb given orally, then repeat in two to three weeks.

For birds: The dose here varies with the exact parasite being treated for. Have a stool sample checked and follow your veterinarian's guidance.

For reptiles: The known dosages vary with the preparation being used. Check with your veterinarian.

Side effects are quite rare with pyrantel, but vomiting may be seen.

Overdosing is again uncommon, but a pet overdosed with pyrantel may show panting or staggering. If you feel your pet has overdosed with pyrantel, contact your veterinarian and the National Poison Control Center.

Puppies can receive parasites from their dam while in utero, and both puppies and kittens can receive parasites from their dam while nursing. Pyrantel is very often used as the first dewormer medication for young pups and kittens. Since these parasites (ascardis and hookworms) can be zoonoses, it is important that *all* puppies and kittens be treated.

COMMON BRAND NAMES: Nemex; Strongid

Pyrethrin

Pyrethrins are derived from the flower of the *Chrysanthenum cinerariaefolium*. Along with the natural product pyrethrin, the synthetic pyrethroids allethrin and permethrin are also covered here. These are all medications that act on outside infestations and are insecticides used to treat flea and tick infestations as well as ear mites.

The pyrethrins act by paralyzing the parasites and killing them. While they are known for low toxicity, some products are approved only for dogs, and dog products should *not* be used on puppies or cats unless specified that they are safe for those animals. Some permethrins have proven fatal when used on cats, and there have also been cases where cats in the household of a dog using certain permethrins became ill.

Pyrethrins are often combined with other medications. They may be combined with some of the insect growth regulators for more complete parasite coverage. They are sometimes combined with piperonyl butoxide or N-acetyl-bicycloheptene dicarboximide (MGK264), which act synergistically by inhibiting the enzyme fleas produce to degrade the insecticide. It should be noted that cats should not be treated with the combination products with piperonyl butoxide, as neurologic signs have been seen in cats using these treatments.

The pyrethrins are regulated by the EPA (Environmental Protection Agency), as they are considered to be insecticides. They are toxic for aquatic life and should be disposed of properly.

Pyrethrins come in many different forms—shampoos, powders, sprays, dips, spot-on topicals, collars, ear drops, and premise sprays.

ROUTINE DOSAGES: These totally depend on the individual product. Read instructions carefully, including package inserts and ingredients. Do *not* use products only approved for dogs on cats, kittens, or puppies.

The most common side effect seen with pyrethrins is salivation (drooling). Rarely, pets will show gastrointestinal upsets as well.

Overdosing can show up as seizures, gastrointestinal upsets, and a loss of coordination. If you feel your pet has overdosed on a pyrethrin product, contact your veterinarian and the National Poison Control Center.

Many of the pyrethrin products are considered to be safe for use in pregnant or nursing pets (though keep topicals away from the mammary glands). Always check the guidelines for the individual product!

COMMON BRAND NAMES: Biospot; some Defend products; some Duocide products; Cerumite; Mita Clear; some Ovitrol products

Pyramethamine

Pyramethamine is an aminpyrimidene that acts as a folic acid antagonist (so it lowers folic acid). This is a medication that is primarily used to fight outside infestations but may influence normal body functions somewhat, too. Pyramethamine is primarily used in pets to treat toxoplasmosis infections, such as *Toxoplasma gondii.*

Toxoplasmosis is the notorious zoonosis associated with pregnant women and cats, particularly cat litterboxes. This organism can infect dogs as well, however. Pyramethamine may be combined with sulfonamides to improve efficacy. Since pyramethamine may influence the bone marrow, pets receiving this medication should have regularly scheduled blood tests to screen for anemia and low blood counts. This medication comes in tablets.

ROUTINE DOSAGES: Pyramethamine is not an FDA-approved drug for pets, so it should be used only under the direct guidance of your veterinarian.

> **For dogs:** 0.2–0.4 mg/lb given orally once daily for two days, then 0.1 mg/lb once daily for two weeks.
>
> **For cats:** 0.2–0.4 mg/lb given orally once daily for two days, then 0.1 mg/lb once daily for two weeks.

Note: The above dosages are for pyramethamine alone. If combined with a sulfonamide, the dosage will change. Check with your veterinarian for guidance.

Some of the side effects seen with pyramethamine include gastrointestinal upsets, depression, and bone marrow suppression. Cats are more likely to show side effects than dogs.

Overdosing can lead to severe bone marrow problems, such as anemia and low blood cell counts. As noted previously, pets receiving pyramethamine should have regularly scheduled blood tests to screen for anemia and low blood cell counts. If you feel your pet has overdosed on pyramethamine, you should contact your veterinarian and the National Poison Control Center.

COMMON BRAND NAME: Daraprim

Selegiline (Deprenyl)

Selegiline is a monoamine oxidase inhibitor (MAOI) medication. This is a medication that influences a normal body function—in this case, by increasing the dopamine in the brain.

Currently selegiline is FDA approved for use in dogs to treat Cushing's disease (hyperadrenocorticism) caused by pituitary tumors and for treating canine cognitive dysfunction and senile dementia. Pet owners are warned to be patient because the true effect of selegiline may not be seen for up to two months. Selegiline is not a miracle drug that can totally reverse aging changes, but has been helpful in improving quality of life for some older dogs.

Selegiline should not be used with other antidepressant medications or any narcotics. These combinations can have severe side effects.

Selegiline comes in tablet form and is normally given with some food.

ROUTINE DOSAGES: Note that this drug is FDA approved for use only in dogs.
  For dogs: 0.5 mg/lb given once daily for two months (dosages may be customized).

Side effects commonly seen with selegiline include gastrointestinal upsets and lethargy. Rarely, some dogs will show behavior changes, increased drooling, and itching. Overdosing is not common but may result in behavior changes and neurologic problems. The results of an overdose may not show up until up to twelve hours later. If you feel your pet has overdosed on selegiline, you should contact your veterinarian and the National Poison Control Center.

COMMON BRAND NAMES: Anipryl; Eldepryl

Spectinomycin

Spectinomycin is an aminocyclitol antibiotic derived from *Streptomyces spectabilis* bacteria. This is a drug that is used to fight outside infestations. Spectinomycin is effective against many gram-positive and gram-negative bacteria, but only aerobes (bacteria that need oxygen to survive). This is a bacteriostatic antibiotic, so it interferes with bacterial growth but does not outright kill bacteria. As such, it should not be combined with a bactericidal antibiotic as you will reduce the efficacy of both medications. Spectinomycin should not be combined with chloramphenicol or tetracycline, as well.

While spectinomycin is used for some infections in dogs and cats, it is primarily used for commercial birds like poultry and adapted to pet birds as needed. It is safer than many antibiotics of its class, causing less ototoxicity (hearing loss) and nephrotoxicity (kidney damage). Spectinomycin is not well absorbed, so it is quite safe from overdosing problems.

Spectinomycin is available both as an oral solution and an injectable.

ROUTINE DOSAGES: Spectinomycin is not FDA approved for use in dogs and cats. If it is used in these pets, it should be only under the guidance of your veterinarian. Since it is most often used short term in the hospital for pets, it is usually given as an injection by your veterinarian.

For dogs: 2–4 mg/lb given intramuscularly twice daily or 10 mg/lb given orally twice daily.

For cats: 2–5 mg/lb given intramuscularly twice daily.

For birds: Check with your veterinarian as the dosage may vary with species.

Side effects are minimal and chances of overdosing are low due to the poor absorption orally.

If you feel your pet has overdosed with spectinomycin, contact your veterinarian and the National Poison Control Center.

COMMON BRAND NAME: Spectam

Stanozol

Stanozol is an anabolic steroid—a synthetic derivative of testosterone, the primary male hormone. This is a medication that influences normal body functions. Stanozol acts to increase appetite, fight debilitation, and may be used as an adjunctive therapy for chronic anemia. Unlike pure testosterone, there are minimal masculinizing effects and those are mainly noted with long-term usage. This is an excellent drug for older cats to "perk them up" and increase their eating.

Care should be taken if using stanozol in pets with kidney or heart problems, based on some human situations. It should not be used in pets with prostate cancer or breast cancer. Do not use stanozol in combination with any anticoagulant medications such as warfarin.

Stanozol may influence the care of diabetic pets as well. Diabetic pets taking stanozol may need their insulin dosages adjusted and may show variations in their blood glucose tests.

Stanozol comes in regular and chewable tablets as well as an injectable form. This is a controlled drug due to the potential for abuse by humans.

ROUTINE DOSAGES:

For dogs: 1–4 mg given orally twice daily or 25–50 mg given intramuscularly once weekly.

For cats: 0.5–0.2 mg given orally twice daily or 10–25 mg given intramuscularly once weekly.

For birds: 25–50 mg/kg given intramuscularly once weekly. Do not treat birds with kidney problems with this medication.

For reptiles: 5 mg/kg given intramuscularly once weekly. Stanozol is used in reptiles primarily to treat chronic debilitation or for a postsurgical boost.

Side effects seen in pets are masculinizing, if stanozol is used long term. Other problems are possible, as seen from human use. If you feel your pet has overdosed with stanozol, you should contact your veterinarian and the National Poison Control Center.

Stanozol should not be used in pregnant pets, as it may masculinize the fetuses, or in young growing pets.

COMMON BRAND NAME: Winstrol

Sucralfate

Sucralfate is an aluminum salt which coats the mucosal lining of the esophagus and stomach and decreases stomach acid. It influences normal body functions and has only a local effect. Sucralfate puts a barrier on ulcers and is used to treat ulcers and erosions of the gastrointestinal tract.

There is minimal absorption of sucralfate into the bloodstream. That minimizes the risk of any aluminum toxicity.

Sucralfate may be combined with histamine blockers, such as cimetidine, but if it is to be combined with any antacids, the medications should be given at different times. Sucralfate may decrease the action of phenytoin and many antibiotics, as it changes the acidity of the stomach and it does bind some other drugs. Always make sure your veterinarian is aware that your pet is taking other medications if he adds sucralfate to your pet's regimen.

Sucralfate can be found as liquid or easy-to-dissolve tablets. It is best if given on an empty stomach.

ROUTINE DOSAGES: Sucralfate is not an FDA-approved medication for pets, so it should be given only under the guidance of your veterinarian.

For dogs: 0.5–1 g given orally two or three times daily.

For cats: .250 mg given orally two or three times daily.

For reptiles: 50–100 mg/kg given orally three or four times daily.

Side effects seen with sucralfate include gastrointestinal upsets such as constipation. Overdosing is extremely uncommon, but if you feel your pet has overdosed on sucralfate, contact your veterinarian and the National Poison Control Center.

COMMON BRAND NAME: Carafate

Sulfadimethazine

Sulfadimethazine is a medication that can act as an antibiotic and an antiprotozoal. As such, it is a drug that acts against outside infections. Alone it may be used for skin infections, but more commonly, it is combined with other medications to make a bactericidal treatment. There is some resistance developing among bacteria.

The most common use of sulfadimethazine is for treating coccidia even though, in pets, it is FDA approved only for use against bacteria. Puppies and kittens with coccidia are often treated with sulfadimethazine.

Pets taking sulfadimethazine or any other sulfa drug should have plenty of fresh water available and be encouraged to drink. This reduces the likelihood of developing sulfa crystals in the kidney and urinary tract.

Sulfadimethazine may increase the action of phenytoin, phenylbutazone, and the thiazide diuretics.

This medication comes in liquid and tablet forms.

ROUTINE DOSAGES: Note that sulfadimethazine is FDA approved only to treat bacterial infections in pets, even though it is routinely used to treat coccidiosis.

For dogs: 25 mg/lb given orally on day one, then 12.5 mg/lb given orally for four days.

For cats: 25 mg/lb given orally on day one, then 12.5 mg/lb given orally for four days.

For rabbits: 50 mg/kg given orally on day one, then 25 mg/kg given orally for four days.

Sulfadimethazine is considered to be a very safe medication though there are some cautions. Pets should be well hydrated and have plenty of fresh water available to reduce the chances of sulfa crystals forming in the urine. Some pets may develop keratoconjunctivitis sicca (KCS, also known as "dry eye") if on this medication long term. Pets receiving sulfadimethazine for more than a short course should have frequent Schirmer tear tests scheduled to evaluate the tearing capability of the eyes. If you notice your pet squinting or having a discharge from her eyes, you should contact your veterinarian.

Rare side effects may include gastrointestinal signs, in particular diarrhea. Rarely some dogs will show acute hypersensitivity. Large-breed dogs are more prone to this—in particular, Doberman pinschers. Overdosing is rare, but if you feel your pet has overdosed on sulfadimethazine, you should contact your veterinarian and the National Poison Control Center.

Cleft palates in newborns have been noted in laboratory studies, so ideally sulfadimethazine should not be given to pregnant or lactating pets.

COMMON BRAND NAMES: Albon; Bactrovet

Sulfasalazine

Sulfasalazine is a sulfa antibiotic, a medication that acts against outside infections. It also has actions as an anti-inflammatory and immunosuppressive, which makes it also a medication that influences normal body functions.

Sulfasalazine is used to treat colitis, inflammatory bowel disease, and immune-mediated joint diseases (some of the arthritis conditions). Ideally, sulfasalazine should not be used in pets with liver, kidney, or bleeding problems.

Sulfasalazine should not be combined with aspirin or bismuth subsalicylate (Pepto-Bismol®). Other drugs that should not be used at the same time include warfarin, phenylbutazone, the thiazide diuretics, or any of the salicylates. Sulfasalazine is a powerful drug and you should be sure your veterinarian is aware of any other medications or supplements your pet may be taking if he adds sulfasalazine to your pet's regimen. Pets taking sulfasalazine should be well hydrated with plenty of fresh water available to reduce the likelihood of sulfa crystals forming in the urine. Any pet taking sulfasalazine for anything but short-term treatments should also have frequent Schirmer tear tests done to evaluate the tearing capability of his eyes.

ROUTINE DOSAGES:
  For dogs: 10–15 mg/lb given orally twice daily.
  For cats: Sulfasalazine is not routinely used in cats due to gastrointestinal side
     effects.

Side effects to the use of sulfasalazine range from mild vomiting to serious jaundice, autoimmune hemolytic anemia, and keratoconjunctivitis sicca (KCS, or dry eye).

Overdosing can cause any of those problems, as well as sulfa crystals in the urine and electrolyte disorders. Pets on sulfasalazine should be well hydrated and should have regularly schedule Schirmer tear tests to evaluate their eyes. If you feel your pet has overdosed on sulfasalazine, you should contact your veterinarian and the National Poison Control Center.

Ideally sulfasalazine would not be used in pregnant or nursing pets.

COMMON BRAND NAME: Azulifidine

Tetracycline (Oxytetracycline)

Tetracycline is the parent drug of a family of bacteriostatic antibiotics (drugs that inhibit the growth of bacteria, but do not kill them outright). For this reason it should not be used with a bactericidal drug as the effectiveness of both medications is reduced. They are effective against many types of organisms, from gram-positive and gram-negative bacteria to rickettsia, such as the ones that cause many of the tick fevers. Unfortunately, resistance is growing, so new tetracyclines are constantly being developed.

Tetracyclines are considered the first line of defense against rickettsial drugs and for many mycoplasma problems.

Tetracyclines have been used in turtles and other reptiles and are often used as eye or ear preparations for rabbits and other pocket pets. The same concerns about using these medications in young, growing animals do apply, though risks are lowered with external use.

Tetracycline is excreted in the urine and the stool (via bile from the liver), so caution should be used in pets with liver or kidney problems. Pets taking digoxin should be carefully monitored if also getting tetracycline. The same is true if your pet is on any anticoagulants. Tetracyclines bind to calcium, which can cause problems in young, growing animals. The tetracycline can get into the enamel on teeth and also into bones. For these reasons, it should not be used in pregnant pets or young growing pets, if at all possible.

Tetracyclines have been mentioned as influencing the insulin dosage of diabetics and possibly interfering with the glucose values on urine test strips. Please check with your veterinarian if your pet is a diabetic and is on this medication.

Most tetracyclines are given in oral (pill) form though there are injectable forms available, which your veterinarian may use. Some tetracyclines come in liquid formats or pelleted feeds for use in birds.

This is a class of drugs that can bind with calcium, so it is important to avoid vitamins and antacids with large amounts of calcium while giving this medication, as well as avoiding dairy products. Ideally you would give this antibiotic on an empty stomach. Tetracyclines may also be used in eye, ear, and skin preparations or ointments.

ROUTINE DOSAGES:

   For dogs: 12 mg/lb given orally three times a day.
   For cats: 8.25 mg/lb given orally three times a day.
   For birds: 200–250 mg/kg given orally once or twice daily (there are also medicated pellets, which may be fed as directed).
   For reptiles: 10 mg/kg given orally once daily.
   For rabbits: 50 mg/kg given orally two or three times daily.
   Side effects may include nausea and vomiting or even fever and depression in some pets (cats seem to be affected more than dogs).

Overdosages are rare, but could cause vomiting or diarrhea. If you have concerns, you should contact the National Poison Control Center or your veterinarian.

Tetracyclines are not recommended for use in young growing pets or pregnant pets due to the effects on bones and teeth (see previous).

COMMON BRAND NAMES: Terramycin; Panmycin

Thiabendazole

Thiabendazole is a parasiticide of the benzimidazole family. As such, it is a medication that acts against outside infections. In dogs it has been used against various ascarids (roundworms), strongyloides species of intestinal worms, and nasal aspergillosis (a fungal infection). Some resistances have been developing, particularly among the intestinal parasites.

Thiabendazole comes in tablets, liquid, and paste versions and is more commonly used in large animals (livestock) than in pets today.

ROUTINE DOSAGES:
>**For dogs:** 20 mg/lb orally given once for intestinal parasites; 10mg/lb given orally for aspergillosis on a customized schedule for your individual pet.
>**For cats:** Thiabendazole is not routinely used in cats.
>**For birds:** Thiabendazole is used to treat ascarids (roundworms) and *Syngamus trachea*. The exact dosage varies with the species being treated so you need to consult pet's own veterinarian.
>**For reptiles:** 50–100 mg/kg given orally once, then repeat in two weeks.

Thiabendazole can cause some side effects. Possible problems seen are gastrointestinal problems and hair loss. The hair loss is generally associated with long-term usage and Dachshunds may be especially prone to this problem. Overdosing is not common with thiabendazole, but if you feel your pet has overdosed with this medication, you should contact your veterinarian and the National Poison Control Center.

Thiacetarsamide

Thiacetarsamide is an arsenic compound that is used to treat heartworm disease in dogs. This is a medication that attacks outside infestations, but is powerful enough to possibly influence normal body functions and needs to be used with care. This is definitely a medication where care has to be used to poison the parasite and not the pet!

In heartworm disease adult parasites may live in the lungs and the heart chambers themselves. Dogs can have varying degrees of heartworm disease—ranging from Class I, which is mild and with few adult heartworms, to Class IV, where there are heartworms right in the portacava. Class IV dogs do best with surgery and have a very grave prognosis. Class III dogs have some serious clinical signs from the heartworms, including pulmonary and cardiac illnesses.

Dogs who are receiving thiacetarsamide should have their illness stabilized first. This medication is quite powerful, with serious side effects, and should be used only in dogs with Class I and Class II heartworm disease. (Many veterinarians simply use the safer melarsomine.) There is always a risk of pulmonary embolism with heartworm disease treatment, and pets need to have restricted exercise for weeks posttreatment to minimize this risk.

Thiacetarsamide is given as a careful intravenous injection via a catheter. This is a very irritating drug if it gets out into the tissues and can even cause tissue sloughs. Most pets are hospitalized for at least the treatment and the first few days posttreatment.

ROUTINE DOSAGES: Thiacetarsamide is FDA approved for use in dogs only though it is used for cats on rare occasions.

> **For dogs:** 1.1mg/lb given intravenously twice in one day for two days total (this may need to be repeated in 4 months). Restricted exercise for six to eight weeks is recommended.

Side effects of thiacetarsamide may include gastrointestinal symptoms. Many dogs vomit directly from the medication, but this is not considered to be a reason to halt treatment, unless it is severe. Many problems are due to the death of the adult heartworms. Dogs may show liver damage or throw clots from the dead worms. Some coughing and gagging is common. Death is possible.

Thiacetarsamide is a drug with a very small safety margin and can easily be overdosed. Signs can include all of the side effects mentioned, plus depressions and death. If you feel your dog has overdosed on thiacetarsamide, contact your veterinarian and the National Poison Control Center immediately.

COMMON BRAND NAME: Caparsolate

Thyroxine, Levothyroxine, L-Thyroxin

Thyroxine is a synthetic form of thyroid hormone, so it is used to influence a normal body function that has failed. It is primarily used in dogs to treat hypothyroidism, a very common problem leaving dogs with low levels of thyroid hormones. The signs seen in hypothyroid dogs can vary but include weight gain, poor haircoats, and lethargy. In birds, thyroxine may be used to help treat respiratory clicks, vomiting in budgerigars, and thyroid problems.

Thyroxine supplementation should be done with care in pets with heart problems. It does increase metabolism and could put a strain on the heart. Thyroxine can also interact with digoxin and warfarin, so care should be taken with pets on these medications. Since thyroxine does influence metabolism, diabetic pets may need their insulin dosages adjusted if they start taking thyroxine.

Thyroxine does have other drug interactions, and your veterinarian should be aware that your pet is taking this supplement (which is lifetime usually). Pets should have their T4 (thyroid hormone) levels checked on a regular basis as the dose may need to be customized. Also, it is recommended that your pet stick with one brand of this medication as there can be variations between brands. Thyroxine comes in tablets and a chewable form.

ROUTINE DOSAGES:

For dogs: 0.1 mg/10 lb given once daily (this may be adjusted quite a bit for your individual dog—regular blood tests to establish the best dose and to check thyroid levels are important).

For cats: 0.04 mg given once daily (this may be adjusted quite a bit for your individual cat—regular blood tests to establish the best dose and to check thyroid levels are important).

For birds: 0.1 mg in 30–120 ml water daily. Offer this for a short time and remove—exact dose will vary with species of bird and problem being treated.

For turtles: 0.02 mg/kg given orally every other day.

Side effects seen with thyroid medications are not common. If a pet should overdose, however, the increased metabolic effect can show up in serious heart changes, increased respiration, excitability, panting, and nervousness. If you feel your pet has overdosed on thyroxine, you should contact your veterinarian and the National Poison Control Center.

COMMON BRAND NAMES: Thyro-Form; Thyro Tabs; Soloxine

Ticarcillin

Ticarcillin is a synthetic penicillin antibiotic. This is a medication that is used to treat outside infections of the body. Ticarcillin is often used for *Pseudomonas* bacterial infections. It may be combined with an aminoglycoside antibiotic for greater efficacy or another synthetic penicillin such as carbenicillin.

Ticarcillin is metabolized and eliminated through the kidneys, so it should be used with care in any pets with kidney problems. Some bacteria are showing resistance (as with all the penicillins), so if no response to treatment is seen, you may need to change antibiotics.

Ticarcillin is found in injectable form and can be given intravenously or intramuscularly. Most likely your pet would receive this while in the hospital under your veterinarian's care.

ROUTINE DOSAGES:
  For dogs: 6–10 mg/lb given by injection intravenously or intramuscularly three times daily.
  For cats: 6–10 mg/lb given by injection intravenously or intramuscularly three times daily.
  For birds: 200 mg/kg given by injection intravenously or intramuscularly three times daily. Note that bird dosages may vary quite a bit depending on the species being treated.

Side effects to the use of ticarcillin include hypersensitivity reactions and allergic reactions. This drug should be avoided in pets with known penicillin allergies. It is possible that clotting problems may also occur.

Overdosing would be unusual, but if you feel your pet has overdosed on ticarcillin, you should contact your veterinarian and the National Poison Control Center.

This medication will pass the placenta and into the milk, so it should be used in pregnant or nursing pets only if absolutely necessary.

COMMON BRAND NAMES: Ticar; Ticillin

Timolol

Timolol is a beta-adrenergic blocker. As such, this is a medication that influences normal body functions by acting on the nervous system. Timolol is used primarily in the treatment of glaucoma in pets and is given as an eye drop.

Timolol acts to decrease the production of intraocular fluid (fluid in the eye) and also decreases ocular pressure.

Timolol should not be used in pets with asthma or other allergic respiratory conditions and only with care in pets with congestive heart failure.

ROUTINE DOSAGES: Timolol is not an FDA-approved medication for pets and should be used only under the guidance of your veterinarian. If your pet is receiving multiple eye medications, such as an antibiotic, as well, you should give the medications at separate times, allowing at least five minutes in between treatments.

For dogs: 1 drop of 0.5 percent solution put in the eye twice daily.

For cats: 1 drop of 0.5 percent solution put in the eye twice daily.

Side effects are extremely rare, since the dose given is so small and is given topically on the eye. If your pet ate the bottle, an overdose could occur with signs of changes in heart rate and respiratory rate, and in extreme cases, seizures. If you feel your pet has overdosed on timolol, you should contact your veterinarian and the National Poison Control Center.

COMMON BRAND NAME: Timoptic

Trimethoprim-Sulfa

Trimethoprim and sulfadiazine are antibiotics combined for a more efficacious effect and the resulting mixture is known as trimetophorim-sulfa. They are often labeled as potentiated sulfas. These are drugs that fight outside infections and are effective against many staphylococci, streptococci, some gram-negative bacteria, and a few protozoa. These are bactericidal antibiotics, which kill the bacteria outright. Trimethoprim-sulfa is commonly used to treat skin infections and urinary tract infections in pets. This is a combination drug that in birds is used primarily for gastrointestinal and respiratory infections. It is safe enough to use in handfed baby birds.

As with all sulfa drugs, this combination should be used with care in pets with liver or kidney problems. Since sulfa crystals may form in the urine, pets taking trimethoprim-sulfa should be well hydrated and have fresh water available at all times.

Sulfa drugs may interact with diuretics and some pain medications such as phenylbutazone. If antacids are also being given to your pet, they should be dosed two to three hours before or after this antibiotic combination.

Trimethoprim-sulfa comes in oral suspensions, tablets, and injectable forms.

ROUTINE DOSAGES: Trimethoprim-sulfa is FDA approved only for use in dogs and should be used in other pets only under the guidance of your veterinarian.

For dogs: 8–15 mg/lb given once or twice daily.

For cats: 8–15 mg/lb given once or twice daily.

For birds: 0.1 ml/30 g given orally two or three times daily.

For reptiles: 15–25 mg/kg given orally once daily.

For rabbits: 30 mg/kg given orally once or twice daily.

Side effects seen with trimethoprim-sulfa include a decrease in thyroid hormones and keratoconjunctivitis sicca (dry eye) with long-term usage. Sulfa crystals in the urine are common. Overdosing can lead to the abovementioned problems and, rarely, to anemia. This is a safe drug, but it is not recommended that it be used for more than two weeks. If you feel your pet has overdosed on trimethoprim-sulfa, you should contact your veterinarian and the National Poison Control Center.

Ideally, trimethoprim-sulfa should not be used in pregnant or nursing pets.

COMMON BRAND NAMES: Tribrissen; Di-Trim

Tylosin

Tylosin is a macrolide antitibiotic so it is a medication that attacks outside infections. It comes from the bacteria *Streptomyces fradiae* and is a bacteriostatic antibiotic—meaning it inhibits the growth of bacteria but does not usually kill them outright. There is minimal bacterial resistance to tylosin and it is safe for normal gastrointestinal bacteria, which makes it quite safe and unlikely to be toxic.

Tylosin is best known for treating *Clostriium perfringens* toxicities. It has been used in both dogs and cats for long term or even lifetime treatment of chronic diarrhea problems. It is also very effective against mycoplasma organisms, including canine genital mycoplasma, and many respiratory infections. In birds and reptiles, it is used mainly for respiratory problems.

Tylosin may interfere with digoxin levels, so it should be used with care in pets receiving digoxin for their heart problems.

Currently tylosin comes in an injectable form and also a powder. It is quite bitter tasting, but can be mixed with foods.

ROUTINE DOSAGES: Tylosin is FDA approved only in the injectable form, but is most commonly used in dogs and cats in the oral form. Since owners are not likely to be giving injections of this, only the oral dosages are included here for dogs and cats.

For dogs: 10–20 mg/lb given orally with food twice daily.

For cats: 2.5–5 mg/lb given orally with food twice daily.

For birds: 10–40 mg/kg given by intramuscular injection two or three times daily.

For tortoises: 5 mg/kg given by intramuscular injection once daily for ten days.

Tylosin has a very low record of side effects or overdose symptoms. Pets may show some soreness at injection sites or mild gastrointestinal problems, such as mild diarrhea. Overdosing is quite rare, but if you feel your pet has overdosed on tylosin, you should contact your veterinarian and the National Poison Control Center.

COMMON BRAND NAME: Tylan

Vinblastine

Vinblastine is a vinca alkaloid derived from the plant *Cantharanthus roseus*. This is a drug used in cancer chemotherapy protocols, and so it influences normal body functions. Vinblastine acts by preventing cell division and interfering with amino acids in the body. These effects may interfere with normal cells as well as cancer cells.

The cancers vinblastine is most commonly used to treat include lymphomas, carcinomas, mastocytomas, and splenic tumors. This drug is usually part of a chemotherapy protocol—being used with other chemotherapy drugs and in a set pattern.

Vinblastine is metabolized in the liver, so caution should be used in pets with liver problems. Since it does reduce the white blood cells (cells that fight infection), it should not be used in pets that already have reduced numbers of those cells.

Vinblastine comes in powders or solutions and is administered by very careful intravenous injection. This drug can cause a great deal of tissue damage (even sloughs) if it gets outside the vein. Your veterinarian will be administering this drug.

ROUTINE DOSAGE: Vinblastine is not FDA approved for use in pets, so it should be used only under the guidance of your veterinarian. This is a powerful drug and the dose is established by m^2 (meters squared—so directly related to size). The dose will be customized to your pet depending on condition being treated for, exact protocol of all the drugs involved, your pet's overall health, etc.

Side effects of vinblastine use may include vomiting, nausea, constipation, jaw pain, and a depression of bone marrow activity—lowering the red and white blood cell numbers. In general, vinblastine causes more bone marrow suppression than neurologic signs, while vincristine does the opposite. Overdoses will cause the above signs as well as decreased tendon reflexes, other neurologic signs, possibly bleeding, and even death. If you feel your pet has overdosed with vinblastine, contact your veterinarian and the National Poison Control Center.

COMMON BRAND NAME: Velban

Vincristine

Vincristine is a vinca alkaloid made from the plant *Cantharanthus roseus*. This is a chemotherapy drug, which is used to treat cancers and interferes with normal body functions. Vincristine acts by preventing cell division and interfering with amino acids. These effects can influence normal cells as well as cancer cells.

Vincristine is used for tumors of the lymphoid system and the hematopoietic system (blood and blood vessels), usually as part of a chemotherapy protocol. It may also be used alone to treat canine transmissible venereal tumors and possibly for immune-mediated thrombocytopenia (low numbers of platelets).

This is metabolized by the liver, so it should be used with extreme caution in pets with liver problems.

Vincristine comes as a powder and is given by very careful intravenous injection. This drug would be given by your veterinarian. If any vincristine gets outside the vein, it can cause serious tissue damage, including sloughing.

ROUTINE DOSAGES: Vincristine is not FDA approved for use in pets, so it should be used only under the guidance of your veterinarian. This is a powerful drug and the dose is established by m² (meters squared—so directly related to size). The dose will be customized to your pet depending on the condition being treated for, exact protocol of all the drugs involved, your pet's overall health, etc.

Side effects of vincristine may include constipation, jaw pain, inflammation of the tongue and mouth, and neurological signs. Vincristine tends to cause more neurological signs and less bone marrow suppression than vinblastine. Overdoses may show neurologic signs including seizures, hair loss, gastrointestinal signs, and even death. If you feel your pet has overdosed with vincristine, you should contact your veterinarian and the National Poison Control Center.

COMMON BRAND NAME: Oncovin

Warfarin

Warfarin is a derivative of coumarin that influences normal body functions by interacting with clotting mechanisms. It is considered to be an indirect anticoagulant and acts by interfering with vitamin K_1.

Warfarin is used to help combat thromboembolism (clots thrown off in the blood vessels). This can be short term as part of heartworm treatment, for example, or long term as in the case of cats with hypertrophic cardiomyopathy.

Warfarin should be used with caution in pets with liver problems and not in pets with bleeding disorders, including von Willebrand's disease, or with upcoming surgery, as it would increase the risk of hemorrhaging.

There are many drug interactions with warfarin, and your veterinarian should be aware of any supplements or medications your pet is receiving if warfarin is to be added to your pet's medication regimen. Warfarin is generally given as an oral tablet to pets.

ROUTINE DOSAGES: Warfarin is not an FDA-approved drug for use in pets so it should be used only under the guidance of your veterinarian. Dosages need to be customized to the pet and to the disease condition being treated. Frequent monitoring of either PT (prothrombin time) or PIVKA (proteins induced by vitamin K antagonists) by blood tests is important.

Side effects of warfarin can include dose-related hemorrhaging such as nosebleeds, bleeding into the gastrointestinal tract, urinary bleeding, or hematomas in muscles. Overdoses have severe cases of the above symptoms and can even lead to death. If you feel your pet has overdosed on warfarin, you should contact your veterinarian and the National Poison Control Center.

Warfarin should not be used in pregnant pets.

COMMON BRAND NAME: Coumadin Tabs

Xylazine

Xylazine is an alpha 2 adrenergic agonist. This is a drug that influences normal body functions by acting on the central nervous system as a sedative and analgesic (pain reliever), with some muscle relaxant properties as well.

Xylazine is used as a sedative and as part of some anesthetic protocols, being used as a preanesthetic. It often causes emesis (vomiting), especially in cats, and is occasionally used to cause vomiting in cats that have eaten toxic substances.

Xylazine should be used with caution in pets with liver, kidney, or cardiac problems, and ideally not in pets with seizures. It can lower heart rates. Xylazine should not be combined with other central nervous system depressants, or only with great care. The effects of xylazine can be partially reversed by yohimbine.

Xylazine is commonly used as an injectable medication.

ROUTINE DOSAGES: Xylazine is FDA approved for dogs and cats, basically as a preanesthetic. This is a drug that should be used only by your veterinarian.

Side effects of xylazine can include cardiac arrthymias and central nervous system and respiratory depression. Overdoses show severe cases of these symptoms and may also have seizures. If you feel your pet has overdosed with xylazine, you should contact your veterinarian and the National Poison Control Center.

COMMON BRAND NAMES: Rompun; Gemini

Yohimbine

Yohimbine is an indolealkylamine alkaloid that influences normal body functions. It can get into and act on the central nervous system, causing central nervous system stimulation. Yohimbine also increases heart rates and blood pressure.

Yohimbine is considered to be an alpha 2 adrenergic antagonist and can be used to partially reverse the effects of xylazine. It may be somewhat antagonistic to acepromazine and ketamine as well.

Yohimbine should be used with caution in pets with kidney problems or that have seizures. This medication is used as an injectable treatment.

ROUTINE DOSAGES: Yohimbine is only FDA approved for use in dogs. It has been used in other species, including rabbits, and pocket pets. This is a medication that should only be used by your veterinarian.

Side effects of yohimbine can include central nervous system excitement, muscle tremors, drooling, and increased respiratory rates. Overdoses may show those signs to a severe degree and even seizures. If you feel your pet has overdosed on yohimbine, you should contact your veterinarian and the National Poison Control Center.

COMMON BRAND NAME: Yobine

Appendixes

Additional Recommended Reading

———◆———

Please note this is *not* an exhaustive or all-inclusive list, but merely intended to get you started on reading about the care and well-being of your pets.

Pet Medications—Traditional

Just What the Doctor Ordered by Race Foster, DVM, and Marty Smith, DVM. Howell Book House, 1996.

The Pill Book Guide to Medication for Your Dog and Cat by Kate A.W. Roby, VMD, and Lenny Southam, DVM. Bantam Books, 1998.

Small Animal Clinical Pharmacology and Therapeutics by Dawn Merton Boothe, DVM, MS, PhD, DACVIM, DACVP. W. B. Saunders Company, 2001.

Veterinary Drug Handbook by Donald C. Plumb, Pharm.D. Iowa State University Press, 1999.

Pet Medications—Nontraditional

Emerging Therapies—Using Herbs and Nutraceutical Supplements for Small Animals by Susan G. Wynn, DVM. AAHA Press, 1999.

Natural Health Bible for Dogs and Cats by Shawn Messonnier, DVM. Prima Publishing, 2001.

New Choices in Natural Healing for Dogs & Cats by Amy D. Shojai and the Editors of Prevention Pets. Rodale Press, 1999.

Pet Care in the New Century by Amy D. Shojai. New American Library, 2001.

Pet Care

Cats for Dummies by Gina Spadafori and Paul D. Pion, DVM, DACVIM. John Wiley & Sons, 2000.

Complete Bird Owner's Handbook by Gary A. Gallerstein and Heather Acker. John Wiley & Sons, 1994.

Cornell Book of Cats, edited by Mordecai Seigel and James R. Richards. Villard Books, 1997.

Dog Health and Nutrition for Dummies by M. Christine Zink, DVM, PhD. Hungry Minds, Inc., 2001.

U C Davis Book of Dogs, edited by Mordecai Seigel. HarperCollins, 1995.

House Rabbit Handbook by Marinell Harriman. Drollery Press, 1995.

Reptile Care: An Atlas of Disease and Treatments by Fredric Frye, MRCVS. TFH Publications, 1992.

Glossary

———◆———

Aerobe—a microorganism, such as a bacterium, that needs oxygen to survive.

Amino acid—an organic compound that is important for metabolism and growth.

Anaerobe—a microorganism, such as a bacterium, that can survive without oxygen and in fact some may not grow with oxygen present.

Antibiotic—a compound that inhibits the growth of or kills microorganisms—sometimes used just in reference to destroying bacteria.

Antifungal—a compound that inhibits the growth of or kills fungae.

Ataxia—incoordination, a loss of balance.

Bactericidal—describes a compound that kills bacteria.

Bacterin—a vaccine developed to stimulate immunity against bacteria.

Bacteriostatic—describes a compound that inhibits the growth of bacteria.

Cardiac—referring to the heart.

Efficacy—the effectiveness of a medication.

Emetic—a substance to cause vomiting.

Euthanasia—technically "beautiful death," used for ending the life of a pet in a merciful way.

Gastric—referring to the stomach.

Gastrointestinal—referring to the stomach and intestines.

Hepatic—referring to the liver.

Intramuscular—in the muscle, usually referring to a vaccination or injection site.

Intravenous—in the vein, usually referring to giving fluids or medications.

Oral—referring to the mouth; oral medications are given to your pet by mouth.

Ototoxicity—damage to the ears (*oto*).

Prognosis—an estimate of the chances of recovery.

Pulmonary—referring to the lungs.

Nephrotoxicity—damage to the kidneys (*nephro*).

Renal—referring to the kidneys.

Respiratory—referring to breathing and the lungs.

Vaccine—a suspension designed to stimulate immunity.

Zoonoses—a disease or parasite that can be passed from animals to people.

Helpful Organizations

———◆———

Drug/Medication-Related Organizations

For animal drugs and foods:
"Veterinary Adverse Experience, Lack of Effectiveness or Product Defect Report." This form (which comes with a preaddressed prepaid postage envelope) can be obtained by writing to:

> ADE Reporting System
> Center for Veterinary Medicine
> U.S. Food and Drug Administration
> 7500 Standish Place
> Rockville, MD 20855-2773

Phone the Center for Veterinary Medicine at:
1-888-FDA-VETS [322-8387]
Phone the Food and Drug Administration at:
1-301-443-4095 (collect), or after hours, leave a message at 1-301-443-1209.

For vaccines, bacterins, and diagnostic tests:
Phone the USDA at:
1-800-752-6255
1-515-232-5789 (collect). Leave a message after hours.

For pesticides (including externally applied parasiticides):
Phone the US EPA at:
1-800-858-PEST [7378]

Another possibility is utilizing the USP Veterinary Practitioner's Reporting Network, which is sponsored by the United States Pharmacopeia. This is an independent, nongovernment program. For veterinary products, call:

1-800-4-USPPRN [487-7776]

For information on drug compounding and the FDA regulations on drug compounding, see: www.fda.gov/fdac/features/2000/400_compound.html

Veterinary Organizations

American Animal Hospital Association
PO Box 150899
Denver, CO 80215-0899
303-986-2800
www.healthypet.com

American Association of Feline Practitioners
530 Church Street, Suite 700
Nashville, TN 37219
800-204-3514
615-259-7799
www.aafponline.org

American Holistic Veterinary Medicine Association
2218 Old Emmorton Road
Bel Air, MD 21015
410-569-0795
AHVMA.org

American Veterinary Medical Association
Public Information Division
1931 North Meacham Road, Suite 100
Schaumburg, IL 60173-4360
847-925-8070
www.avma.org

Association of Avian Veterinarians
PO Box 811720
Boca Raton, Fl 33481-1720

561-393-8901

www.aav.org

Association of Reptile and Amphibian Veterinarians
PO Box 605
Chester Heights, PA 19017
610-358-9530
www.arav.org

Animal Health Care and Research Organizations

AKC Canine Health Foundation
251 West Garfield Road, Suite 160
Aurora, OH 44022
888-682-9696
www.akcchf.org

CERF (Canine Eye Registry Foundation)
1248 Lynn Hall
Purdue University
West Lafayette, IN 47907
765-494-8179
www.vet.purdue.edu/~yshen/cerf/html

Morris Animal Foundation
45 Inverness Drive East
Englewood, Co 80112-5480
800-243-2345
303-790-2345
www.morrisanimalfoundation.org

Optigen
Cornell Business and Technology Park
33 Thornwood Drive, Suite 102
Ithaca, NY 14850
607-257-0301
www.optigen.com

OFA (Orthopedic Foundation for Animals)
2300 East Nifong Boulevard
Columbia, MO 65201-3856
573-442-0418
www.offa.org

PennGen Laboratories
3850 Spruce Street
Philadelphia, PA 19104-6010
215-898-3375
www.vet.upenn.edu/researchcenters/penngen

The Winn Feline Foundation
1805 Atlantic Avenue
PO Box 1005
Manasquan, NJ 08736-0805
732-528-9797
www.winnfelinehealth.org

Leash = Love = Life

———◆———

Every day many dogs die, often painful deaths, due to the lack of a leash. A leash could be as simple as parachute cord or as fancy as custom tooled leather. What is important is that the leash is attached to a caring owner. A dog on a leash attached to a responsible person has a much greater likelihood of a long, healthy life than a dog running free.

While on a leash, your dog has a greatly reduced risk of being hit by a car, being injured in a dog fight, getting lost, or being stolen. Disease risks drop as you can limit your dog's contact with other dogs and with their areas of elimination. Your dog won't be in contact with wild animals. A leash can even stop a dog from picking up dangerous trash or eating rotten litter or food left around.

Leashed dogs make good neighbors and good ambassadors both for their breed and for dogdom in general. No trash raids, no eliminating on lawns or urinating on prized bushes. No digging up gardens or chasing cats. Joggers and bike riders are safe from pursuit. Your canine companion can't be accused of biting anyone or of siring or whelping an unintended litter.

A dog on a leash is a law-abiding citizen. Virtually all communities have some sort of leash law. This can range from restrictions for certain areas or certain times of year (most communities outlaw dogs running loose during the winter months when they might harass deer and other wildlife in the deep snow). New York has a state-mandated leash law going back to the rabies epidemic, which states that a dog that is off its owner's property must be on leash—it cannot be "at large."

Many people move to a suburban or rural area figuring that now they can truly give Rover "room to run" and a chance "to be free." It is equally, if not more, important that rural dogs be leashed or confined. Dogs seen running deer or harassing or worrying livestock can be destroyed on sight with no liability to the person defending the livestock or deer.

I would like to share with you a personal tragic story of two cute pet dogs allowed to run free. We have animals on our small farm—horses, ducks, sheep, and my son's pet goat along with our house pets. To keep my animals safe, I put up four-feet-high, tightly woven stock fence (literally so tight and so close to the ground that my ducks can't squeeze under or through it). I did this after a neighbor's dog killed a number of my ducks last year.

Picture two cute pet dogs—about thirty to thirty-five-pounds each, breed is not important as it could be *any* breed or any mix. Dogs who slept in the house that night and were fed that morning in a bowl in the kitchen. Not feral dogs, not coy dogs, not hungry dogs, not big "tough" dogs. Pet dogs who someone did not quite care enough about to leash or confine. Pet dogs left to run free and enjoy the day while the family went off to work or school. Pet dogs who had been spotted chasing deer and undoubtedly killing some.

Now picture a gorgeous fall day—bright blue sky, beautiful leaves. A small flock of mixed-breed sheep and one lovely young dairy goat named Molly. Molly was more of a pet than many dogs—she came to her name, knew some tricks, walked on hikes with us. She loved Cheerios and sliced apple. She was my seven-year-old son's pet and a beloved family member.

I was at the barn around 10 A.M. and all was well. At 11 A.M., I took my Belgian Tervuren, Beep, and headed to the barn to do some herding practice. I immediately knew something was wrong. The sheep were all tightly flocked together and there was no sign of Molly. As I ran and turned the corner of the barn, I saw something that will remain in my nightmares for the rest of my life.

Molly had positioned herself between two dogs and the sheep, whom she lived with and considered part of her family. She was fighting desperately. These two dogs were savagely mauling her. Her left front leg was partly torn off, her tail ripped almost off, her nose bitten right through the bridge. In less than an hour, those cute little pet dogs had put over two hundred punctures in Molly.

I rushed Molly to my clinic, put in an IV and treated her for shock, then raced her to Cornell, where she went into the Intensive Care Unit. Molly fought for thirty-six hours, then the brave little goat lost her battle. The dogs were lucky—they had quick, fairly painless deaths.

We have three innocent victims here. A brave little goat and two dogs who deserved some training and responsible ownership. Those dogs had obviously killed before. They had to be extremely determined to climb/jump that fence and then to persist attacking in the face of a one-hundred-twenty-pound goat who was trying to fight them off. Once dogs have run deer or killed livestock, they continue to do so. It is next to impossible to break that habit. If their owner had just confined them or used a leash, three wonderful animals would be alive today.

I can only hope that Molly's legacy will be that everyone who reads this passes it on, encourages puppy buyers, training class students, people at public demonstrations, shelter workers, all dog owners, to leash or confine their dogs. The life they save could be their own dog's.

(Free to reprint courtesy of *GoodDog!*)

Information Sources

———◆———

Avian health care

www.aav.org/basic_care

www.multiscope.com/hotspot

Clinical Avian Medicine and Surgery by Greg J. Harrison, D.V.M., and Linda R. Harrison, B.S. W. B. Saunders, 1986.

Bach Flower Essences

www.gcci.org/ciah/articles/flower.html

Dog health

Dog Health and Nutrition for Dummies by M. Christine Zink, D.V.M., Ph.D. Hungry Minds, 2001.

Drugs and medications

Small Animal Clinical Pharmacology and Therapeutics by Dawn Merton Boothe, D.V.M., M.S., Ph.D., D.A.C.V.I.M., D.A.C.V.P. W. B. Saunders, 2001.

Just What the Doctor Ordered by Race Foster, D.V.M., and Marty Smith, D.V.M. Howell Book House, 1996.

Reptile Clinician's Handbook by Fredric Frye, B.Sc., D.V.M., M.Sc. Krieger, 1995.

The Exotic Animal Drug Compendium by Keath L. Marx, D.V.M., and Margaret A. Rosten, B.S., R.N. Veterinary Learning Systems, 1996.

Natural Health Bible for Dogs & Cats by Shawn Messonnier, D.V.M. Prima, 2001.

Veterinary Drug Handbook by Donald C. Plumb, D. Pharm. Iowa State University Press, 1999.

The Pill Book Guide to Medication for Your Dog and Cat by Kate A.W. Roby, V.M.D., and Lenny Southam, D.V.M. Bantam, 1998.

Feline health

www.aafponline.org/about/guidelines_vaccine.pdf

Herbal treatments

www.healthypet.com/Library/petcare-37.htm

www.gcci.org/ciah/articles/botanicalmedicine.html

tempestwolf.com/animals/pets/health/herbs/c.htm

www.kcweb.com/herb/arnica.htm

www.altvetmed.com/herb_med.html

Natural Health for Dogs & Cats by Richard H. Pitcairn, D.V.M., Ph.D., and Susan Hubble Pitcairn. Rodale Press, 1995.

Emerging Therapies—Using Herbs and Nutraceutical Supplements for Small Animals by Susan G. Wynn, D.V.M. AAHA Press. 1999.

Vet Prac News, June 2002. "Herb-Drug Interaction Awareness" by Kathleen M. Carson, D.V.M.

Ivermectin and Loperamide

American Journal of Vetinary Research, vol. 63, no. 4, April 2002. "Frequency of the mutant MDR1 allele associated with ivermectin sensitivity in a sample population of Collies from the northwestern United States." Katrina L. Mealey, D.V.M., Ph.D., Steven A. Bentjen, M.S., and Denise K. Waiting.

Rabbit care

House Rabbit Society at www.rabbit.org

www.therabbitcharity.freeserve.co.uk

www.morfz.com/rabref.htm

Reptile and amphibian care

www.arav.org/Journals/CaptiveCare.htm

Reptile Medicine and Surgery by Douglas R. Mader, M.S., D.V.M., D.A.C.V.P. W. B. Saunders, 1996.

Veterinary care, including rabbits, reptiles, birds, and pocket pets

www.merckvetmanual.com

Measures and Equivalents

Liquids

1 milliliter (ml) = 1 cubic centimeter (cc)
1 liter = 1,000 ml
1 teaspoon = 5 ml
1 tablespoon = 3 teaspoons = 15 ml
1 cup = 8 fluid ounces = 16 tablespoons = 237 ml
1 pint = 2 cups = 16 fluid ounces = 473 ml
1 quart = 2 pints = 32 fluid ounces = 946 ml
1 gallon = 4 quarts = 8 pints = 128 fluid ounces = 3,785 ml

Weights

1 milligram (mg) = 1,000 micrograms (mcg)
1 grain = approx. 65 mg
1 gram = 1,000 mg = 15.43 grains
1 ounce = 28.4 grams (g)
1 pound (lb) = 16 ounces = 454 g
1 kilogram = 1,000 grams = 2.2 pounds

Medical Abbreviations and Terms for Prescriptions

———◆———

The medical fields have almost their own language when it comes to writing out treatment directions and prescriptions. If you don't understand an abbreviation or symbol or can't clearly read the writing, make sure you find out before you treat your pet. Ideally, treatment directions should be written out in "plain English" and legibly. A prescription should include the name of the medication, the amount (number of pills or amount of liquid or powder), the pet it is intended for, the name of the doctor who prescribed it, clinic or pharmacy where you purchased it, and the expiration date. Instructions as to dose amount and frequency should be clearly marked. Liquid medications should be clearly labeled as to whether they should be given by mouth, in the eye or ear, or possibly topically on the skin. I personally also try to include what the medication is for—is it an antibiotic, antihistamine, whatever.

A number of common abbreviations are included below. Many of these are derived from Latin, such as *sinistra,* "for the left," abbreviated by *s.*

a.d.—right ear.

a.s.—left ear.

a.u.—both ears.

BID—twice daily.

c.—with (this might be used to indicate that you should give this pill with food, for example).

DAW—dispense as written—seen on prescription forms to indicate if the generic form of a medication might be acceptable.

disp.—dispense.

gm—gram (might also be represented by plain "g").

IM—intramuscular—refers to injections in the muscle—normally done by the veterinarian.

IU—international units.

IV—intravenous—refers to injections in the vein—normally done by the veterinarian.

lb—pound.

mg—milligram.

ml—milliliter.

o.d.—right eye.

o.s.—left eye.

o.u.—both eyes.

PO—by mouth (to give this medication orally).

PRN—as needed (this would most likely be on pain medications or sedatives, possibly allergy medications).

q.—every—for example q6h would mean every 6 hours.

SID—once daily.

SQ, SC, Subcut—refers to injections given under the skin—subcutaneously.

TID—three times daily.

tab—tablet.

tsp—teaspoon.

Permanent Identification Systems

———◆———

Having a way to permanently identify your pet is a major plus. Tattoos and micro-chips are the current standard permanent methods of identifying your pet. Tattoos involve permanent ink embedded in tissues. Microchips involve small chips being injected under the skin that are read off with special scanners. Microchips have even been used in some birds as well as cats, dogs, and rabbits.

While both of these methods do permanently identify your pet, the tattoo or microchip should be registered with one of the organizations that will then trace the pet back to you. Most shelters now have scanners on site.

Tattoo Registries

Tattoo A Pet
6571 S. W. 20th Court
Fort Lauderdale, FL 33317
1-954-581-5834
1-800-828-8667
www.tattoo-a-pet.com

National Dog Registry
1-800-NDR-DOGS [637-3647]
www.natldogregistry.com

Microchip Companies

AVID
3179 Hamner Avenue
Norco, CA 92860
1-800-336-AVID [2843]
www.avidid.com

Home Again
c/o Destron Fearing Corporation
490 Villaume Avenue
South St. Paul, MN 55075-2445
1-800-2FIND-PET [234-6373]

Pet Recovery Registry
(registers both tattoos and microchips)

AKC—Companion Animal Recovery
5580 Centerview Drive, Suite 250
Raleigh, NC 27606-3389
1-800-252-7894
www.akc.org/registration/index.htm

Poisonings, Including Poisonous Plant Listings

---◆---

Protect Your Bird from Poisons and Toxic Chemicals

Use this chart as a reminder of what poisonous plants and chemicals can harm your pet bird.

POISONOUS PLANTS THAT ARE HARMFUL TO BIRDS

Amaryllis	Holly	Oleander
Avocado	Hyacinth	Philodendron
Azalea	Hydrangea	Poison Ivy and Oak
Balsam Pear	Indian Turnip	Poinsettia
Baneberry	Iris	Pikeweed
Beans: Castor, horse,	Ivy **—all types	Potato
peas, navy, glory	Java Bean	Privet
Bird of Paradise	Jerusulem Cherry	Rhododendron
Black Locust	Jimsonweed	Rhubarb
Blue-Green Algae	Juniper	Rosary Peas
Boxwood	Larkspur	Sandbox Tree
Calla Lily	Lily of the Valley	Skunk Cabbage
Cherry Tree	Lobelia	Snowdrop
Christmas Candle	Locoweed	Sweet Pea
Coral Plant	Marijuana	Tobacco
Daffodil	Mayapple	Virginia Creeper
Dieffenbachia	Mistletoe	Wisteria
Eggplant	Mock Orange	Yam Bean
Elephant's Ear	Morning Glory	Yew
Foxglove	Narcissus	
Hemlock	Oak	

*** most poisonous; ** moderately poisonous; * least poisonous

SOURCES OF FUMES THAT ARE TOXIC TO BIRDS

This is by no means a complete list. If you are unsure, read the label, seek more information from maker. When in doubt, don't use!!

Asbestos	Kerosene	Permanent Wave
Bleach / Chlorine	Matches	Solution
Carbon Monoxide	Moth Balls	Pesticides
Cigarette Smoke	Nail Polish and Remover	Shoe Polish and Cleaners
Diazanon	Oil Paint	Spot Removers
Flea Bombs and Collars	Oven Cleaner	Spray Starch
Floor Polishes	Overheated Nonstick	Suntan Lotions
Formaldehyde	Cookware **Teflons**	Surgical Acrylics
Hair Dye and Spray	Paint Remover	Toilet Cleaners
House Paint	Perfume	Wax

Thanks to BOB and LYNNETTE STEWART. Information from www.multiscope.com/hotspot.

Here are some of the toxic plants you should keep away from your pets. If you suspect that your dog might have eaten any plant that might be toxic, contact his/her vet immediately. Many common house and garden plants can be toxic to animals if swallowed. The symptoms can be diarrhea, nausea, or skin allergies.

Our list is limited and if you need further information about a particular plant, please contact your pet's vet and local Poison Control Center.

TOXIC PLANTS

Name	Poisonous Parts	Clinical Signs
Apricot	Stem, bark, seed pits	
Azalea (Rhododendron spp.) *	All parts, mostly leaves	Stomach irritation, abdominal pain, abnormal heart rate and rhythm, convulsions, coma, death.
Bird of Paradise	Fruit, seeds	

Name	Poisonous Parts	Clinical Signs
Boston Ivy	All parts	
Caladium	All parts	
Creeping Charlie (Glecoma hederacea L.)	All parts	Sweating, drooling, usually not fatal.
Castor Bean (Ricinus communis) ***	All part but mostly seeds, if chewed	Nausea, abdominal pain, bloody diarrhea, tenesmus, dehydration, shortness of breath, excessive thirst, weakness, muscle twitching, convulsions, coma.
Choke Cherry (Prunus virginiana) ***	Leaves, seed pits, stems, bark	
Daffodil (Narcissus spp.)	Bulbs	
Daphne	Berries, bark, leaves	
English Ivy (Hedera helix L.) ***	Leaves, berries	Stomach irritation, diarrhea, troubled breathing, coma, death.
Foxglove (Digitalis purpurea L.) *	Leaves, seeds, flowers	
Glacier Ivy	Leaves, berries	
Heartleaf	All parts	
Hemlock, Water (Cicuta maculata L.) ***	All parts, root and root stalk	Dilated pupils, frothing at the mouth, muscles spasms, restlessness, convulsions, and death (within 15 min to 2 hours).
Hyacinth (Hyacinth orientalis)	Bulbs, leaves, flowers	Colic, vomiting and diarrhea, usually not fatal.
Hydrangea (Hydrangea spp.)	Leaves, buds	Irritation and inflammation of the digestive tract, diarrhea, bloody stool.
Jerusalem Cherry (Solanum pseudocapsicum L.)	All parts, unripe fruit	
Johnsongrass (Sorghum halepense) ***	Leaves and stems, especially young plants.	Breathing problems, severe anxiety, convulsions, coma, death. Intravenous antidote exists.

Toxic Plants, continued

Name	Poisonous Parts	Clinical Signs
Jimson Weed (Datura stramonium L.) ***	All parts	Rapid pulse, rapid breathing, dilated pupils, restlessness, nervousness, twitching, frequent urination, diarrhea, depression, weight loss, weak pulse, convulsions, coma, death.
Jonquil	Bulbs	
Lantana (Lantana camara L.) ***	Leaves and berries	Sluggishness, weakness, bloody diarrhea. In severe cases, death may occur in 2 to 4 days.
Lily-of-the-Valley (Convallaria majalis)	All parts	
Mandrake	Roots, foliage, unripe fruit	
Mistletoe	Berries	
Morning Glory	Seeds	
Marble Queen	All parts	
Nightshade (Solanum spp.) ***	All parts	Hallucinations, severe intestinal disturbances, diarrhea, drowsiness, numbness, dilated pupils, trembling, labored breathing, nasal discharge, rapid heartbeat, weak pulse, incoordination, paralysis or severe shaking of the rear legs, rapid heart rate, bloat, can be fatal.
Nephthytis, Arrowhead Vine	All parts	
Oats, (Avena sativa)	All parts	Breathing difficulty, skin irritation, paralysis, convulsions, death (rare).
Pigweed, Redroot (Amaranthus retroflexus) ***	Leaves, stems, roots	Troubled breathing, trembling, weakness, coma, death.

Name	Poisonous Parts	Clinical Signs
Poinsettia (Euphorbia pulcherrima) *	Leaves, flowers	Skin, mouth, eye, and stomach irritation.
Pokeweed, Inkberry **	All parts	Colic, diarrhea, blood in stool, rare cases anemia, and possible death.
Parlor Ivy	All parts	
Red Sage	Green berries	
Rhubarb (Rheum rhaponticum) ***	Leaves	Staggering, trembling, breathing difficulties, weakness, diarrhea, increased drinking and urinating, death.
Red Princess	All parts	
Saddleleaf	All parts	
Tulip (Tulipa spp.)	Bulbs	
Umbrella Plant	All parts	
Yew, English (Taxus baccata) and Japanese (Taxus cuspidata Sieb. & Zucc.) ***	n/a	Breathing problems, trembling, weakness, heart problems, stomach upset, very sudden death.

All information provided at CyberCanine.com is for educational purposes only. This information is not intended as medical advice and can never replace medical care and treatments.

Preventive Care: Prevent Poisonings

Have you taken inventory of your medicine cabinets lately? Now that summer lawn and garden care is in full swing, are you properly storing pesticide containers? When you tidy up around the house, do you put food, liquor, and tobacco products safely out of harm's way? These precautions are second nature to households with children, but homes with animals must be just as secure. Let's tour a typical home and see what we find.

If you suspect your animal may have ingested any of the substances on this list or if you pet shows any of the following symptoms, you should consider the situation a medical emergency and should contact your veterinarian immediately. Be sure to bring any containers or the remains of any substance you think your pet may have swallowed with you.

Organophosphates, identified as malathion, diazinon, and fenthion, and carbamates, most commonly known as carbaryl and carbofuran, are *neurological* poisons found in lawn and garden pesticides and flea and tick products. Signs of toxicity include apprehension, excessive salivation, urination, defecation, vomiting and diarrhea, and pinpoint pupils. If an animal has absorbed enough of any neurological toxin, sudden death may be the only sign.

Pyrethrins and pyrethroids, both natural and synthetic, are also neurological poisons. Natural names include pyrethrin I and II. Synthetic compounds include allethrin, resmethrin, and permethrin. They are found in insecticidal aerosols, dips, shampoos, and house and garden products. Signs of ingestion include excessive salivation, vomiting, diarrhea, tremors, and hyperexcitability or depression.

Coumarins, most recognizable as D-Con®, a rat and mouse poison, affect the ability of the blood to clot. Mice that consume the poisoned grain essentially bleed to death. Your pets will be affected the same way, and the severity of the symptoms often depends on the amount ingested. Even cats who eat poisoned mice can become ill. If you find an empty box, look for labored breathing, anorexia, nosebleeds, bloody urine or feces, and pinpoint hemorrhages on the gums.

Tobacco products cause excitement, salivation, vomiting, muscle weakness, and coma or death, and the toxic effects can develop within minutes. Marijuana causes involuntary muscle movements, depression or excitability, trembling, and salivation. Large amounts can be fatal.

Aspirin and other pain relievers are in every home, and these poisonings can be severe. When aspirin is prescribed for animals, the dosage must be strictly followed. Too much aspirin can lead to anemia and gastric hemorrhage. Ibuprofen and naproxen will cause painful gastrointestinal problems. One 200 mg ibuprofen tablet is toxic to a small dog.

Never give acetaminophen to a cat or dog. In cats the drug affects oxygen in the blood, and it produces severe depression and abdominal pain in dogs. If not quickly eliminated from the body, just two extra-strength tablets in twenty-four hours will most likely kill a small pet. Clinical signs in cats develop within one or two hours and include excessive salivation, paw and facial swelling, depression, and ash-gray gums. In dogs watch for anorexia, vomiting, depression, and abdominal pain. High doses are usually fatal.

Garbage is not often regarded as poisonous. After all, many animals find compost attractive. But toxins are produced by bacteria fermenting the garbage. Rapid and severe signs include vomiting, bloody diarrhea, painful abdominal distention, shivering, shock, and collapse.

How should pets be protected from these poisons? Some very simple rules to follow are:

Properly dispose of and store all pesticide containers up and out of sight of your pets. Make sure the lids are tight, the containers undamaged.

Use cords or locking lids for garbage cans. Put them in a heavy frame to prevent knock-down.

Keep pets off lawns sprayed with chemicals. Consult with the lawn care company for proper information on drying time and compounds used. Wash pets' feet with mild soap and water if exposed.

Keep your pets out of vegetable and flower gardens.

Encase compost piles or use commercially made containers.

Never assume that a human drug is applicable to an animal unless a *veterinarian* instructs you to use it.

WHAT IS POISONOUS?

Here is a quick reference guide to the more common house and garden plants and foods that are toxic to almost all animals and children. If you have these plants or foods, you need not dispose of them—just keep them away from pets and children.

C   cardiovascular toxin
GI   gastrointestinal toxin
R   respiratory toxin
N   neurological toxin
KO   kidney/organ failure
★   Substance is especially dangerous and can be fatal.

Alcohol (all beverages, ethanol, methanol, isopropyl)	N
Almonds★ (kernel in the pit contains cyanide)	R
Amaryllis bulb★	GI, N
Anthurium★	KO
Apricot★ (kernel in the pit contains cyanide)	R
Autumn crocus (Colchicum autumnale)★	GI, C, very poisonous
Avocado (leaves, seeds, stem, skin)★	C, KO, fatal to birds

Azalea (entire rhododendron family)	C, GI, N
Begonia★	KO
Bird of Paradise	GI
Bittersweet	GI
Bleeding heart★	C
Boxwood	GI
Bracken fern	N
Buckeye	GI, N
Buttercup (Ranunculus)	GI
Caffeine	GI, N
Caladium★	KO
Calla lily★	KO
Castor bean★ (can be fatal if chewed)	GI, C, N
Cherry (kernel in the pit contains cyanide)	R
Chinese sacred or heavenly bamboo★	R, contains cyanide
Chocolate★	GI, N
Choke cherry, unripe berries★	R, contains cyanide
Chrysanthemum (a natural source of pyrethrins)	GI, N
Clematis	GI
Crocus bulb	GI, N
Croton (Codiaeum sp.)	GI
Cyclamen bulb	GI
Delphinium, larkspur, monkshood★	N
Dumb cane (Dieffenbachia)★	GI, R, severe mouth swelling
Elderberry, unripe berries★	R, contains cyanide
English ivy (All Hedera species of ivy)	GI
Fig (Ficus)	General allergen, dermatitis
Four-o'clocks (Mirabilis)	GI
Foxglove (Digitalis)★	C, can be fatal
Garlic★ (raw or spoiled)	GI
Hyacinth bulbs	GI
Hydrangea★	R, contains cyanide
Holly berries	GI
Iris corms	GI
Jack-in-the-pulpit★	KO

Jimson weed*	R
Kalanchoe*	C, can be fatal
Lantana*	KO (liver failure)
Lily (bulbs of most species)	GI
Lily-of-the-valley*	C, can be fatal
Lupine species	N
Marijuana or hemp (Cannabis)*	N, GI, can be fatal
Milkweed*	C
Mistletoe berries*	N, C, shock
Morning glory*	N, Seeds toxic to birds
Mountain laurel	C
Narcissus, daffodil (Narcissus)	GI
Oak* (remove bark for use as a bird perch)	KO
Oleander*	C, very poisonous, can be fatal
Onions* (raw or spoiled)	GI
Peach* (kernel in the pit contains cyanide)	R
Pencil cactus/plant* (Euphorbia sp.)	GI, dermatitis
Philodendron (all species)*	KO
Poinsettia (many hybrids, avoid them all)	GI, dermatitis
Potato (leaves and stem)	GI, N
Rhubarb leaves*	KO
Rosary Pea (Arbus sp.)*	GI, C, N, can be fatal if chewed
Scheffelera (umbrella plant)*	KO
Shamrock (Oxalis sp.)*	KO
Spurge (Euphorbia sp.)	GI
Tomatoes (leaves and stem)	GI, N
Yew*	C, fatal to most animals

Pet Care Tips:
Ten Tips for a Poison-Safe Household

1. Be aware of the plants you have in your house and in your pet's yard. The ingestion of azalea, oleander, mistletoe, sago palm, Easter lily, or yew plant material, by an animal, could be fatal.

2. When cleaning your house, never allow your pet access to the area where cleaning agents are used or stored. Cleaning agents have a variety of properties. Some may only cause a mild stomach upset, while others could cause severe burns of the tongue, mouth, and stomach.

3. When using rat or mouse baits, ant or roach traps, or snail and slug baits, place the products in areas that are inaccessible to your animals. Most baits contain sweet-smelling inert ingredients, such as jelly, peanut butter, and sugars, which can be very attractive to your pet.

4. Never give your animal any medications unless under the direction of your veterinarian. Many medications that are used safely in humans can be deadly when used inappropriately. One extra-strength acetaminophen tablet (500 mg) can kill a seven-pound cat.

5. Keep all prescription and over-the-counter drugs out of your pets' reach, preferably in closed cabinets. Painkillers, cold medicines, anticancer drugs, antidepressants, vitamins, and diet pills are common examples of human medications that could be potentially lethal even in small dosages. One regular-strength ibuprofen (200 mg) could cause stomach ulcers in a ten-pound dog.

6. Never leave chocolates unattended. Approximately one-half ounce or less of baking chocolate per pound, body weight can cause problems. Even small amounts can cause pancreatic problems.

7. Many common household items have been shown to be lethal in certain species. Miscellaneous items that are highly toxic even in low quantities include pennies (high concentration of zinc), mothballs (contain naphthalene or paradichlorobenzene, one or two balls can be life threatening in most species), potpourri oils, fabric softener sheets, automatic dish detergents (contain cationic detergents which could cause corrosive lesions), batteries (contain acids or alkali, which can also cause corrosive lesions), homemade play dough (contains high quantity of salt), winter heat source agents like hand or foot warmers (contain high levels of iron), cigarettes, coffee grounds, and alcoholic drinks.

8. All automotive products such as oil, gasoline, and antifreeze should be stored in areas away from pet access. As little as one teaspoon of antifreeze (ethylene glycol) can be deadly in a seven-pound cat and less than one tablespoon could be lethal to a twenty-pound dog.

9. Before buying or using flea products on your pet or in your household, contact your veterinarian to discuss what types of flea products are recommended for your pet. Read *all* information before using a product on your

animals or in your home. Always follow label instructions. When a product is labeled "For use in dogs only," this means that the product should *never* be applied to cats. Also, when using a fogger or a house spray, make sure to remove all pets from the area for the time period specified on the container. If you are uncertain about the usage of any product, contact the manufacturer or your veterinarian to clarify the directions *before* use of the product.

10. When treating your lawn or garden with fertilizers, herbicides, or insecticides, always keep your animals away from the area until the area dries completely. Discuss usage of products with the manufacturer of the products to be used. Always store such products in an area that will ensure no possible pet exposure.

These helpful tips were compiled by:

Jill A. Richardson, D.V.M.
Veterinary Poison Information Specialist
ASPCA National Animal Poison Control Center
1717 Philo Road, Suite #36
Urbana, IL 61801
(217) 337-5030

Prescription Diets

———◆———

The dietary compositions included here were generously provided by Purina. Remember that prescription diets are included as part of an overall treatment regimen to help your pet. Most pets will still need medications or supplements to treat their problems. This is *not* an all-inclusive listing of prescription diets, not even all of Purina's—but rather an overview of some of the most commonly used diets. *Please note:* The compositions listed here are as of this writing. Pet food manufacturers often adjust or update formulas as more information is researched into dietary management.

For Heart Disease

Diets for heart problems are formulated with lower sodium and sometimes added potassium, B vitamins, and taurine or carnitine. They are most commonly used for pets with congestive heart failure and hypertension.

Purina CV Cardiovascular Canine Formula—Canned

AVERAGE NUTRIENT COMPOSITION		
	As Fed	**Dry Matter**
Protein %	5.84	17.82
Carbohydrate %	16.32	49.81
Fat %	10.44	31.88
Fiber %	0.45	1.38
Calcium %	0.24	0.73
Phosphorus %	0.13	0.40
Sodium %	0.04	0.12

Average Nutrient Composition, continued

	As Fed	Dry Matter
Potassium %	0.40	1.21
Chloride %	0.42	1.27
Magnesium %	0.02	0.06
Taurine %*	0.08	0.24
Carnitine %	0.005	0.015

Purina CV Cardiovascular Feline Formula—Canned

AVERAGE NUTRIENT COMPOSITION

	As Fed	Dry Matter
Protein %	12.48	42.53
Carbohydrate %	6.77	23.07
Fat %	7.86	26.79
Fiber %	0.29	0.99
Taurine %	0.09	0.31
Calcium %	0.36	1.23
Phosphorus %	0.27	0.92
Sodium %	0.06	0.20
Potassium %	0.39	1.33
Chloride %	0.32	1.09
Magnesium %	0.02	0.07
Carnitine %	0.01	0.34

*In the Average Nutrient Composition tables, this symbol indicates calculated values.

For Gastrointestinal Problems

Pets with gastrointestinal problems often require either very easy-to-digest diets and low- or soluble-fiber diets. They will have special sources of fatty acids and easy-to-digest proteins and fats. These diets are used for pets with pancreatitis, inflammatory bowel disease, gastritis, or diarrhea. These diets are appropriate for some liver problems in pets as well. Some pets will need these diets long term, while others may just use them short term to get over a temporary health problem. In this category I have included diets for diabetes mellitus and colitis. These diets will have special fiber sources and complex carbohydrates.

Purina DCO Diabetes Colitis Canine Formula—Dry

AVERAGE NUTRIENT COMPOSITION		
	As Fed	Dry Matter
Protein %	23	25.26
Carbohydrate %	43.51	47.79
Fat %	11.30	12.41
Fiber %	6.95	7.63
Calcium %	1.11	1.22
Phosphorus %	0.85	0.93
Sodium %	0.31	0.34
Potassium %	0.64	0.70
Chloride %	0.75	0.82
Magnesium %	0.11	0.13
Omega 6:3 ratio	8.8:1	8.8:1
Total dietary fiber %	20.20	22.18
Soluble fiber %	3.65	4.01
Insoluble fiber %	16.60	18.23
Vitamin E IU/kg*	192	213

Purina DM Diabetes Management Formula Feline—Dry

AVERAGE NUTRIENT COMPOSITION		
	As Fed	Dry Matter
Protein %	14.80	56.90
Carbohydrate %	2.10	8.08
Fat %	6.20	23.80
Fiber %	0.95	3.65
Calcium %	0.30	1.15
Phosphorus %	0.29	1.10
Sodium %	0.10	0.39
Potassium %	0.21	0.82
Chloride %	0.20	0.76
Magnesium %	0.03	0.10
Taurine %	0.09	0.34
Vitamin E IU/kg*	62	214
Total omega-6 %	0.87	3.35
Total omega-3 %	0.23	0.88
Omega 6:3 ratio	3.8:1	3.8:1

Purina EN Gastroenteric Canine Formula—Canned

AVERAGE NUTRIENT COMPOSITION		
	As Fed	Dry Matter
Protein %	9.03	30.52
Carbohydrate %	14.46	48.87
Fat %	4.07	13.75
Fiber %	0.27	0.91
Calcium %	0.26	0.88
Phosphorus %	0.16	0.54
Sodium %	0.11	0.37

Purina EN Gastroenteric Canine Formula—Canned, continued		
	As Fed	Dry Matter
Potassium %	0.18	0.61
Chloride %	0.23	0.78
Magnesium %	0.02	0.07
Zinc mg/kg*	72	260
Vitamin E, IU/kg*	145	505
Vitamin C, mg/kg*	40	139
Omega 6:3 ratio	11:1	11:1
Total omega-6 %	0.33	1.11
Total omega-3 %	0.03	0.10

Purina EN Gastroenteric Formula Feline—Canned

AVERAGE NUTRIENT COMPOSITION		
	As Fed	Dry Matter
Protein %	26.10	41.89
Carbohydrate %	20.02	32.13
Fat %	10.60	17.01
Fiber %	0.67	1.08
Calcium %	1.05	1.69
Phosphorus	1.25	2.01
Sodium %	0.20	0.32
Potassium %	0.50	0.80
Chloride %	0.34	0.55
Magnesium %	0.08	0.13
Taurine %	0.12	0.19
Omega 6:3 ratio	5:1	5:1
Total omega-6 %	1.38	2.21
Total omega-3 %	0.28	0.45

For Allergy Problems

One of the best developments for pets and their owners in prescription diets have been the diets that help with allergy problems. These may use "novel" or unusual protein sources, such as duck or venison, or may actually modify the protein sources to make them less reactive. While pets can have allergies to many different substances, food allergies often contribute to chronic skin and ear problems. Having a less allergenic diet can keep other allergy problems to a minimum.

Purina HA Hypoallergenic Formula Canine—Dry

AVERAGE NUTRIENT COMPOSITION		
	As Fed	Dry Matter
Protein %	19.30	21.33
Carbohydrate %	53.80	59.45
Fat %	9.54	10.54
Fiber %	1.43	1.58
Calcium %	1.28	1.41
Phosphorus	0.96	1.06
Sodium %	0.22	0.24
Potassium %	0.62	0.69
Chloride %	0.62	0.69
Magnesium %	0.10	0.11
Omega 6:3 ratio	9.7:1	9.7:1

For Kidney Diseases

Kidney or renal problems are quite common in older pets or young pets with congenital problems such as cystic kidneys. These pets do much better if put on prescription diets and will be on these diets long term. Pets with short-term kidney problems can also benefit. These diets tend to have lower sodium; less, but top-quality protein; and may have other electrolyte adjustments.

Purina NF Kidney Failure Formula Canine—Dry

AVERAGE NUTRIENT COMPOSITION		
	As Fed	Dry Matter
Protein %	14.40	15.89
Carbohydrate %	56.94	62.84
Fat %	14.20	15.67
Fiber %	0.82	0.90
Calcium %	0.69	0.76
Phosphorus	0.26	0.29
Sodium %	0.20	0.22
Potassium %	0.78	0.86
Chloride %	0.52	0.57
Magnesium %	0.06	0.07
Total omega-6 %	2.51	2.77
Total omega-3 %	0.27	0.30
Omega 6:3 ratio	9.4:1	9.4:1

Purina NF Kidney Failure Formula Feline—Dry

AVERAGE NUTRIENT COMPOSITION		
	As Fed	Dry Matter
Protein %	28.50	30.78
Carbohydrate %	46.88	50.63
Fat %	11.90	12.85
Fiber %	1.14	1.23
Calcium %	0.64	0.69
Phosphorus	0.38	0.41
Sodium %	0.18	0.20
Potassium %	0.81	0.88
Chloride %	0.59	0.64
Magnesium %	0.09	0.10

Average Nutrient Composition, continued		
	As Fed	**Dry Matter**
Taurine %	0.17	0.18
Total omega-6%	1.87	2.02
Total omega-3%	0.29	0.31
Omega 6:3 ratio	6.5:1	6.5:1

For Weight Management

Just as our human population has tended to gain weight in recent years, so have our pets. Prescription diets have been developed that help our pets to lose weight in a healthy manner, by adding fiber and lowering fat to lower calories overall while still leaving our pets feeling full and satisfied. Exercise is important as well.

Purina OM Overweight Management Formula Canine—Dry

AVERAGE NUTRIENT COMPOSITION		
	As Fed	**Dry Matter**
Protein %	28.25	32.00
Carbohydrate %	38.25	43.30
Fat %	5.88	6.70
Fiber %	9.43	10.70
Calcium %	1.30	1.46
Phosphorous	1.29	1.46
Sodium %	0.19	0.21
Potassium %	0.73	0.82
Chloride %	0.28	0.32
Magnesium %	0.17	0.19

Purina OM Overweight Management Formula Feline—Dry

AVERAGE NUTRIENT COMPOSITION		
	As Fed	Dry Matter
Protein %	34.77	38.40
Carbohydrate %	34.09	37.60
Fat %	7.72	8.50
Fiber %	7.29	8.00
Calcium %	1.16	1.28
Phosphorus	1.06	1.17
Sodium %	0.24	0.26
Potassium %	0.63	0.69
Chloride %	0.80	0.88
Magnesium %	0.09	0.10
Taurine %	0.25	0.28

For Urinary Problems

Diets have been a major help in pets with urinary problems, primarily the development of bladder stones and crystals. These may contribute to urinary infections and even cause urinary blockages, which are emergencies. Different urinary diets are designed for different stones, so you need to clearly diagnose your pet before putting them on one of these diets. These diets influence urinary pH as one of their actions and you need to be sure what type of crystal your pet is producing so you adjust pH in the proper direction.

Purina UR Urinary Formula Feline—Dry

AVERAGE NUTRIENT COMPOSITION		
	As Fed	Dry Matter
Protein %	32.36	35.43
Carbohydrate %	41.63	45.58
Fat %	10.60	11.61
Fiber %	1.36	1.49
Taurine %	0.19	0.20
Calcium %	1.02	1.12
Phosphorus %	0.77	0.84
Sodium %	0.22	0.24
Potassium %	0.77	0.84
Chloride %	1.02	1.12
Magnesium %	0.07	0.08

Zoonoses

Zoonoses are diseases that can pass from animals to people (and most of them go vice versa as well). The list is provided here to make you aware of the primary zoonoses. Some of these diseases are passed on via parasites such as fleas and ticks; some directly infect us from contaminated urine, feces, or blood. Keeping your pet parasite free and healthy is the best way to avoid these diseases. You should discuss these with your veterinarian or your physician if your pet is diagnosed with one of these problems.

(See opposite, for an article from the CDC on intestinal parasites.)

Brucellosis	Plague
Campylobacter	Q fever
Chlamydiosis	Rabies
Ear mites	Ringworm
E. coli enteritis	Rocky Mountain
Ehrlichiosis	spotted fever
Fleas	Roundworms
Giardiosis	Salmonellosis
Histoplasmosis	Sarcoptic mange
Hookworms	Ticks
Leptospirosis	Toxoplasmosis
Mycoplasmosis	Tularemia

Intestinal parasites are one of the most common zoonotic disease problems we see in the United States. Keeping puppies and kittens parasite free, practicing basic good hygiene, and deworming *all* young pets can go a long way toward eliminating this problem. The following article is graciously included through the generosity of the Centers for Disease Control. This article also appears on their website at: www.cdc.gov/ncidod/diseases/roundwrm/roundwrm.htm.

Prevention of Zoonotic Transmission of Ascarids and Hookworms of Dogs and Cats: Guidelines for Veterinarians

ASCARIDS AND HOOKWORMS

Ascarids *(Toxocara canis, T. cati)* and hookworms *(Ancylostoma* spp.) are common intestinal parasites of dogs and cats (referred to here as pets). Not only can ascarids and hookworms cause disease in their respective hosts, they are also well-known causes of larva migrans syndromes in humans, especially children. While ascarids and hookworms are most commonly diagnosed in puppies and kittens, infections can occur in dogs and cats of all ages. Dogs can also become infected with *Baylisascaris procyonis,* the common raccoon ascarid, which can cause serious disease in other animals and humans.[1]

Ascarids Because of the occurrence of both transplacental and transmammary transmission of *T. canis,* puppies are usually born with or acquire ascarid infections early in life.[2] Kittens do not become infected in utero, but like puppies, can acquire ascarids *(T. cati)* through the queen's milk.[3] The tissue-migrating and early intestinal stages of these worms may cause severe, sometimes life-threatening, disease in the first few weeks of life. Patent intestinal infections can develop within the first 2½–3 weeks of life. Left untreated, this can lead to widespread contamination of the environment with infective eggs.

Hookworms Both puppies and kittens acquire hookworm infections *(A. caninum, A. braziliense,* and *A. tubaeforme)* through ingestion of or skin penetration by infective larvae, or from infective larvae passed in their dam's milk *(A. caninum).*[2] Hookworms suck large amounts of blood from their hosts and while infected animals may look healthy in the first week of life, they can develop a rapidly severe, often fatal, anemia.[4] Patent intestinal infections can occur as early as 2- (dogs) to 3- (cats) weeks of age, leading to environmental contamination with infective larvae.[5,6]

The prevalence of these infections varies with climatic conditions; however, they are present in all parts of the United States and must be viewed as a potential public health hazard.[6-9]

ZOONOTIC TRANSMISSION AND HUMAN DISEASE

The growing popularity of dogs and cats in the United States, together with high rates of ascarid and hookworm infections, has resulted in widespread contamination of the soil with infective eggs and larvae. Epidemiologic studies have implicated the presence of dogs, particularly puppies. in a household, and pica (dirt eating) as the principal risk factors for human disease. Children's play habits and their attraction to pets put them at higher risk for infection than adults.

Humans become infected with ascarids *(Toxocara* spp., *Baylisascaris* spp.) through ingestion of infective eggs in the environment. When a human ingests infective eggs, the eggs hatch and release larvae that can migrate anywhere in the body, a condition known as visceral larva migrans. The signs and symptoms seen in humans are determined by the tissues or organs damaged during larval migration. Organs commonly affected are the eye, brain, liver, and lung, where infections can cause permanent visual, neurologic, or other tissue damage. The common dog ascarid, *T. canis,* has long been recognized as a cause of larva migrans syndromes in children. The cat ascarid, *T. cati,* can also cause disease in humans, although for reasons partly related to the defecation habits of cats, it does so less frequently. The raccoon ascarid, *B. procyonis,* is increasingly being recognized as a cause of human disease.[10]

Humans can become infected with hookworms through ingestion of infective larvae or through direct penetration of the skin.[7] When infective larvae penetrate the skin, they undergo a prolonged migration that causes a condition known as cutaneous larva migrans. These larval migrations are characterized by the appearance of progressive, intensely pruritic, linear eruptive lesions, which are usually more extensive with *A. braziliense* infections. *A. caninum* larvae may also penetrate into deeper tissues and induce symptoms of visceral larva migrans, or migrate to the intestine and induce an eosinophilic enteritis.[11,12]

THE PUBLIC HEALTH PROBLEM

Larva migrans syndromes are not reportable in the United States, so the actual number of human cases is unknown. However, many human cases continue to be diagnosed and a recent national survey of shelters revealed that almost 36 percent of dogs nationwide, and 52 percent of dogs from southeastern states harbored helminths capable of causing human disease.[13] Every year at least 3,000–4,000 serum specimens from patients with presumptive diagnoses of toxocariasis are sent to the Centers for Disease Control and Prevention (CDC), state public health laboratories, or private laboratories for serodiagnostic confirmation.[14] Zoonotic hookworm infections are more geographically restricted than toxocariasis, with most cutaneouslarva migrans and other hookworm associated syndromes diagnosed in southeastern and Gulf Coast states. Persons likely to come in contact with larvae-contaminated soil include electricians, plumbers, and other workers who crawl beneath raised buildings, sunbathers who recline on larvae-contaminated sand—as well as children who play in contaminated areas. While most hookworm infections are self-limiting, massive infections can lead to infection of deeper tissues.[15]

VETERINARIANS CAN HELP PREVENT HUMAN DISEASE

Most cases of human ascarid and hookworm infections can be prevented by practicing good personal hygiene, eliminating intestinal parasites from pets through regular deworming, and making potentially contaminated environments, such as unprotected sand boxes, off limits to children.[9,10,14] It is also important to clean up pet feces on a regular basis to remove potentially infective eggs before they become disseminated in the environment via rain, insects, or the active migration of the larvae.[16] Hookworm eggs can develop into infective stage larvae in the soil in as little as 5 days, and ascarid eggs within 2 weeks, depending on temperature and humidity.[4] To illustrate the extent of environmental contamination that can occur as the result of one infected puppy, a single female ascarid can produce more than 100,000 eggs/day, resulting in millions of potentially infective ascarid eggs per day spread throughout the area the puppy is allowed to roam.[10] Once the eggs become infective, they can remain infective in the environment for years.[4,10]

Most pet owners do not know that their pets may carry worms capable of infecting people. Therefore, practicing veterinarians can provide an important public service by recommending regular fecal examinations, providing well-timed anthelmintic treatments, counseling clients on potential public health hazards, and advising them on any precautionary measures that may be undertaken. Veterinarians are in an ideal position to provide pet owners with this service because of their access to the pet-owning public, their knowledge and training, and their role in the human-animal bond.[17,18]

PREVENTIVE ANTHELMINTIC TREATMENT

Because puppies, kittens, and pregnant and nursing animals are at highest risk for these infections, and therefore responsible for most of the environmental contamination and human disease, anthelmintic treatments are most effective when they are initiated early and targeted at these populations.[4,15]

While it has long been recognized that transplacental and transmammary infection of ascarids and hookworms could be prevented through prophylactic treatment of pregnant dogs, no drugs are currently approved for this use. However, the effectiveness of this approach with different drugs approved for parasite control in dogs has been well documented. Daily treatment of pregnant dogs with fenbendazole from the 40th day of gestation through the 14th day of lactation has been shown to inhibit *T. canis* larvae in tissues, thereby preventing or greatly reducing the incidence of infection in puppies.[19] Alternatively, studies have shown that treatment with ivermectin on day 0, 30, 60 of gestation and 10 days post whelping, reduced the adult *T. canis* worm burden in pups by 100 percent and prevented the shedding of eggs.[20] In yet another study, treatment with selamectin at 10 and 40 days both before and after parturition was effective in reducing *T. canis* fecal egg counts in both pups and their dams, and adult worms in the pups.[21]

If the mother did not receive prophylactic treatment, puppies and kittens must be treated early and repeatedly in order to prevent patent infections.[22] In areas where both ascarids and hookworms are common, begin treating both puppies and their mothers with an age-appropriate anthelmintic at 2, 4, 6, and 8 weeks of age. Some recommend extending this to 12 weeks and then treating monthly until the pet is 6 months old. To treat for ascarids alone, begin by 2½–3 weeks and treat every 2 weeks for at least three additional treatments. Because prenatal infection does not occur in kittens, preventive treatment should begin at 3 weeks of age, and be repeated at 5, 7, and 9 weeks. Nursing dogs and queens should be treated concurrently with their offspring because they often develop patent infections along with their young.

Because most puppies and kittens are not routinely brought to a veterinarian before 6–8 weeks of age, they will already have patent infections and be actively contaminating the environment. For this reason, it is important to reach out to clients who have pregnant or newly born animals at home, and provide these animals with early prophylactic treatment for intestinal parasites. Early identification of these high-risk animals will provide the veterinarian with the opportunity to educate the owners on the public health risks, provide them with an appropriate anthelmintic, and advise them on how and when to administer it to their pets at home. This approach to treatment is justified by the frequency with which puppies and kittens acquire intestinal parasites from their mothers, and the difficulties that exist in early diagnosis. Because young animals may continuously acquire new infections from nursing and from the environment, they may develop a serious illness or even die before a prenatally or lactogenically acquired infection becomes patent and can be diagnosed by fecal examination.

While intestinal parasites are usually less of a problem in young adult and adult animals, they too can develop patent infections and contaminate the environment. Therefore, they too should be regularly monitored or treated for intestinal parasite infections. While all adult animals are at risk, those that are allowed to roam or spend most of their time outside run a greater risk of becoming infected. There are a variety of anthelmintic drugs available that are safe and effective against ascarids, hookworms, and other intestinal helminths of dogs and cats (Table 1). Mature animals can also be monitored through biannual or yearly diagnostic stool examinations and treated with anthelmintics directed at specific intestinal nematodes. For animals that live in areas where heartworm *(Dirofilaria immitis)* infection is enzootic, many of the heartworm preventives are also effective against intestinal parasites (Table 1).[23]

TABLE 1.

Drugs for the Treatment of Ascarid and Hookworm Infections in Dogs and Cats

| Name | Route of Administration/ Frequency/Dose | Range of Efficacy | FDA Approved in: | |
			Species	Minimum Age/Weight
Diethylcarbamazine citrate[1, 10]	Oral 6.6 mg/kg daily	DI	Dog	≥ 8 weeks
	55-110 mg/kg once; repeat in 10-20 days	A		
Diethylcarbamazine/ oxibendazole[1, 3, 4, 10]	Oral/daily 6.6 mg/kg DEC 5.0 mg/kg OXI	A, H, W, DI	Dog	≥ 8 weeks and ≥ 1 lb
Fenbendazole	Oral/daily for 3 days 50 mg/kg	A, H, W, T	Dog	None
Ivermectin[4, 10]	Oral/monthly 24µg/kg	H, DI	Cat	≥ 6weeks
Ivermectin/pyrantel pamoate[1, 7, 10]	Oral/monthly 6µg/kg IVM 5mg/kg PYR	A, H, DI	Dog	≥ 6weeks
Milbemycin oxime[1, 4, 7, 10]	Oral/monthly Dog: 0.5 mg/kg	A, H, W, DI	Dog	≥ 4 weeks and ≥ 2 lbs
	Cat: 2.0 mg/kg	A, H, DI	Cat	≥ 6 weeks and ≥ 2 lbs

Table 1, continued

Name	Route of Administration/ Frequency/Dose	Range of Efficacy	FDA Approved in: Species	FDA Approved in: Minimum Age/Weight
Milbemycin oxime/ lufenuron [1, 4, 7, 10, 11]	Oral/monthly 0.5 mg/kg MO 10 mg/kg LUF	A, H, W, DI	Dog	≥ 4 weeks and ≥ 2 lbs
Moxidectin [1, 4, 6, 10, 12]	SC/twice yearly 0.17 mg/kg	H, DI	Dog	≥ 6 months
Piperazine [5]	Oral/discretionary See label for dose	A	Dog/cat	≥ 6 weeks
Pyrantel pamoate [14]	Oral/discretionary 5 mg/kg	A, H	Dog	≥ 2 weeks
Pyrantel pamoate/prazi- quantel [4, 13]	Oral/discretionary 5 mg/kg PRA 20 mg/kg PYR	A, H, T, D	Cat	≥ 1 month and ≥ 1.5 lbs
Pyrantel pamoate/prazi- quantel/febantel [2, 9]	Oral/discretionary 5 mg/kg PYR 5 mg/kg PRA 25 mg/kg FEB	A, H, W, T, D, E	Dog	≥ 3 weeks and ≥ 2 lbs
Selamectin [1, 4, 7, 8, 10]	Topical/monthly 6mg/kg S	Dog: DI	Dog	≥ 6 weeks
		Cat: A, H, DI	Cat	

A = ascarids *(Toxocara* and *Toxascaris* spp.); H = hookworm *(Ancylostoma* and *Uncinaria* spp.); W = whipworm *(Trichuris vulpis)*; T = Taeniid tapeworms *(Taenia pisiformis, Taenia taeniaeformis, Taenia* spp.) D = Flea tapeworm *(Dipylidium caninum)*; E = *Echinococcus granulosus, Echinococcus multilocularis;* DI = *Dirofilaria immitis.*

Contraindications: [1]Not for use in animals with established heartworm infections. [2]Do not use in pregnant animals. [3]Do not use in dogs with hepatic dysfunction. [4]Not effective against *Uncinaria.* [5]Some salts not for use in unweaned animals. [6]See package insert for injection technique. [7]Safe in collies at label dose. [8]Also effective against fleas, flea eggs, ticks, and mites (including ear mites). [9]Repeat every 21–26 days for control of *Echinococcus multilocularis.* [10]Effective against tissue stage of heartworm larvae. [11]Not a flea adulticide—contains an insect growth regulator. [12]Effective against hookworm larvae and adults at time of injection only. [13]Consult with veterinarian before using in pregnant animals. [14]Approved for use in lactating dogs (administer 2–3 weeks after parturition).

Educating and Counseling Pet Owners

Pet owner education regarding intestinal parasites and their effects on the health of both their pets and family members should be included in a well-pet exam. Pet owner education should focus on prevention and include the following:

- Description of ascarids and hookworms that infect dogs and cats, early signs of illness, and when pets are at greatest risk for infection (in utero and when nursing).
- How ascarids and hookworms cause disease in humans, especially in children whose play habits and attraction to pets put them at increased risk.
- How prophylactic treatment of pregnant and nursing pets and their offspring can protect their pets from becoming infected, thus preventing them from shedding eggs into, and contaminating, the environment.
- The need for regular diagnostic fecal examinations of pups or kittens or prophylactic treatment of older pets.
- The need for prompt collection and disposal of pet feces, especially in areas where children play, to remove eggs from the environment before they can become a problem.
- The need to keep children away from areas that may be contaminated with pet feces.

References

1. Samuel WM, Pybus MJ, Kocan AA. Parasitic diseases of wild mammals. Second ed. Ames: Iowa State University Press. 2001; 301-41.
2. Burke TM, Roberson EL. Prenatal and lactational transmission of *Toxocara canis* and *Ancylostoma caninum*: experimental infection of the bitch before pregnancy. Int J Parasitol 1985; 15:71-5.
3. Swerzcek TW, Nielsen SW, Helmbolt CF. Transmammary passage of *Toxocara cati* in the cat. Am J Vet Res 1971; 32:89-92.
4. Bowman DD. Georgis' parasitology for veterinarians. Seventh ed. Philadelphia: WB Saunders Company. 1999; 178-84.
5. Hendrix CM, Homer SB, Kellman NJ, Harrelson G, Bruhn BF. Cutaneous larva migrans and enteric hookworm infections. J Am Vet Med Assoc 1996; 209(10): 1763-76.
6. Kalkofen VP. Hookworms of dogs and cats. Vet Clin North Am Small Anim Pract 1987; 17:1341-54.

7. Glickman LT, Schantz PM. Epidemiology and pathogenesis of zoonotic toxocariasis. Epidemiol Rev 1981; 3:230-50.

8. Parsons JC. Ascarid infections in cats and dogs. Vet Clin North Am Small Anim Pract 1987; 17:1307-39.

9. Kazacos KR. Visceral and ocular larva migrans. Semin Vet Med Surg (Small Anim) 1991; 6:227-35.

10. Kazacos KR. Protecting children from helminthic zoonosis. Contemp Pediatr 2000; 17(3)(Suppl):1-24.

11. Little MD, Halsey NA, Cline BL, Katz SP. *Ancylostoma* larva in muscle fiber of man following cutaneous larva migrans. Am J Trop Med Hyg 1983; 32:1285-88.

12. Prociv P, Croese J. Human eosinophilic enteritis caused by dog hookworm *Ancylostoma caninum*. Lancet 1990; 335:1299-1302.

13. Blagburn BL, Lindsay DS, Vaughan JL, et al. Prevalence of canine parasites based on fecal flotation. Comp Contin Educ Vet Pract 1996; 18:483-509.

14. Schantz PM. Toxocara larva migrans now. Am J Trop Med Hyg 1989; 41(3)(Suppl):21-34.

15. Schantz PM. Zoonotic ascarids and hookworms: The role for veterinarians in preventing human disease. Compendium on continuing education for the practicing veterinarian 2002; 24(1)(Suppl):47-52.

16. Beaver PC. Biology of soil-transmitted helminths: The massive infection. H. L. S. 1974; 12(2):116-25.

17. Harvey JB, Roberts JM, Schantz PM. Survey of veterinarians' recommendations for the treatment and control of intestinal parasites in dogs: Public health implications. J Am Vet Med Assoc 1991; 199:702-7.

18. Barriga OO. Rational control of canine toxocariasis by the veterinary practitioner. J Am Vet Med Assoc 1991; 198:216-21.

19. Duwel D, Strasser H. Birth of helminth-free canine pups through maternal fenbendazole therapy. Dtsch Tierarztl Wochenschr 1978; 85(6):239-41.

20. Payne PA, Ridley RK. Strategic use of ivermectin during pregnancy to control *Toxocara canis* in greyhound puppies. Vet Parasitol 1999; 85(4):305-12.

21. Payne-Johnson M, Maitland TP, Sherington J, Shanks DJ, Cements PJ, Murphy MG, McLoughlin A, Jernigan AD, Rowan TG. Efficacy of selamectin administered topically to pregnant and lactating female dogs in the treatment and prevention of adult roundworm *(Toxocara canis)* infections and flea *(Ctenocephalides felis felis)* infestations in the dams and their pups. Vet Parasitol 2000; 91(3–4):347–58.

22. Stoye M. Biology, pathogenicity, diagnosis and control of *Ancylostoma caninum*. Dtsch Tierarztl Wochenschr 1992; 99(8):315–21.

23. Reinemeyer CR, Faulkner CT, Assadi-Rad AM, Burr JH, Patton S. Comparison of the efficacies of three heartworm preventatives against experimentally induced infections with *Anycylostoma caninum* and *Toxocara canis* in pups. J Am Vet Med Assoc 1995; 206(11):1710–5.

Index

———◆———

About the Author

Debra Eldredge, D.V.M., works at Burrstone Animal Hospital in New Hartford, New York. In addition to her veterinarian duties, she is a consultant for Canine Working Companions, and is the winner of the Central New York Veterinary Medical Association Award. An award-winning writer on veterinary issues, her articles focus primarily on health care, training, and human interest. She is married with two children, five dogs, four cats, one house bunny, two guinea pigs, nineteen ducks, six horses, sixteen sheep, and three goats.